Opium, Soldiers and Evangelicals

Also by Harry G. Gelber

NATIONS OUT OF EMPIRES

AUSTRALIA, BRITAIN AND THE EEC, 1961–1963

THE AUSTRALIAN-AMERICAN ALLIANCE

NATIONAL POWER, SECURITY AND ECONOMIC UNCERTAINTY

NUCLEAR WEAPONS AND CHINESE POLICY

PROBLEMS OF AUSTRALIAN DEFENCE (ed.)

TECHNOLOGY, DEFENSE AND EXTERNAL RELATIONS IN CHINA 1975–1978

THE COMING OF THE SECOND WORLD WAR

THE ROLE AND FUNCTION OF UNIVERSITIES

SOVEREIGNTY THROUGH INTERDEPENDENCE

Opium, Soldiers and Evangelicals

Britain's 1840–42 War with China, and its Aftermath

Professor Harry G. Gelber
Visiting Research Fellow, London School of Economics

First published 2004 by
PALGRAVE MACMILLAN
Houndmills, Basingstoke, Hampshire RG21 6XS and
175 Fifth Avenue, New York, N.Y. 10010
Companies and representatives throughout the world

PALGRAVE MACMILLAN is the global academic imprint of the Palgrave
Macmillan division of St. Martin's Press, LLC and of Palgrave Macmillan Ltd.
Macmillan® is a registered trademark in the United States, United Kingdom
and other countries. Palgrave is a registered trademark in the European
Union and other countries.

ISBN 1–4039–0700–5 hardback

This book is printed on paper suitable for recycling and made from fully
managed and sustained forest sources.

A catalogue record for this book is available from the British Library.

Library of Congress Cataloging-in-Publication Data

Gelber, Harry Gregor.
  Opium, soldiers and evangelicals : England's 1840–42 war with China and
its aftermath/Harry G. Gelber.
    p. cm.
  Includes bibliographical references and index.
  ISBN 1-4039-0700-5
    1. China—History—Opium War, 1840–1842. 2. Great Britain—Foreign
relations—China. 3. China—Foreign relations—Great Britain. I. Title:
England's 1840–42 war with China and its aftermath. II. Title.

DS757.5.G45 2004
951' .033—dc22   2003063052

10 9 8 7 6 5 4 3 2 1
13 12 11 10 09 08 07 06 05 04

Printed and bound in Great Britain by
Antony Rowe Ltd, Chippenham and Eastbourne

To my grandchildren

Contents

Introduction

The Anglo-Chinese War of 1840–42, usually known as the 'First Opium War' has received a good deal of modern attention. It has, for the last hundred years or so, been discussed and analysed very largely with the Chinese as the injured party and with British views and policies thought to be in various ways deplorable. Arguably the most important strands have been two linked ones. The first has had to do with admiration of China and its civilization together with growing understanding of the problems of the nineteenth-century Chinese empire. Some works also went on to point out something which had been recognized quite early on – the sheer confusion of purposes between the Chinese and the British. Not only over opium but, at least equally, over equality of treatment between states and governments, over systems of justice and the appropriate treatment by sovereign states and empires of foreign residents.

The other line of criticism has come from the broad stream of anti-imperialism. That, in turn, has its roots in two widely divergent views of the world. These are in principle incompatible, though Christian Socialism has made valiant attempts to link them. One is Marxism, which sees imperialism as a combination of class oppression and, as both Lenin and J.A. Hobson have famously argued, economic exploitation. The other is the view from Christian evangelism, most strongly expressed through the extremely effective propaganda conducted over decades by the Christian missionaries in China and their churches in Britain and America.

The result has been a combination of ideas of uncommon power. There is the suspicion on the political Left of all notions of 'profit'; the view that all modern economic and industrial organization has always been likely to result in the unfair exploitation of workers – in this case in the exploitation of the Chinese by cynical British merchants and statesmen. Together with this sympathy for the 'working man' (or his equivalent) have gone notions of the brotherhood of man and therefore, given the sheer political and industrial power of the West, its responsibility for the poorer and less advanced.

In addition, from the late nineteenth century and, more forcibly still from early in the twentieth, came quite novel views about the evils of drugs and the drug trade. The view took hold – encouraged by the

Chinese – that Britain had been in the business of persuading, even forc-ing, opium on the Chinese, with hugely harmful social consequences and purely in the interests of vile profit. And when China tried to resist, the British used superior firepower to get their way. Here, it was argued, was one important contribution to the growing disintegration of the Chinese empire from the middle of the nineteenth century, with all the suffering and hardship which that entailed.

In all that, rather less attention has been paid to the question of what the British government, and London opinion, thought they were doing and why. Hence this book. It regards the 1840–42 war as the focus of Anglo-Chinese relations for virtually the whole period from the 1830s to the Chinese revolution of 1911. In that discussion it stresses British per-spectives and the points of view of the government and of Parliament in London; and points to the low priority which Chinese affairs had in a foreign policy far more urgently concerned with a dozen other issues. And how, quite clearly, the British saw themselves as very much the injured party before and during the war that ended with the 1842 Treaty of Nanjing. The point is not, of course, to discount or play down the Chinese point of view. It is simply to sketch why the British did what they did, and how China and the world, and British responsibilities in that world, looked to people in London at the time.

It therefore tries to deal with three questions. First, what is the evi-dence for saying that the 1839–42 conflict was an 'opium war'? Second, how did the conflict come to be known by that title? Why did a later generation in Britain – and America – come to accept as conventional wisdom that the British had been wicked, sinful and grasping, and had even forced opium on the Chinese? Third, what role did that war play in the difficult and painful transition of China, in the period 1830–1911, from the condition of a somewhat antiquated empire to the threshold of modern nation-statehood?

I am grateful to the London School of Economics and to friends and colleagues in the Department of International Relations, which has been my academic home during the writing of this book.

1
Mission to Canton

On 15 July 1834 a trim Royal Navy frigate, the *Andromache*, cast anchor at Macao, on the South China coast, and put ashore William John, the 8th Baron Napier, the British Government's first-ever representative in the Chinese Empire. His task was to supervise British merchants at the nearby trading port of Canton (new Guangzhou); but his arrival triggered disputes that led to war a mere six years later.

He landed in his splendid blue-and-gold uniform of a captain of the Royal Navy. A local merchant described him as a 'tall, raw Scotchman with light hair',[1] with a trim figure, fine features and a prominent nose. He had started as a midshipman in the last days of the old century and served under Nelson at Trafalgar. He was not a particularly sharp or subtle fellow, but even his early contemporaries thought him strong, brave and not easily rattled. After Napoleon's defeat at Waterloo he found the notion of peacetime service unattractive, so he went on half pay to look after his estate in Scotland and the family he had barely seen in his years at sea. Then, in 1830 an old ship-mate, a royal prince who had just become King William IV, took him away from breeding sheep and brought him to London as a lord-in-waiting.

Three years later, in August 1833, the British East India Company's legal monopoly of the China trade came to an end by Act of Parliament. That threw the trade open to all comers, and it became necessary to appoint official superintendents to look after the traders. Napier, after his time in the social whirl of London, decided that the new post of Chief Superintendent, at the very handsome salary of £6000 per annum (Today's values [tv] £291,000)[2] would be just the thing for an unemployed naval officer with a large brood of children to care for. With the king's support, he applied to the Prime Minister, Lord Grey. By December 1833 he was duly appointed,[3] and on 7 February 1834 he

sailed from Devonport, accompanied by his wife, two daughters and two maids. This being just before the age of steamships, he travelled under sail, and since the Suez Canal did not yet exist either, it took him the best part of six months to reach Macao.

That rocky peninsula, south of Canton, had been held by the Portuguese for some 300 years and boasted a lovely little town with 12 churches and four, largely ornamental, forts. It had a population of some 4500 Portuguese and perhaps 40,000 Chinese. European women not being allowed at Canton, the British merchants' wives and daughters lived there, too, mostly in lovely, large houses on a ridge overlooking the water, and with lots of servants. So, during the summer, did the traders themselves, since they were not allowed to stay at Canton either, except for the six months' trading season. Napier, too, had to leave his wife and daughters at Macao, so he accepted the loan of a large house there from William Jardine, perhaps the most senior, and certainly the most determined, of the non-East India Company, or 'country', traders.

Napier spent the first day or two ashore, dealing with staff appointments. He confirmed John Davis and Sir George Robinson as Second and Third Superintendent respectively. Both were former East India Company men, Davis having been chairman of the company's group of supercargoes. He appointed a secretary and an interpreter, in the person of Robert Morrison, who had served as missionary in China for the best part of thirty years. Morrison's son John, also a competent translator, came along as well. And another ex-Navy captain became Master Attendant, a minor post dealing with ships and crews operating between Macao and Canton itself. This officer, of whom much more would be heard, was Charles Elliot who, together with his wife Clara and two children, had also come from England together with the Napiers.

Napier found that his staff agreed with the idea of moving on to Canton at once, and he duly sailed on in *Andromache* across the sparkling blue waters of the Bay of Canton, dotted with occasional jagged rocks of islands and alive with junks and other ships from around the world. They anchored off Chuenbi (Chuenpi),[4] a fort guarding the mouth of the Bogue, or Bocca Tigris (the Tiger's Mouth). Here was the narrow channel through which the waters of Canton's Pearl River flowed into the sea. From there Napier went on in the cutter *Louisa*, a 75-ton ship equipped with three-pounder guns that he had bought from the Company at Macao. He sailed through the Bogue, upstream to the harbour of Whampoa. From there he went on in a smaller boat, between green rice fields and scattered villages and through thundery rain showers. He reached Canton on 25 July, and promptly ran the

Union Jack up the flagstaff of the British 'factory', one of a group of such foreign depots. Others belonged to the Americans, Austrians, Dutch, French, Spaniards and Swedes. Each factory housed its foreign merchants, living in very modest comfort, and doubling as a place of business, where goods were stored and trading was done. All these factories were grouped, outside the gates of Canton itself, next to the Pearl River from which they were separated by an enclosed gravel square and a riverside walk.

The foreigners were confined in more ways than one. To enter the teeming city itself they needed special permission, which was rarely given. As for the wider countryside, between Canton and the White Cloud Mountains that could be glimpsed in the North through the morning mists, it was a region full of villages that detested strangers. Chinese poets might go to the mountains to hold wine-drinking contests but for Europeans, going for a stroll could mean quite serious dangers to life and limb. Even within the maze of Canton's narrow streets there would surely be shouts and insults, while strolling along the pathway on top of the city walls might mean dodging stones hurled at the foreign 'barbarians'.

Unfortunately for Napier, his mission was doomed to an unhappy start. To have a British government representative take charge of the merchants, instead of a mere East India Company officer, was sure to make trouble. China had no formal, regular diplomatic relations, in the Western sense of that term, with any other state. From Beijing's point of view, it was the centre of the world and of civilization, and if foreigners came to trade, they must simply do so on China's terms. In fact, back in 1831, when the Chinese were given their first intimation that the Company's monopoly might not last, they had suggested informally that a senior merchant, or manager of foreign merchants and trade, should be sent out instead. A new Canton Viceroy, Lu Kun, said it again in 1834. A British government representative was something else entirely.

The omens for Napier's arrival were therefore gloomy, as people who knew something of China understood well enough. As much as a year before Napier sailed from England, the *Quarterly Review* in London was uncannily prescient. He will, it said,

> go probably in a ship of war, to save his dignity, which the Chinese will not care one farthing about, and do not in the least understand; she will proceed up to Whampo [sic] ... and the *King's Representative* will demand an interview with the Viceroy [i.e., the Chinese Governor of Canton and its province] to deliver his credentials. The

Viceroy in the first place will order the ship immediately to leave the river, and the Superintendent may be told that whatever he may have to deliver must come through the hong [group of Chinese merchants] ... His dignity will probably be offended, and remonstrances made, accompanied by a demand to present his credentials in person. This will be peremptorily refused – perhaps Chinese courtesy may go so far as to allow the King's Representative to wait an hour at the city gate, and then hand his credentials over to the Viceroy's runners; As a last resort he may, perhaps, be driven to invite the captain of the ship of war to bring up a party of seamen, and then all trade will be forthwith suspended. Something of this kind will probably happen unless the Chinese are previously prevailed on by negotiation to concede the point of a personal interview, which we do not think they will do. In what a lamentable situation, then, will a King's Representative be placed, a stranger to the customs and the language of the people, and appealed to on all sides by the disappointed and dissatisfied [British] free-traders?[5]

Yet London's motives in sending out a government representative were neither acquisitive nor malign; least of all were they – to use twenty-first-century language – 'imperialist'. They had simply to do with some limited control over British traders, with freeing up trade, and perhaps with establishing more 'normal' relations between Britain and the Chinese Empire. It had long been quite clear that London had no designs on China beyond trade. Sir James Graham, the First Lord of the Admiralty in London – that is, the Minister in charge of the Navy – wrote about that to the Governor-General of India a year before Napier sailed: 'Trade with China is our only object; conquest would be as dangerous as defeat ... Our grand object is to keep peace, and by the mildest means ... to extend our influence in China with a view to extending our commercial relations.'

However, the pessimism of the Canton traders continued, the more so as the Chinese stepped up military preparations as soon as Napier arrived. 'The Chinese,' said one message to England,[6] 'were totally unable to comprehend what was meant by the opening of trade, and some imagined that the British were going to set up an independent government in Canton ... The attempts ... it was known would not be tolerated ...' Yet once any British subject, and not just Company people, could trade at Canton – and there were rapidly increasing numbers of them[7] – they were bound to look to their own government for protection and support. The more so as these brash new men were impatient with the older, ceremonial ways of dealing with the Chinese. Manufacturers at home, looking for export markets, were sure to join them in pushing for free trade. On terms and conditions, naturally, that met normal Western international practice.

The Foreign Secretary in London, Lord Palmerston, felt the same. But sending out an official British representative meant that the power of the English state was for the first time brought to bear directly on all British affairs at Canton. For London, that naturally meant a fresh push for inter-governmental relations, the diplomatic relations with Beijing that Britain had vainly sought for forty years or more. The appointment of a Chief Superintendent must mean just such governmental contacts with the Chinese authorities.

The reality, however, was more complicated than London imagined and the Chinese were not always easy to deal with. Napier's interpreter, Robert Morrison, knew something of his Chinese. He noted that 'The Chinese are specious, but insincere; jealous, envious and distrustful, to a high degree. They are generally selfish, cold-blooded and inhumane.' In any case, the Empire was governed by extremely strict and detailed rules and procedures, and in the Chinese official world, every tiny or trivial detail of ceremonial mattered as an indicator of power and status. Administration was by highly educated, often skilled and subtle mandarins who were responsible, through an elaborate chain of command, directly to the throne. This complex structure suddenly found itself confronted by a British naval captain, claiming to have some authority from his government, which lay dimly beyond the pale of civilization. Yet the man had no credentials, let alone a *laissez-passer* from competent Chinese authorities. For them Napier, whether he belonged to his nation's nobility or not, was simply a trader, and therefore by definition a much lower form of life than a government official.

Napier had, in fact, been warned before sailing that he should get a hand-written letter from his king to the Chinese emperor. He had at least asked that London should inform the Chinese of his appointment; but Palmerston thought that unnecessary. So he came to China not only without credentials but without any warning or prior notice. Even so, he assumed that he had the rights and privileges of an envoy of the British crown.

However, his instructions were confused. The king told him to wear his naval uniform and behave as the crown's representative. Lord Grey advised caution and quiet, while Palmerston said he must announce his arrival at Canton by letter to the Viceroy and take control of British subjects there. In his dealings with the Chinese, wrote Palmerston, he should be moderate and circumspect. He should help along British mercantile activities, explore possibilities for extending trade to other regions of China, and urge traders to conform to Chinese laws. So long, that is, '... as such laws shall be administered ... with justice and good faith in the same manner ...' to Chinese as well as foreigners.[8] Also, Napier must not endanger England's existing good relations with the Chinese empire, either by threatening language or by asking for British military or naval help. Unless, of course, that should be required 'in extreme cases (by) the most evident necessity.' He was given clearly to understand that direct communication with Beijing would be desirable eventually; but in the meantime he was not to enter into anything smacking of formal negotiations. In passing, he should also survey the Chinese coast and look for places where warships could safely operate.

There was also the potentially critical matter of legal authority. The Superintendent's own powers over the British on the China coast were strictly limited. London's 1833 arrangements for the China trade provided for a court with criminal and admiralty jurisdiction, presided over by the Chief Superintendent and sitting either at Canton or on board a British ship. However, Palmerston's detailed instructions of 25 January 1834 warned Napier not to do anything about setting up courts until he had 'most serious[ly]' thought about it. That limitation was especially important for the many British who were breaking Chinese laws by smuggling opium. Though opium was quite legal and in fairly common use in Britain, no one in London much liked the smuggling business in China. The government had already said that 'it was as anxious as anybody' to get rid of it. But Napier was now told, confusingly, that 'it is not desirable that you should encourage such adventures, but you must never lose sight of the fact that you have no authority to interfere with them or prevent them.'

That obviously created a dilemma. Superintendents were to urge obedience to Chinese laws and discourage opium trading. But the Superintendents had no power of arrest or punishment of their own. And, of course, London could hardly give it to them without establishing a system of enforcement by courts, policing and penal arrangements. Trying to establish that would be a clear and highly provocative violation of Chinese sovereignty. Which would, at minimum, bedevil just those good relations with the Chinese that London was keen to maintain. On the other hand, the British as well as other foreigners refused to submit their nationals to Chinese legal and police procedures which they regarded as erratic, arbitrary and thoroughly unjust. They objected especially to the Chinese system of collective rather than individual responsibility.

From a Chinese point of view, though, Napier's very arrival at Whampoa, in a foreign warship and without prior permission, was itself a clearly hostile act and his unauthorized entry to Canton, at minimum, an impertinence. There were immediate signs of serious displeasure at this way of doing things. On 21 July Viceroy Lu Kun, having heard of Napier's arrival at Macao, issued orders to the Hong group of merchants, the only ones licensed to do business with the foreigners. They were also the people who guaranteed the foreigners to the Chinese mandarinate and the only ones through whom the foreigners and the Chinese authorities could communicate with each other. These merchants were now instructed to hurry to Macao and ask why this new headman had come and whether, with the end of the East India Company arrangements, he had any proposals for changing existing procedures. If he did, decisions would of course have to be made in Beijing. Meanwhile, existing laws must be observed and if the new headman wished to come to Canton he must apply for permission in the normal way. Lu was evidently determined not to let Napier change or circumvent the regulations. The two senior Chinese merchants, Howqua and Mowqua, hurried to Macao, but missed Napier who was by then on his way to Canton. They caught up with him there, and explained their mission, just as his letter to the Viceroy, informing him of his arrival, was being translated into Chinese.

For Napier, irascible, proud and with all the stubbornness of his Scotch Presbyterian upbringing, what they were saying was quite unacceptable. Here he was, a nobleman of ancient lineage, a senior officer of the world's greatest navy, the representative of its greatest power, an emissary and personal friend of its king, being asked to send obsequiously worded petitions to the provincial official of a large but decrepit and notoriously corrupt empire; and not even to send them directly but through some private merchants. It was worse than absurd. It was an intolerable insult to the King of England. So he simply said he would only communicate with the Viceroy direct. The Chinese politely insisted: Napier was not a merchant, so the existing arrangements for traders to approach the authorities did not apply. Napier must return to Macao until Beijing decided what was to be done. Politely but firmly, he sent them away.

For any mandarin, Napier's insistence on writing directly to the Viceroy was yet another impertinence. It was bad enough for him to go to Canton without a pass and to stay there without the required additional permit. But now, even worse, he had tried to write directly to the Viceroy, and in thoroughly inappropriate terms. It was a firm rule throughout the empire that every communication had to start with a clear indication whether it was addressed to a subordinate, an equal or a superior. And Napier's note was headed with the character meaning 'Letter', implying equality between sender and recipient. But as had often been explained to foreign barbarians, direct contact with Chinese officials by foreigners involved with mere trade was strictly forbidden. Not only must all documents from or about the foreigners reach the Viceroy through the Hong merchants, but they must carry the normal heading of 'Petition'. Yet here was Napier, a man without accreditation, who seemed to be some kind of chief of merchants, calmly assuming an official relationship of diplomatic equality. For the Chinese, that was not only unacceptable, it was incomprehensible. To cap this list of offences, his secretary, accompanied by a group of foreign merchants, carried Napier's letter to the city gates. Although the rule was that only two persons could present a communication.

The upshot was a diplomatic pantomime. At the city gate, the secretary tried to hand the letter to a mandarin, who refused to accept it. Various other Chinese officials arrived and also declined to take it. After three hours of this, the foreigners trudged back to their factory. Two days later Napier was informed that the Viceroy would not accept the letter unless it was labelled a 'petition'. The Viceroy himself, as usual, blamed the Hong merchants for the incident and threatened condign punishment if they did not make the foreigners behave themselves in future.

A day after this stalemate at the gate, on 27 July, Viceroy Lu issued revised orders about this obstreperous foreigner, again through the Hong merchants. He began with the precedents, pointing out that the English had traded at Canton for a hundred years under imperial regulations. Only if they obeyed them could they trade in peace. Traders had been allowed to live at Macao and if they wanted to come to Canton they needed a permit from the *hoppo*, the administrator of Canton customs with the status of a direct representative of the Emperor. Now that Napier had illegally come to Canton he would, since he was obviously ignorant of the law, be generously allowed to stay to look into the conditions of trade, but he must then return to Macao and not come back without a permit. Lu went on to outline the general principles under which Chinese officials dealt with foreigners:

The Celestial Empire appoints officials – civilian to rule the people, military to intimidate the wicked; but the petty affairs of commerce are to be directed by the merchants themselves. The officials are not concerned with such matters ... The great ministers of the Celestial Empire are not permitted to have private intercourse by letter with outside barbarians. If the said barbarian headman throws in private letters, I, the Viceroy, will not at all receive or look at them. [The factory] is a place of temporary residence for barbarians coming to Canton to trade. They are permitted to eat, sleep, buy and sell in the factories. They are not permitted to go out and ramble about ... [In sum] the nation has its laws. It is so everywhere. Even England has its laws: how much more the Celestial Empire! How flaming bright are its great laws and ordinances! More terrible than the awful thunderbolt! Under this whole bright heaven none dares to disobey them. Under its shelter are the four seas. Subject to its soothing care are ten thousand kingdoms....[9]

Or again: 'There has never been such a thing as foreign barbarians sending a letter ... It is contrary to all dignity and decorum. The thing is most decidedly impossible.' The Hong merchants would be held responsible for ensuring that Napier understood these orders and would obey them. Or, as Lu explained to all concerned, 'Say not that you were not forewarned ... These are the orders. Tremble hereat! Intensely tremble!'[10] It was hardly the kind of language to which Napier was accustomed.

Three days later, on 30 July, Lu sent further orders saying the Chinese merchants must be held strictly to account for the recent breaches of regulations. Napier's arrival at Canton raised novel questions and he must return to Macao at once, pending decisions by the Emperor. A day later, on 31 July, he sent yet another order, telling his own merchants that the *hoppo* had laid formal charges against them for allowing Napier to come to Canton. On 4 August the *hoppo* himself weighed in, ordering an even more rigorous enforcement of the rules. Since the barbarians were forbidden to bring firearms to Canton, all ships and boats must henceforth stop at customs posts and be searched for arms and contraband. Since bringing women to Canton was equally forbidden, any who might be brought in would be removed, if necessary by force. Nor were foreigners allowed to come to the city itself to present petitions. If Napier did not return to Macao immediately, the Hong merchants would be severely punished. The formal repetition of these standing orders caused considerable alarm and many of the Chinese servants, office staff or watermen employed by the British promptly fled. By this time, too, wise old Robert Morrison had become very ill and died.

The Hong merchants found themselves in a cleft stick. For half a century or more they had been the accepted conduit for orders to the foreigners,

and for securing compliance. Now, suddenly, they had to deal with someone who was not a British trader and flatly refused to accept them as
a proper channel of communication. So, on 8 August Howqua and
Mowqua called on Napier once more to persuade him to return to Macao.
In vain. Two days later the Chinese merchants invited their English
colleagues to a meeting to consider what might be done. To forestall them,
Napier called an even earlier meeting at which the British unanimously
decided not to act independently of the Chief Superintendent.

On 16 August the Chinese merchants, apparently on their own initiative and to mollify the authorities, stopped doing business with or for
the British. That was followed by yet further instructions from the
Viceroy, conveyed to William Jardine.[11] The complaints against the
English headman were repeated. The circumstances of Napier's arrival
had been seriously discourteous. So was his demand for direct access to
officials: '...the barbarians...coming to or leaving Canton, have,
beyond their trade, not any public business and the commissioned officers of the Celestial Empire never take cognizance of the trivial affairs of
trade.' The existing rules had worked very well for a hundred years or
more and there had never been direct correspondence between officials
and a 'barbarian eye' (that is, foreign headman). Official intervention
would be undignified and actually hamper trade. Moreover, it was
hinted, China had real leverage. Trade, and British products, including
textiles, were of no interest to the empire. If Napier refused to behave
himself, it would be clear that he did not want a proper marketing system and trade would have to be stopped altogether, including the export
of China's own tea, rhubarb and silks, which were so essential for the
British. Here was only the first of many quaint Chinese illusions. As far
as the Viceroy was concerned, 'the tea, the rhubarb, the silk of the inner
dominions, are the sources by which ... [the English] ... live and maintain life.'[12] Five years later, as Sino-British relations slid towards war, a
new Chinese Commissioner warned again that if trade were stopped,
foreign nations would suffer. 'Yet more, our tea and our Rhubarb; if you
are deprived of them, you lose the means of preserving life ...'[13] A dozen
years later, the Chinese public was given the fuller explanation:

> The foreigners from the West are naturally fond of milk and cream;
> indulgence in these luxuries induces costiveness, when there is
> nothing but rhubarb and tea will clear their system and restore their
> spirits; if once we cut off the trade of the barbarians, turbulence and
> disorder will ensue in their own countries; and this is the first reason
> why they must have our goods.[14]

Clearly, even allowing for the political correctness of official pronouncements or the usual disparagement of barbarians, some Chinese views of the British were seriously absurd. Five or six years later, one Chinese woman recalled that the first time she saw 'the tall man with the black beard I had thought he was a devil and ... squatted in the road and hid my head in my arms.' And even Imperial Commissioner Lin had to agree 'they do really look like devils' and added that in their tight-fitting clothes these people 'look like actors playing the parts of foxes, hares and other such animals on the stage'.[15]

However, Napier remained firmly convinced that trade was as necessary to the Chinese as to the British, and continued to seek direct talks with the Viceroy. He was encouraged to be told on 22 August that three senior officials, headed by the Prefect of Canton, would visit him next day. As usual in China, formalities and protocol proved to be critical. The Hong merchants prepared ceremonial chairs and places of honour for the officials in the reception room of the English factory. There were visibly lesser chairs for the merchant representatives and lesser chairs still for the English, who were placed with their backs to the portrait of their own sovereign. Napier promptly rearranged things so as to put himself in the position of host, and sat in the central ceremonial chair. He flatly refused the entreaties of senior Chinese merchants not to change the original arrangements, lest deep offence be caused to the officials. The three arrived two hours late, having awaited the outcome of the 'battle of the chairs', and to follow custom when calling on a lesser person. But they would have broken rules of decorum, and lost face, if they had shown irritation at the revised arrangements.

Lord Napier began by rebuking their unpunctuality: they were no longer dealing with the officials of a private company but with officers of the British crown, who would not accept indignities. The officials listened without comment. Napier asked why they had come. The senior of the three said they had been instructed to find out why he had travelled to Canton, what he expected to accomplish and when he proposed to leave. Napier explained that he had been sent as official Superintendent, to manage the commerce of the free merchants of Canton. As the Viceroy had himself originally requested. As to the nature of his business, it was set down in his letter to the Viceroy, which the officials could now accept and transmit. He would leave Canton when it was convenient to him.

The Chinese replied that what had originally been asked for, back in 1831, was the dispatch of a head merchant, 'for the general management of the commercial dealings'. (The word used to denote the headman, at least in the Viceroy's memorial of 8 September 1834 to the Emperor, seems to have been 'taipan', carrying no official or political meaning.[16]) The status of such a person would fit the existing regulations, whereas the presence of an official would require their fundamental revision. If the King of England desired a change in these regulations, he should have put a request to the Viceroy, which would have been submitted to the Emperor, instead of sending a representative who assumed privileges that had never been sought, let alone granted.

On 25 August the British merchants formed a Chamber of Commerce and shortly afterwards Napier issued a general proclamation entitled 'State of Relations between China and Great Britain at Present', had it translated into Chinese, printed and circulated through Canton. He insisted that trade benefited the Chinese as much as anyone and that his aim was to open 'the wide field of the Chinese Empire to the British spirit and Industry.'[17] He accused the Governor-General of 'ignorance and incompetence'[18] and identified the interests of the foreign merchants with those of the '…thousands of industrious Chinese who must suffer ruin and discomfort through the perversity of their government.' Many people in London shared that view. Already, back in 1830, the Canton merchants had told the House of Commons that, while the China trade was potentially the most important in the world, nothing was to be gained by diplomacy, and force would have to be used. In fact, the merchants genuinely believed that their interests were the same as those of ordinary Chinese and trade expansion was only blocked by a corrupt and obdurate Chinese officialdom. Now, four years later, the *Gentleman's Magazine* was also sure that the Chinese very much wanted to trade with foreigners but were 'repressed' by the mandarins.[19] It was all, of course, deeply offensive to the Chinese officials, who were not remotely prepared to open up their country to foreign trade, still less to do it at foreign urging. They were even less prepared to have foreigners address the Chinese public. A number of Cantonese found themselves caned or gaoled on charges of helping Napier to publicize his impertinent and, indeed, seditious notice. The authorities pointed out to 'the lawless foreign slave … the barbarian dog …' that inciting people against their rulers was a capital offence.[20]

By now, a number of Western merchants were becoming queasy about Napier's tactics. The old hands and Company men had always wanted the 'softly, softly' approach that had served them so well in the past. The new, assertive private traders might want a much stronger line, but even some of Napier's staff began to doubt the wisdom of what he was doing. Even Clara Elliot, to whom Napier had been kind, and whose husband he had commended to Palmerston in strong terms, remarked in a private letter that 'The Chinese are the most industrious clever beings I ever read or heard of but such abominable cheats that it is painful to have anything to do with them,' adding 'I do not like to say a word of ill nature about him (that is, Napier) but I fear much he is unfit to negotiate with the Chinese they are so cunning and clever.'[21]

The increasingly agitated Viceroy now sent a series of fresh orders. On 27, 30 and 31 August he told Napier once more to obey the laws and to return to Macao; and reprimanded the merchants for not getting Napier to behave properly. On 2 September came a joint proclamation from the Viceroy and the Governor ordering Napier to return to Macao and instructing that all trade with the British be stopped in the meantime. In fact, just before that, the Hong merchants had got together with Jardine and agreed a compromise. If the British merchants petitioned the Viceroy, he would allow a resumption of trade; Napier would return to Macao now, but if he wanted to come back to Canton later on, he could come for a few days without fuss, and the Chinese would look the other way.[22] But the Viceroy rejected the compromise. His proclamation repeated all the complaints against Napier, referred to his 'stupidity and obstinacy' and ordered all Chinese support staff to leave the British. More ominously still, not only were servants and porters told to leave, and shopkeepers forbidden to sell provisions to the factory, but it was surrounded and isolated by a cordon of soldiers. A copy of the proclamation was fixed to the factory gate, though Napier had it removed.

By this time Lord Napier had become enormously exasperated with the mismanagement and corruption so obvious in every part of the local Chinese administration. How could one do serious business with such people and how could the endless prevarications be brought to an end? He concluded that a firmer hand was needed. He had begun to refer to the Viceroy as a 'presumptuous savage' and wrote to London that the government's aim should be to 'get a settlement on the same terms that every Chinaman, Pagan, Turk or Christian sits down in England.' The Chinese, he wrote home, displayed an 'extreme degree of mental imbecility and moral degradation, dreaming themselves to be the only people on earth, and being entirely ignorant of the theory and practice of international law.'

He went further. Within a month of arriving in Canton he actually suggested to London what turned out to be an eventual solution to trading in southern China: he recommended that Britain should seize what was then the fairly empty rock of Hong Kong. As early as 14 August he pointed out to London that, while his instructions had forbidden him to

enter into negotiations with the Chinese, any attempt to conduct negotiations directly between London and Beijing would lead to enormous
delays. In any case, talks not backed by the threat of force would be
pointless. Pressure by even a small force would achieve much more. If
Britain acted firmly, the Emperor would punish the Viceroy, who had
behaved outrageously.[23] A week later, on 21 August, he asked London
again to accept 'the urgent necessity of negotiating with such a government, having in your hands at the same time the means of compulsion;
to negotiate with them otherwise would be an idle waste of time.'[24] His
view was simply that if the Chinese rejected British terms, the forts and
batteries along the river and coast should be destroyed. 'Three or four
frigates or brigs, with a few steady British troops' would settle the thing.
'What can an army of bows and arrows, and pikes, and shields, do
against a handful of British veterans? ... The batteries at the Bogue are
contemptible ...' That view of Chinese military and naval capacity was
widely held. Back in 1830 the East India Company had said that a war
could be very easily won, and two years after that Captain Hugh
Lindsay, ordered to verify coastal observations originally made some
forty years earlier, sailed his frigate along the Chinese coastline and
concluded that 'The best ports – such as Amoy [Xiamen] or Ningpo
[Ningbo] – are still protected only by derisory batteries incapable of
interdicting access.'

   In any event, by the start of September there was considerable alarm
among the British civilians at Canton. Here they were, surrounded by
soldiers and completely defenceless. Napier sent a message down river to
order two Royal Navy frigates – the *Andromache* and also the *Imogene*,
which had in the meantime arrived – to sail up the Pearl River to protect
British people and goods; and to send some marines by cutter ahead to
Canton itself, to protect the factory. While the frigates must not fire
first, they could certainly defend themselves if attacked. He also, for
good measure, asked Calcutta to have some Indian troops dispatched to
China. On 6 September some 13 marines commanded by a Lieutenant
duly reached the factories and a day later the frigates, together with
the cutter *Louisa*, started to force the passage of the Bogue under fire.
There is some doubt about who started things. According to one seaman
on the *Imogene*, the forts began by firing blanks – presumably as a
warning – and only used round shot once the British ships moved on.[25]
In any case, it was remarked that during the entire action Charles Elliot
lounged under an umbrella on the deck of the *Louisa* and the British
lost only two men to some very poor Chinese gunnery. The frigates
arrived at Whampoa on the 11th. By now Napier was very thoroughly

contravening Palmerston's instructions about maintaining good relations with China. But he was also, in the humid weather of Canton, feverish and quite ill.

However, he tried to hold out, and on 8 September issued a manifesto in the form of a letter to the new British Chamber of Commerce. He refuted the Viceroy's charges, threatened to bring the 'false and treacherous conduct' of the Viceroy directly to the attention of the Emperor, warned that the Chinese had 'opened the preliminaries of war', and asserted the power of his own sovereign. On the same day the Viceroy and the Governor, in consultation with the *hoppo* and the generals commanding the Manchu garrrison, sent a memorial to the Emperor outlining the actions taken. On 11 September the Viceroy responded to Napier, saying it was entirely for the Chinese to decide the way communications should pass between the foreigners and the Chinese authorities; that there had never been direct relations between the officials and foreigners; that London had given Napier no credentials nor sent to China any official notice of his appointment. He had totally broken the laws of the empire by having armed ships force a passage into the Pearl River and firing at Chinese forts.

Moreover, Viceroy Lu had learned something of military tactics, and secured the Emperor's agreement to the use of force. Back in 1806 he had served against Moslem rebels in Xinjiang (Sinkiang) and been in charge of supplies and finance for some 36,000 troops. He had again shown military talent against Yao rebels in 1831–32, a campaign in which the Canton governor, Chi Kung, had also been decorated.[26] So now, once the British frigates reached Whampoa, Lu had the river blocked up both above and below them, so that they could neither proceed nor retreat to the open sea. They had to sit tight, with stone barriers blocking their exit to the sea, and Chinese soldiers and fire-rafts ready for action. On 15 September Lu and Chi sent a joint memorial to the Emperor telling him of the entrance of the frigates into the river and of their military preparations. Three weeks later the Emperor reprimanded them for not stopping the British vessels, and punished the Viceroy by depriving him of his office, his rank and his insignia while keeping him at his post.

By this time, in early September, a group of English merchants petitioned the *hoppo* for a resumption of trade. The response was: certainly, as soon as Napier leaves Canton. On the 9th, the tension, the heat and rain – not to mention the growing impatience of Napier's own people with him – had begun to undermine his health and he went down with a sharp attack of malarial fever. Though he claimed to be protecting the merchants and their property, the East India Company agents at Macao later reported to London that the goods, chattels and buildings at Canton had never really been at risk. Nor had there been a genuine shortage of supplies: the European quarter had plenty and Chinese shopkeepers were quite willing to ignore the Viceroy's orders and go on supplying the foreigners. One anonymous correspondent wrote to the *Morning Post* in London saying it was sad that the predictions of the *Quarterly Review* a year and a half earlier[27] should have been 'so literally fulfilled.'[28] 'It is to be regretted that a person so inexperienced and ignorant of Chinese usage should have been sent to China ...' What Napier should have done was to comply with the maxim so appositely quoted by the Viceroy – 'when you enter the frontiers inquire about the prohibitions – when you enter into a country inquire into its customs.' The Chinese government was bound to be offended by having Royal Navy ships go to Chuenbi and Canton without a pass. Altogether it was 'evident that his Lordship has fallen into the hands of that violent faction which predominates amongst the British free and independent merchants at Canton, whose turbulent spirits have for some years past been bent upon involving the two countries in a rupture ...'

Captured or not, Napier was now suffering from a raging fever, which made it necessary for him to leave Canton, and possible to do so without seeming to have been forced out. He applied, through his doctor, for permission to sail to Macao, but the Viceroy insisted that the frigates had to quit the river before permission could be given. Jardine managed to negotiate the terms of Napier's retreat and on Sunday, 21 September a very sick Napier finally boarded his boat, at the same time ordering the Royal Navy frigates to withdraw beyond the river, to Lintin island. A few days later the Chinese resumed trading. At the Viceroy's insistence, Napier travelled to Macao by a very slow Chinese boat, with many holdups and under military guard, accompanied by beating gongs and firework explosions: the worst possible treatment for a sick man. He managed to reach Macao on 26 September and died there shortly afterwards, on 11 October 1834, at the age of 48. He was buried with due ceremony in the Protestant cemetery and his widow and daughters sailed sadly for Scotland on 10 December.

The outcome of the mission was unfortunate for all concerned. It convinced the Chinese that the Superintendent's behaviour, without regard for proper law and government, proved how truly barbaric these British strangers were. More ominously still, they concluded that the only thing the British were interested in was profit, and they could always be brought to heel by stopping trade. Peaceful pressures such as blockading the factories would always make the foreigners cave in. They also thought they had been justified in holding the English 'chief' responsible for 'his' ships and crews anywhere in China, though in reality Napier had no legal authority over his countrymen, nor any way of enforcing 'orders'.

For the British, on the other hand, it had always been an illusion to suppose that the arrival of a single Scots Navy captain could overturn centuries-old traditions of protocol and official behaviour. Since that was not understood, the affair seemed to demonstrate that there was unlikely to be a middle way between quiet acquiescence to Chinese rules and forcing change by the threat of force, or even its use. In fact, the unofficial American consul at Canton reported to Washington towards the end of the Napier affair that a Sino-British war was about to start. He even suggested that it might be in America's interests to take part, or at least to deploy a US naval force in Chinese waters and demand that any terms granted to the British should be extended to the United States.[29] In London, however, the immediate reaction to Napier's death was to revert to the first course, keeping trade moving by Chinese rules. The Duke of Wellington got it right, as usual.[30] When he saw the Canton files during the brief hundred-day Peel government of 1835, he noted that Napier had gone to Canton '...without previous permission and insisting upon direct communication with the Viceroy...' when it would have been far better to seek commercial intercourse by the 'conciliatory methods' formerly used by the experienced officers of the East India Company.[31] 'It is quite obvious...that the attempt to force upon the Chinese authorities at Canton an unaccustomed mode of communication with an authority, with whose powers and of whose nature they had no knowledge, which commenced its proceedings by an assumption of powers hitherto unadmitted, had completely failed...'[32] If tried, it would fail again. While the existing arrangements for trade might not be ideal, things could have been worse. 'That which we now require is not to lose the enjoyment of what we have got.' Time, Wellington must have thought, would take care of things, as time almost always does. Even Palmerston spoke in retrospect of 'poor Napier' playing 'his foolish Pranks.'[33] There were similar criticisms in news-sheets. The *Gentleman's Magazine*, for instance, thought Napier had shown 'pugnacity and defiance'. It was the Chinese who had been reasonable.[34]

Accordingly, the Cabinet appointed Napier's assistant, John Francis Davis, to succeed him. Davis had accompanied Lord Amherst's fruitless embassy to Beijing in 1816, then spent twenty years in China for the East India Company, and now advocated a policy of being 'perfectly quiet'. Others were promoted, too, Charles Elliot advancing from Master

Attendant to Secretary, with a salary increased from £800 to one of £1500 per annum (tv: £38,850 to £72,850). By the end of April 1835, he had been promoted again and was earning twice that as second Superintendent.

But William Jardine and his partner, James Matheson, the most important and influential of the 'country' traders, differed entirely from Davis. Matheson promptly took ship for England, shortly after the newly widowed Lady Napier sailed home. He intended to make himself known at Westminster and to urge altogether less 'quiet' policies.

2
Palmerston's England, the World and China

One tends to forget how unimportant China was in the higher reaches of British politics. At the beginning of the 1830s England – as the United Kingdom was universally known – was one of the greatest powers in the world, at the centre of global politics, economics and finance. Victory in war, industrialism and its skills, invention, trade and financial innovation had made her the world's richest nation and greatest trader. London was the heart of an empire stretching over large parts of Asia, smaller parts of Africa, Canada and other territories in the Americas and the Pacific, with influence far beyond the lands actually under the English flag.

The guiding spirit in England's foreign affairs throughout the 1830s and beyond was Henry John Temple, Viscount Palmerston. Tall, athletic, popular, impossibly handsome even into middle age, he became by common consent one of the greatest Foreign Secretaries of modern times. He was, all his life, fond of the outdoors and of sport, especially at his country seat where he went rowing or shooting or rode to hounds. He was very much a man of fashion, too, and for two decades was a notable Regency beau, playing, dancing, seducing and being seduced. Not that he was alone. In 1822 we find one lady of fashion writing to another '...does it strike you that vices are wonderfully prolific among the Whigs? There are such countless illegitimates among them, such a tribe of children of the mist...'.[1] Women, and highly formidable ones at that, played a major role in Palmerston's life, politics and diplomacy. He spent some 25 years being captivated, maddened, teased and charmed by his fascinating, beautiful and entirely unfaithful mistress, Emily Lamb, Countess Cowper; probably fathered at least one of her children and, when her husband obligingly died, spent another 25 years happily married to her. 'Lord Cupid' was just one of his nicknames with a public which increasingly warmed to him. When he was in his seventies, and cited as co-respondent in a divorce action by a Mrs Cain, the word went round London 'She is Cain but is he Abel?' His political opponents wearily decided that to make an issue of the divorce would only make him even more popular.

Of course, there was much more to him than that. In the manner of his class and station he assumed, as a matter of course, that it was his right and duty to help govern the state. Having an Irish peerage, he could sit in the House of Commons and steadfastly refused suggestions that he should take an English title, which would have obliged him to go to the Lords. He had strong opinions, moral as well as physical courage, vast energy and stamina. After schooling at Harrow he went to Edinburgh University and later to St John's College, Cambridge. He was probably lucky in starting off at Edinburgh, which around 1800 was at the height of its fame. Many thought it the leading institution of its sort in the world. With liberal opinion sympathetic to French revolutionary principles, but Napoleon keeping young Britons out of France, liberal-minded youngsters flocked to Edinburgh. Young Palmerston was fortunate again in lodging with Professor Dugald Stewart, a famous and popular teacher of philosophy and political economy, who supervised his studies and social life. The habits of hard work, concentration and logical thinking that the young man acquired in the Stewart household stayed with him for the rest of his life. Certainly he learned a good deal more in Edinburgh than he did later at Cambridge.

His record in office was quite remarkable. Born in 1785, he sat in the Commons for 58 years and was therefore in office for most of his adult life. After some lesser posts he was Secretary at War from 1808 to 1827, a post which gave him plenty of time for social life and amusements. He twice declined the governor-generalship of India. In 1827, after the death of the great Canning, Palmerston became Foreign Secretary in the new 1830 administration, which was headed by Lord Grey, a man less remembered for being Prime Minister than for giving his name to 'Earl Grey' tea – not to mention as the lover of that famous beauty, Georgiana, Duchess of Devonshire, and the likely father of at least one of her children. In any case, Palmerston remained Foreign Secretary from 1830 to 1834, from 1835 to 1841 and from 1846 to 1851. That was followed by two years at the Home Office from 1853 to 1855, and then a decade as Prime Minister. He died in October 1865, still Prime Minister, a few days short of his 81st birthday, a despatch box at his side and a half-written letter in front of him. That, at least, is the official version. There was also a rather unlikely tale that at the end of his life he reverted to more youthful habits, and died while making love to a parlour-maid on his billiard table.

As Foreign Secretary, Palmerston was uncommonly dominant. He worked very hard and was usually much better informed than his colleagues. He was a forceful debater, a stranger to indecision, a brilliant master of forceful, clear and precise prose, but also a domineering personality and something of a bully with his staff. Formal party allegiance was much less important than being his own spin-doctor. So he was particularly careful to cultivate public opinion, which he described as one of 'the two powers in the country', the other being the government itself. He was even more careful about the newspapers than many of his Whig colleagues, which was just as well in a period when they were quite as vitriolic as modern tabloids. One of his colleagues said that he would 'see any newspaper editor who called on him and often communicate to such persons matters of great delicacy'.[2] In 1837, while electioneering at Tiverton, he arranged for reporters to be taken from and to London, to get local accommodation and, especially, good seats for his speeches.[3] He would even supply news and anonymous leading articles to papers he favoured, especially the *Globe* and the *Morning Chronicle*, which leaned towards the Whig party and defended the Foreign Office against *The Times* and the *Morning Post*. Politically, the fact that his wife, the former Countess Cowper, was the sister of the Prime Minister, Lord Melbourne, did him no harm either.

But his popularity was not merely a matter of spin, nor even of his detailed policies. The public admired what he stood for. He personified the dominant English attitudes of his time and the self-confidence of the mid-Victorian middle classes.[4] He did not have to play the part of John Bull; he lived it. He shared the people's sense of Britain's self-evident superiority, the unquestioning pride in England's power and achievements and their growing sense of destiny. He regarded England as the home of liberty, justice and the rule of law which, like dominant powers before and since, he and his countrymen thought were universally valid. He was strongly patriotic and, contrary to much modern mythology, believed in Englishmen, not class. The story goes that in 1861 on some railway platform the station-master, strongly opposed to smoking, abused someone caught smoking and pulled the cigar out of his mouth. He later discovered that the passenger had been the Prime Minister, and rushed to apologize. To which Palmerston replied: 'Sir, I respected you because I thought you were doing your duty like an Englishman, but now I see you are nothing but a snob. Cut along!'[5] Or in 1850, there was the so-called Don Pacifico affair, in which he was accused of behaving high-handedly by blockading Athens in a dispute over the debts of a Gibraltarian Jew of doubtful reputation.

Palmerston simply told Parliament that anyone who could claim to be a *civis Britannicus* should be free from danger anywhere in the world. (Every member of the House would instantly understand the reference to the proud claim 'I am a Roman citizen' that could be made in the days of the Roman Empire.)

In foreign affairs he was nothing if not a realist. His most famous *bon mot* was that Britain, in seeking to maintain the balance of power, has no eternal friends and no eternal enemies. He also understood that, as he said in 1857, 'No powerful nation can ever be expected to be really loved or liked by any other.' But beyond that, in many ways more important than material issues, were questions about the morality of British policies and their effect on Britain's global position and reputation and the moral standing of British statesmen.

He therefore consistently promoted liberalism and constitutionalism. They were, of course, right and good in themselves, but Palmerston understood that principles are also tools of power. 'There is in nature no moving power but mind... In human affairs this power is opinion; in political affairs it is public opinion; and he who can grasp this power, with it will subdue the fleshly arm of physical strength and impel it to work out his purpose.' Men who know 'how to avail themselves of the passions, the interests and the opinions of mankind' could expect to win influence far beyond the power and resources of their state. They could, in the words of another Foreign Secretary a century and a half later, Douglas Hurd, 'punch above their weight.' In fact, since powers, like people, tend to be taken at their own valuation, English confidence and self-assertion had a huge effect on all concerned, not least the English themselves. So England became the acknowledged champion of liberalism in Europe and beyond. In Italy and Germany, especially, liberal nationalists – in an era when these nationalist ideas meant unity, freedom, popular assertion, progress – strongly admired and sought to imitate English liberal and representative institutions. Palmerston's England played a liberalizing role in Greece, Italy and the Iberian peninsula and, with rather less success, in Poland. That dovetailed neatly enough with Palmerston's conviction of England's pre-eminence among the nations and the sense that the best thing she could do for the world would be to help it to become, in structures, values and civilization, English. He certainly did not accept the right of any backward country to exclude English influence. He might be punctilious about diplomatic and legal state-to-state formalities, but he was unlikely to stand any nonsense from the peripheral or the backward, least of all if they seemed arrogant or likely to harm England's welfare and the expansion of

English power. In tone and general direction it was all very much like the promotion of Western values and 'democracy' by the United States and Britain a century and a half later.

Still, it goes without saying that London's chief concerns were domestic. Britain was in the midst of uncertainty, change and social unrest. Issues like religion or Ireland needed urgent attention. The growing towns produced great social problems. So did new inventions, industrialism and general population growth. Industrial growth had, of course, been stimulated by England's hugely successful and economically profitable wars, and concentrated on supplying wartime demands: textiles for uniforms, metal-working, coal and machinery for weapons and munitions, and shipbuilding. By 1815 England had by far the largest and most powerful navy and merchant fleet in the world. These shifts made the new industrial and commercial centres like Manchester, Leeds, Sheffield and Glasgow much more important. The new industries also produced new men, great wealth and much human misery. At times the economy slumped and unemployed workmen smashed machines. Children of ten and younger were working 12-hour days in Northern factories. In some of the mines, half-naked women could be found pulling carts. Yet the factory masters were a tough, competitive breed, pious, hard-working, innovative, who believed in self-denial, honesty and hard work. They were also, like the merchant classes, inordinately proud about making the opening decades of the nineteenth century a time of unprecedented growth. As the editor of the *Leeds Mercury* wrote in 1843, their skill and enterprise 'constitutes the main spring of all the foreign commerce of England ... which has added more to the wealth, population and power of England than the boldest speculator would have thought possible at the close of the last century.'[6]

At the same time, the new political economists and utilitarian philosophers were steadily becoming more influential. Industrial, commercial and governmental opinion was increasingly influenced by the ideas of economists like Adam Smith, David Ricardo and Jeremy Bentham, which seemed to prove the wisdom of the untrammelled market – *laissez faire*.

Shifts in political power were slower to come. Not until 1830/32 was serious parliamentary reform in England promoted by the example of yet another revolution in Paris and the threat of revolution in England itself. A bill to extend the franchise, and give two seats each to the new industrial towns, became law in June 1832. It created half a million new voters, virtually doubling the electorate. The Duke of Wellington mordantly, but accurately, forecast the results of greater democracy. He told the landowners that 'We shall not have a commotion, we shall not have blood, but we shall be plundered by forms of law.'

In foreign policy, the chief principle naturally remained the European balance of power. Here was the centre of world politics. The fate of the British Isles had been tied to Europe for a thousand years and a system of balance there, with England as one of its central pillars, was the prerequisite for England's security and welfare anywhere. It was European powers which had threatened England's security, from the Spanish armada to Napoleon, just as it had been European diplomacy and alliances which contained or removed these threats. Almost all of England's overseas interests, whether of strategy or trade, were influenced, if not governed, by the activities of other European powers. From North America to India, England's eighteenth-century wars with France had largely been about trade and wealth as a means to power in Europe.

As soon as Waterloo was done, therefore, and Napoleon Bonaparte had been safely exiled to the island of St Helena, London took a lead in transforming the anti-French alliance into a Concert of Europe, to manage the essentials of global power. At its core was the idea that, whatever other differences there might be, maintaining the Concert was an essential interest for everyone. It was in this context that French ambitions or Russian expansion needed to be resisted lest they should threaten England's security, prestige and commerce. For instance, if Russia's yearning for Constantinople, and the gateway to the Mediterranean, were ever achieved, how could the expansion of the Czar's power to the Persian Gulf and into the Mediterranean be prevented? Palmerston's Cabinet thought England should

> ... make a stout stand against [Russia's] systematic encroachments on Peace; as we ought to be convinced that she is always pushing on as far and as fast as she can go without war; but that whenever she finds that perseverance in encroachment will lead to forcible resistance, she will pull up and wait for some more favourable opportunity of carrying on her schemes ... .[7]

The wording was eerily similar to that used a hundred years later by an American diplomat, George Kennan, when he laid the intellectual foundations for America's Cold War policies of Containment of the Soviet Union.[8]

Palmerston also took a lead, from 1830, in promoting the independence of Belgium, that potential launching pad for invasions of Britain herself. (The resulting guarantees of that new country by the major powers would bring England into the First World War a mere 70 years later.) And he had a particular loathing of the slave trade. Slavery itself had been effectively ended in England in 1774, but the Atlantic slave trade had not. So far as Palmerston was concerned,

> ... if all the other crimes which the human race has committed, from the creation down to the present day, were added together in one vast aggregate, they would scarcely equal, I am sure they would not exceed, the amount of guilt which has been incurred by mankind, in connexion with this diabolical Slave Trade.[9]

And it was up England to do something about it. For

> As long as England shall ride pre-eminent on the ocean of human affairs, there can be none whose condition shall be so desperate and forlorn, that they may not cast a look of hope towards the light that beams from hence ... (but if England fell) ... for a long period of time, would the hopes of the African be buried in the darkness of despair ...[10]

And in fact, for much of the first half of the nineteenth century the major duty of the Royal Navy was not to fight wars but to combat the slave trade.

What there was not, was enthusiasm for imperial expansion. The empire was expensive, uncertain and created problems. Most of it seemed a disparate collection of territories only vaguely under control. Almost half a century earlier, Bentham had told the French revolutionaries that colonies were useless and should be emancipated.[11] By the 1830s radicals like Richard Cobden and John Bright thought much the same. And as Thomas Babington Macaulay, the most brilliant essayist and historian of his generation, pointed out: 'The reluctant obedience of distant provinces generally costs more than it is worth.'[12] Colonies of British settlement would anyway want independence, like the new United States. Canada might even slip into union with its southern neighbour. Indeed, some Members of Parliament were quite willing to view US independence, not as a defeat, but rather as a fulfilment of British purposes. As one of them pointed out in March 1838: 'The saying "Emancipate your colonies" means ... a great deal more than the mere words ... What! are we to repent of having planted the thirteen English colonies of North America, which have expanded into one of the greatest, most prosperous and happiest nations the world ever saw?'[13]

Not that the empire was about to go away. Imperialism had, inevitably, begun to affect life in England. Sunburned men were returning from India or the West Indies with strange habits or phrases, bringing wealth into the counties before leaving their names in country churchyards or memorial plaques in great cathedrals. Empire was, as empires always are, an arena for adventure, exploration and derring-do. But it also gave status, some political and strategic advantages, maybe even some economic benefit. At least equally important, it was an arena for spreading enlightenment. As an 1837 House of Commons report put it, the aim of the empire was that England should give to the peoples of the world 'the opportunity of becoming partakers of that civilization, that innocent commerce, that knowledge and that faith with which it has pleased a gracious providence to bless our own country.'[14] At the same time, though, colonies should be as self-supporting as possible, especially those of English settlement. A major turning point was an 1840 Bill making colonial governments and their ministers more accountable to their own electors.

It was, of course, India which, with its multitudes, wealth and resources, quickly became the jewel in the empire's crown. It was governed with a light hand. In effect, the English assumed the role of the Mogul emperors, governing millions through local princes and with tiny numbers of English officials. It was for India's sake that the Foreign Office and the Admiralty worried about places from Morocco to Rangoon and from Cape Town to Persia. In the 1830s the progressive disintegration of the Persian Empire fuelled fears about Russia's advances through Central Asia. That seemed to pose a major threat to India and led to English intervention in Afghanistan. Palmerston insisted that Persia could not 'be allowed to serve Russian purposes'. Altogether, as Lord Melbourne remarked morosely 'The Black Sea and the Caucasus and these great Asiatic Empires inflame imaginations wonderfully.'[15]

Given this enormous palette of actual and potential involvements, London found itself – and did so repeatedly for the next century or more – seriously limited in strategies and resources. Britain had, for instance, two main armies. In the 1830s the British army was some 100,000 strong, half of them usually abroad. There was also the army of the East India Company, some 250,000 strong, manned by Indian sepoys with British officers and at Britain's disposal. For a global empire, it was not enough. In 1840, Palmerston's colleague, Lord John Russell, put the point in a rather unfortunate doggerel:[16]

> The Chinese at Canton
> Prodigiously rant on

Our prospects in Turkey
Are lowering and murky
The Frenchmen will task us
With thoughts of Damascus
But though we have stayed in
The Snug post of Aden
And were not such a fool
As to give up Cabul
By such plagues are we curst
Those of Egypt the worst.

But if 'empire' became in some quarters a rather embattled concept, trade did not. It had, after all, been the engine of England's prosperity since the days of Elizabeth I. In the seventeenth and earlier eighteenth centuries that meant mercantilism – the economic cake is finite; if I take a larger slice, yours has to be smaller. But by the 1820s and 1830s Adam Smith's free trade ideas were spreading and were supported by highly practical needs. The war had created large, machine-based industries that needed lower costs and larger markets, which would necessarily have to be overseas. Demobilization brought a flood of cheap manpower for industrial and trading efforts. Moreover, by the 1820s Britain could no longer feed all her people, and freer trade would stimulate the exports needed to buy food. All of which would encourage an international division of labour, benefit everyone, and strengthen England's role as the 'Workshop of the World'. At the same time, it was increasingly obvious that trade could flourish very well without political entanglements, let alone control of lands far afield. Within a decade of newly independent America's invention of the cotton gin in 1793, her cotton exports multiplied by over forty, and flooded into Lancashire and Cheshire factories. Manchester, for instance, long the centre of England's cotton trade, was by the 1830s producing almost one half of the country's total exports. And where the Lancashire cotton industry had in 1760 supported some 40,000 people, by 1830 or so cotton, and its support services in transport, chemicals and so on, supported some 1.5 millions, or maybe one in eleven of the country's entire population.[17]

It was clear that trade, so largely responsible for England's power and prosperity, had to be protected and promoted. Obstacles to it had to be removed. Since human nature was everywhere essentially the same, trade and capitalism would spread uplift, progress and enterprise around the world. For men like Richard Cobden, free trade was actually 'God's

Diplomacy', which would make war redundant and bring about 'universal and permanent peace.'[18] Palmerston supported much of this. In language which American presidents and British prime ministers could only echo 150 or more years later, he and others saw free trade as not just good for England's power and influence, but as likely to promote commercial expansion and the spread of modernity everywhere. It would naturally help to spread Christianity and civilization. These convictions brought a flush of national self-confidence, a sense of righteousness, a conviction of England's benevolence, of the justice and humanity of English purposes, that has rarely been equalled before or since. As Palmerston told Parliament in 1848: 'I may say without any vain glorious [sic] boast ... that we stand at the head of moral, social and political civilization. Our task is to lead the way and direct the march of other nations.'[19]

Others thought so, too. The German economist Friedrich List was quite overcome with envy and admiration:

> In all ages there have been cities or countries which have been pre-eminent above all others in industry, commerce and navigation; but a supremacy such as that [of Britain] which exists in our days, the world has never before witnessed. In all ages, nations and powers have striven to attain to the dominion of the world, but hitherto not one of them has erected its power on so broad a foundation. How vain do the efforts of those appear to us who have striven to found their universal dominion on military power, compared with the attempt of England to raise her entire territory into one immense manufacturing, commercial and maritime city, and to become among the countries and kingdoms of the earth, that which a great city is in relation to its surrounding territory; to comprise within herself all industries, arts and sciences; all great commerce and wealth; all navigation and naval power – a world's metropolis.[20]

In such a context, China was inevitably marginal. It was a peripheral, isolated and somewhat dilapidated entity whose rulers seemed corrupt, inefficient and untrustworthy. Palmerston's biographer remarks: 'It is doubtful whether the foreign secretary had any passion or deep interest to spare to the China issue from the far more vital matters which were in his hands from 1839 to 1841. It occupied surprisingly little space in his private correspondence for those years.' Chinese affairs '... were but sideshows in Palmerston's eastern policy.' A number of mid- or late nineteenth-century books on English foreign policies scarcely bother to mention the Chinese empire at all.[21]

Still, dilapidated or not, for many eighteenth-century Europeans China was huge, mysterious and romantic. Mystery was encouraged by China's isolation. Its sheer size, its wealth, the strange magnificence of its culture and its attitude of lofty superiority to the outside world intrigued Europeans. Its government was sophisticated, hierarchic and centralized. At its head was the Emperor, the 'Son of Heaven'. By 1830 it was the Daoguang emperor: earnest, dutiful, well-meaning but not very effective in trying to reform a corrupt court and government and to deal with signs of dynastic decline such as growing corruption and peasant unrest. In the Chinese order he was, in constitutional theory and principle, ruler in both spiritual and temporal senses, the guardian of peace and prosperity, the model of morality and justice. The people owed him loyalty and obedience, subject only to the vague but immensely powerful notion that he retained the 'Mandate of Heaven' so long as – but only so long as – he maintained just government and proper behaviour.[22] His empire was meant to be a peaceful and stable order, which defined doctrine, judged behaviour and emphasized mutual and collective responsibility. Its rules and regulations were mostly based on Confucian ideas of social harmony and a co-operative striving for the general good. Reports on everything, from every part of the empire, were brought by an army of couriers, on foot, on horse, directly to the Emperor, who met each day with his Grand Councillors to decide on action. Officials of the imperial service, the mandarins, were directly responsible to him. But their effectiveness depended largely on the local gentry, and they were moved from one province to another to avoid 'going native' and have their loyalty to the centre diluted. They were selected by fiercely competitive examinations based on the classics. They were therefore a corps of literary intellectuals, gentleman-scholars, strong on tradition, and included some of the finest essayists and calligraphers in the empire. It was a system of men rather than of laws, with power only limited, in the end, by the right of rebellion. There was no independent judiciary, no system of reliable property or other rights, certainly no encouragement for private enterprise.

This empire regarded itself as the centre of the civilized universe. For the Chinese scholar-bureaucrat 'China' did not mean a state, in the modern sense, at all. There were the Chinese people and, beyond, there was barbarism. In fact, the tax registers of the Qing empire did not bother to list Manchurian tribesmen, Mongols, Tibetans or Turkic-speaking Moslems.[23] China was simply the entity which comprised civilized society, and civilization was an empire without neighbours, if 'neighbours' are people who are also civilized. The Emperor was therefore a figure of universal significance, the mediator between heaven and earth. His significance was expressed, among other things, by the conventional courtesy of the kow-tow – three separate kneelings and prostrations – expected from all persons received into his presence. And since that supremacy was in principle universal, there were no specific territorial limits to his authority. All other rulers were mere vassals, expected to send tribute; although tribute was met with generous imperial patronage. Indeed, the court had virtually no interest in foreign relations, no foreign ministry and no regular machinery for gathering information about the outside world. For example, relations with Vietnam and the South were handled by the Ministry of Rituals.

Consequently, tributary relations carried no decisive political meaning. Rather, it implied homage not to a person, or even a state, but to civilization itself, and a proper global order. To that extent it implied an international order of sorts. But the concept of a treaty between sovereign states was wholly irrelevant, for it was not possible for such a China to be merely one state among many, and even less possible for the Emperor to be just one ruler among others who, as in Europe, were his equals in status. The Emperor's claim to moral supremacy was the rock on which the entire governmental system rested; for the British to claim 'equality' was therefore an attack on the whole system of loyalty and state cohesion within China. Strangers from unknown regions might indeed appear from time to time to admire Chinese civilization, and perhaps to buy its products. But they could hardly be of much concern to the Celestial Empire. They were 'barbarians' – in popular slang, 'foreign devils'. As late as 1860 Chinese official correspondence spoke of a British envoy as 'The English barbarian chieftain.' That treatment even applied to the use of foreign names.[24]

Yet government policies towards foreigners in the sixteenth and seventeenth centuries were tolerant and hospitable. In the sixteenth century Jesuit missionaries, many of them trained scientists, were welcomed and they introduced Chinese scholarship to Europe. In 1557 the Portuguese won a permanent lease of Macao. There was some British trading with China from 1637. By 1687 the Bodleian Library at Oxford seems to have had some 80 Chinese works, as well as Western writings on China. In the 1770s the British East India Company established agents in China and its trade began to move to Canton by the end of the century. The Americans followed suit immediately after independence, in 1784. The first charter of the Canton colony, in 1720, begins: 'Foreigners and Chinese are members of one family … and must be on an equal footing.'[25] That seemed easy at first, since foreign trade was not very significant for the empire as a whole. Its economy was overwhelmingly agrarian and most trading was done within China's borders. Indeed, officials worried that expanding foreign trade might disturb China's domestic balance and peace. As early as 1717 the Emperor warned that 'there is cause for apprehension lest in centuries or millennia to come China may be endangered by collisions with the nations of the West.'[26]

By 1800 this China had entered a time of troubles. In the previous century China had doubled in area, often by methods as brutal as those used anywhere. By the start of the nineteenth century over half of the area of the empire was composed of lands whose native population was not Chinese. Together with that, though, came China's own population growth; and demography, said Auguste Comte, the nineteenth-century French philosopher, is destiny; its effects going deeper, and lasting longer, than those of most other social or economic forces. China's population increased quickly: from the time that Manchu sovereigns assumed the peacock throne in 1644, to 1850, it grew from maybe 100 to nearly 450 millions. That increased crowding on the land and drove Han Chinese migration into neighbouring native lands, including southern parts of the Manchuria that the dynasty had tried to preserve for Manchus. Economic stagnation and ecological damage brought social difficulties. So did religious discontents and official corruption. So the last decades of the century saw a series of rebellions in various parts of the empire. In addition, the regime worried about the loyalty of the ruling class of mandarins, landlords and scholars. The Manchu sovereigns had always placed special reliance on these elites rather than on popular support. The dynasty, and its Manchu followers, never felt themselves to be 'properly' Chinese, and its Han Chinese subjects did not think they were, either. Yet excessive reliance on the civil service meant indulging the bureaucracy, and increasing the gulf between it and the people. There was general unrest and a series of uprisings. Piracy and brigandage became rife. These things fuelled Manchu fears of disaffection.

As for state security, China had always been threatened by the wild horsemen of Central Asia. But by the eighteenth century an altogether more formidable threat appeared as Russia expanded eastwards. Though the Russians gave up, in the 1689 Treaty of Nerchinsk, formal claims to the Amur valley in the borderlands between China and Siberia, that did not stop their general move to the east and south. For Beijing, that was far more dangerous than minor problems on the southern coasts, which were a long way from anywhere that mattered and where no serious threat had ever before arisen. Beyond that, the empire had very little inkling of the way that Western national and industrial revolutions were totally changing the meaning and balance of power in the world. Even so, by 1830 Chinese views of Britain and the West were becoming more alarmed. Britain, in particular, looked like a positively revolutionary state. Her colonial expansion, including the probes from India into Malaya, Burma and Nepal, was especially worrying. Here was Europe on the march in China's immediate neighbourhood.

It was Britain, the leading Western trading power, that followed others and sent the first major Western embassy to China. It was led by Lord Macartney, an Irishman with some previous diplomatic experience at the Russian court of Catherine the Great. It arrived in Beijing in 1793 to try to expand Sino-British trading opportunities and establish official links, and was a total failure. To be sure, even the best of Britain's sinologists knew almost nothing about China's internal affairs or views of the world. The mission's difficulties began with trying to find interpreters. In the end, since no-one competent could be found in England, the mission recruited two young Chinese language teachers from a Catholic college in Naples. When Macartney reached Beijing, he scandalized the Chinese by refusing to kow-tow before the Emperor, thinking it demeaning to an envoy of the King of England. To be sure, the language of subservience expected of barbarians was formal and traditional; on private or unofficial occasions Qianlong and his people did not treat Macartney as an envoy from a tributary. Still, as far as trade was concerned, the Emperor told Macartney blandly: 'We possess all things. I set no value on objects strange or ingenious, and have no use for your country's manufactures.'[27] As an economic assessment, this was badly mistaken. Still, the Emperor's decision was final and remained so even for the subsequent missions of the Dutch in 1795, of the Russians in 1806 and the second British embassy, headed by Lord Amherst, in 1816.

So foreign trade remained concentrated at Canton, where it was of marginal importance to most parts of the empire, and created no great problems. Foreigners could be kept under strict control there, as they were in the North, and imperial revenues increased. Accordingly, a finely elaborated trading system had more or less crystallized by 1760 and remained in place until 1842. As Lord Napier found, it set out in minute detail the conditions under which trading could be done (although the Portuguese were also allowed to trade at Macao).[28] Among the foreigners, there was a sharp distinction between East India Company men and private merchants. Both bought and sold, exported and imported, via the Cohong merchants, without written agreements, at prices which included, but did not separately identify, all official duties and charges. Since tariffs could vary with the rapacity of the local mandarin, foreigners often did not know what the official charges actually were. The East India Company, conforming to Chinese law, treated the Cohong as a unit and traded solely through its members. It confined itself almost entirely to selling British or Indian goods and buying tea, and acquired such a reputation for honest dealing that its goods, bearing the Company's mark, came to be accepted without question. A private trader, on the other hand, could bargain with any Hong merchant in selling the cargo of any ship. He could even conduct much of his business at the outer anchorages, beyond the reach of the Canton authorities. Clearly, such people did not always have the same reputation for straight dealing as the Company. Many of them were Scots – indeed, Britain's entire Eastern trade was largely developed by family and clan groupings, many of them Scots – an educated and energetic lot who had no difficulty in competing with the comparatively somnolent East India Company. At the same time, the Chinese had a civilized habit of allowing foreign communities, living in their own cantonments, some extraterritorial status.

By the 1820s and 1830s this Canton trading system was coming under pressure. There were four kinds of causes: tea, opium and the balance of payments of British India and of China. To begin with, there was the enormous increase of Britain's consumption of Chinese tea. In 1664 Britain probably imported just 2 lbs 2 oz of tea. A little over a century later, by 1784/85, that had grown to over 15 million lbs. Then, with British tea duties sharply reduced, it doubled again to 30 million lbs a year by the early 1830s. Virtually all of it came from China, for the Company did not start to grow tea in India until the 1820s, and did not begin to ship Indian tea to London until 1858. In 1811–19 alone, total British imports from China were valued at over £72 million (tv: some £2.4 billion) with tea worth £70 million (tv: £2.3 billion) of that.[29] In fact, by the early nineteenth century tea was so important to Britain that the East India Company was required by law to keep one year's supply always in stock. The British exchequer benefited, too. By the 1830s the government in London was harvesting £4.2 million (tv: £184 million) from duties on Chinese products imported into Britain, roughly £3.5 million (tv: over £153 million) of it from tea.[30] The revenue from the Chinese tea trade may have been up to 10 per cent of total British government revenue. It is hardly surprising that London was keen to open up what seemed to be the potentially vast internal China market as well.

As time went by, this thirst for tea raised increasingly acute questions of how to pay for it. The Company began, in the obvious way, by selling

British goods like cottons, lead and wool. But China being so largely self-sufficient, demand for British manufactures was quite slender and there were great difficulties with variable and unstable Chinese money anyway. So the tea had to be paid for with gold and silver, Bolivian, Peruvian or French silver currency but especially those silver dollars minted in old or new Spain that the Chinese craved, and most particularly the Carolus dollar of the reign of Charles IV of Spain (1788–1808). Which created increasingly acute problems as the English trade deficit grew to unsustainable levels. But there were some things the Chinese did want to buy, notably raw cotton and, most especially, opium. The Company was, of course, aware that opium trading was illegal in China. But there were also the country (private) traders, British and others, who had the obvious advantage of not operating under the Company's authority. By 1817 three times as much non-European merchandise as British merchandise was coming into Canton and by 1833 it was six times. The bulk of it was opium.

By then smoking opium was becoming a feature of life in China. Opium had been known there since the seventh century and may have been imported by the Arabs. Before the seventeenth century it was taken medically, by mouth, but then came smoking. The Spaniards had brought tobacco smoking from the Americas to the Philippines and then Formosa. From there, tobacco smoking spread to China and other parts of the East. It seems to have been the Dutch in Java who began to smoke a mixture of tobacco and opium as a cure for malaria and from there brought the practice to Formosa. They started to import Patna opium from Bengal in 1659 and a hundred years later just a single Dutch settlement, Batavia in Java, was buying 100 tons a year of it. In diluted form, it was widely used as a stimulant. In China itself opium, in addition to being grown locally, was a recognized import well before 1600. It was traded by the Portuguese, who controlled its import until the 1770s. So British trade in opium, in and from India, seemed at first quite unremarkable. The subsequent and longstanding Bengal opium monopoly became a prize of British conquest. In 1773 the East India Company took control of opium sales in the English-controlled areas of India and soon afterwards of its production as well. By the end of the century the Company had also monopolized the China trade. By the late 1790s annual imports into China – with opium still a normal article of trade – may have been some 4000 chests, with one chest containing some 130 to 160 pounds of opium, depending on the place of origin.

In China, although some imperial officials fulminated against both opium and tobacco smoking, opium was for long available as a legitimate medicine. It was, for instance, useful against dysentery and the only effective painkiller before the invention of modern synthetics. It was even listed on the official customs tariff. The first anti-opium edict did not come until 1729. At this point, the scale of imports was still very small, perhaps some 200 chests per annum. In the 1760s maybe 1000 chests were coming in via Central Asia and Burma; and by 1782 some 1600 chests reached Macao from India. By the end of the century, however, new and more powerful methods of using the drug were in vogue.[31] So more stringent rules were introduced including, in 1796, a ban not just on trading opium but on growing it. The rules now spoke of opium as a 'destructive and ensnaring vice'. They had little practical effect since, by that time, opium was being produced in fair quantities in China itself, as well as in India, Persia, Greece, Bulgaria, Egypt, Yugoslavia and most especially in Turkey.

In the 1820s, as the Chinese authorities found that the mandarinate itself, and the army, were beginning to be affected, they began to introduce even tougher-sounding rules. Both the East India Company and the official Cohong merchant group stopped trading in the drug and made some ineffectual attempts to stop its import. Yet in practice the Chinese administrative classes, indeed the entire administrative system, as well as many of the great merchant houses, remained more or less involved. Numbers of imperial officials not only allowed the drug traffic to continue, but promoted and exploited it, enriching themselves in the process by imposing a fixed fee per chest of opium. In 1821 came disputes among merchants and Chinese officials about sharing the spoils. The Viceroy of Canton, well aware of what was going on, decided to make an example. He briefly stopped the entire tea trade, warned the British, Americans and Portuguese that the anti-opium edicts would in future be properly enforced, and heavily fined or gaoled some Chinese merchants. Yet almost everyone seemed to connive at continuing as before and the official anti-opium edicts remained quite unenforceable.

The reality, then, was that private traders brought in opium from anywhere to fill a growing local demand. That very much included the Americans, who began to come into the China market in the 1790s, selling European goods in Spanish American ports for Mexican silver which they brought to China to pay for tea, porcelain and silks. They seem to have started their opium operations there in 1811 with opium from Turkey. As early as 1814 the foreign merchants created a 'corruption fund' with a levy of $40 per chest of opium, which meant something like $100,000 per annum. By the 1830s, with regular deliveries being made along China's East coast, the fees payable to officials were even higher. The traffic was quite open and from 1827 the *Canton Register* regularly published opium prices, rather as modern newspapers publish stock exchange movements. Not only that, but the trade relied on the Company's certification even once the Company itself had stopped selling opium into China. All concerned relied on the Company's excellent management of its opium monopoly in India, to the point where its trademark was accepted by the Chinese, even for contraband, as a hallmark of quality.

At the same time, large numbers of Chinese officials pocketed not only bribes and shares of the opium profits, but in many cases even filched the revenue from the legal trade rather than remitting it to the Emperor. The result of all this was that the Chinese state began to have adverse balances even for legal trade, while opium consumption entirely reversed the overall balance of trade and payments. What had been a substantial flow of silver into China, to pay for tea, became an even more substantial, and ultimately insupportable, outflow of payments for opium. By 1831 Chinese imports, including opium, may have totalled $17 million compared with exports of $5 million, leaving the firms with a favourable balance of $12 million. Everyone involved in the tea trade naturally developed a strong interest in the welfare of this opium traffic. But the flows also created a complicated, and almost universally misunderstood, financial network.

It has been estimated that in the eleven years from 1829 to 1840 China may have imported only $7.5 million of silver but exported $56 million worth of cash, silver and gold. Certainly domestic silver prices in China rose sharply and many people were convinced that payments to opium smugglers were to blame. It is hardly surprising that some Chinese officials, in debating opium policy, stressed economic issues rather than moral or social ones.[32] But it is not clear, even now, that they understood the full complexities of the Canton currency system. The cash and bullion that traders earned from their opium sales could be banked locally with the Company in exchange for bills on London or Calcutta. That gave the Company large bullion reserves at Canton. These could be used directly to finance Company purchases of tea. All of which meant that, contrary to what almost everyone believed, much of China's 'exports' of silver – possibly three quarters[33] – may never actually have left China. It has been estimated that from 1818 to 1833 some 20 per cent of total Chinese exports were silver; how much of that actually left the country is much less clear.

In any event, all kinds of benefits flowed from this complex network. The earnings from the China trade helped to support the entire British position in the Far East and, most especially, in British India, whose balance of payments came to depend on it. By the early years of the nineteenth century, India seems to have had an annual trade surplus with Canton of approximately $5 million. Which meant, in turn, that much of India's ability to absorb exports from Britain herself came to depend on funds from China, by way of bills on London. Moreover, at the end of the 1820s a decade-long Indian boom collapsed; and at the same time the flow of American silver to China dried up as Americans turned to inward investment. All of which made the opium trade even more critical. By 1830 the Auditor-General of the East India Company, T.C. Melville, declared that: '...India does entirely depend upon the profits of the China trade',[34] possibly yielding one-sixth of Indian revenue. A House of Commons Select Committee of 48 members reported sagely that 'In the present state of the revenue of India it does not appear advisable to abandon so important a source of revenue, a duty upon opium being a tax which falls principally upon the foreign consumer, and which appears upon the whole, less liable to objection than any other which could be substituted.'[35] No parliamentary committee was likely to lose sight of the fact that, as a practical matter, opium production not only played an essential role in the Indian fiscal system, but employed many thousands and had by now a huge influence on land values there.[36] In 1839, when a new Chinese commissioner at Canton (of whom more later) adopted rougher tactics for dealing with the opium trade, Bombay and Calcutta suffered a good deal. Even Britain was directly affected. Altogether, by the 1830s, though some people in Britain disapproved of trading in drugs, only a minority thought that just because a thing was undesirable, the government should do something about it. The East India Company's position on growing opium in India, and selling it there, had much support. As Parliament and public also became aware of the full financial and commercial ramifications of the trade, it was approved of by a solid and highly respectable body of merchants, and even sanctioned by Parliament.

Not surprisingly, perhaps, somewhere along the line the distinction between legal trade and contraband became blurred. In volume as well as value, contraband became much more important than the ordinary, legal foreign trade monopoly at Canton. And foreigners could see, clearly enough, the gap between official Chinese regulations and the actual behaviour of Chinese officials. The East India Company's role was ambiguous, too. It controlled opium growing in British India, giving it great advantages over rival growers in marketing high-grade opium. But opium supplies could also come from independent Indian princes, from Turkey, Persia and very much from China itself. The Company sold refined Indian opium at annual auctions in Calcutta to private firms, which ended the Company's involvement in trading it. The people who then owned and transported it to China were private merchants, who often consigned it to commission agents in Canton for sale. Consequently most of the opium at Canton did not actually belong to the people doing the selling. The Company had no direct responsibility for, or authority over, the Chinese end of the trade. It could and did insist that its ships did not carry opium, and that its officials were solely concerned with the tea trade on which they paid proper duties at Canton. Company Indiamen sailing to China were strictly prohibited from carrying opium 'lest the Company be implicated' in the eyes of the Chinese authorities. The Company could also argue that it had no authority of any kind over the people or activities at Lintin, though that claim was more doubtful. A few years later the British superintendent at Canton summarized the situation briefly in a letter to London.[37]

> No British subjects are [at Canton] without a license from the Company; and the Committee [of senior East India Company officers] in any case of emergency, had it in their power to apprise the Chinese authorities, that the license had been suspended, and that they would in no respect interfere for the adjustment of any debts the parties complained of might contract subsequently to the date of that notice. The British shipping which resorted to China was under the complete control of the committee; they either belonged to the Company, or were chartered by it; and the country ships were furnished with licenses by the Indian Governments, withdrawable at pleasure, either by these authorities, or, in case of exigency, by the committee itself.

Still, for all its complications and difficulties, this Canton trading system worked extremely well. When the House of Commons Select Committee enquired into the China trade in 1830, almost all the witnesses agreed that 'business could be dispatched with greater ease and facility at Canton than anywhere else in the world.' And much of that ease was clearly due to the Chinese Hong merchants, whose honesty and commercial integrity became a byword both in London and in Bombay. 'As a body of merchants we found them able and reliable in their dealings, faithful to their contracts, and large-minded. The monopoly they enjoyed could not have been in the hands of a more able, liberal or genial class of men.'[38]

Even so, by the 1830s British manufacturers and the private traders were impatient with the system, and especially with the East India Company monopoly there, which seemed altogether too timid *vis à vis* the Chinese. For at least 20 years merchants from Manchester, Glasgow and elsewhere had pleaded with Parliament, demanding 'freedom of commerce as the birthright of all Britons.' By 1830 an even stronger campaign for free trade with China began and gathered pace through 1831 and 1832. A delegation to the Prime Minister, Earl Grey, went so far as to argue that opening up the China trade would be of even greater commercial benefit to Britain than opening up India had been. At the same time, everyone agreed that Britain must on no account be drawn into governing in China, as she had formerly been drawn into governing in India.

By 1834 the East India Company, under fire from both traders and Parliament, gave up its China monopoly almost without a fight,[39] and the trade was duly opened up to all comers. As Palmerston wrote in 1841, after hostilities with China had begun: 'It is the business of Government to open and secure roads for the merchant.'[40] But for the private British merchants – who, by 1834, controlled over half of all British trade with China – the end of the East India Company monopoly was in any case not enough. They also wanted to see an end of those official and unofficial Chinese restrictions, including the arbitrary system of Chinese import charges. They wanted much stronger political support from home. In fact, what they wanted was a whole new commercial code. As Adam Smith had pointed out half a century earlier, a restrictive commercial system was irrational. Similar pressures came from India. In May 1829, for instance, 44 Bombay Parsees petitioned the Governor-General to try to secure better trading conditions with China.

By the early 1830s therefore, there were, for the foreign traders at Canton and their associates in India and London, at least two fundamental issues. One was the need to get China to open up its markets to the manufactures which Britain and the West were producing in increasing quantities. That involved the growing general belief in free trade and the prospective benefits to British industry but equally, great benefits for the Chinese themselves, whom such trade would free from the 'capriciousness and corruption' of the Canton officialdom. The other issue was the dispatch of a senior and powerful British representative to Canton, supported, if necessary, by some threat of force to get the place straightened out.

It was this that brought Napier to the Pearl River.

3
It's More Than Trade, Stupid! Canton 1835–38

It says a good deal about London's 'softly, softly' approach to Chinese issues that there was no reaction at all to Napier's death. Palmerston himself had spoken of Napier's 'foolish pranks'. All the British Cabinet did was to appoint his former assistant, John Francis Davis, to succeed him. Davis had accompanied the Amherst embassy to Beijing in 1816, and then spent twenty years in China for the East India Company. He now promoted a policy of being 'perfectly quiet,' with no attempt to negotiate with the Chinese or even to expand trade. That tallied well enough with Chinese views since, as soon as Napier was dead, the Governor-General ordered the English traders, as usual through the Hong merchants, to send home for a new head man, but 'a commercial man, conversant with business. It is unnecessary again to appoint a barbarian headman, thereby causing friction and trouble.'[1] Here was traditional policy, reinforced by China's experiences on the trading frontiers of Central Asia: taming barbarians like Kazakhs or Mongols by rule through local governors and laws.

But barely two months after taking office, in January 1835, Davis left, to be replaced by his deputy, Sir George Robinson, with Elliot as his number two. The new man's opinion of the Chinese was much the same as Napier's: Robinson wrote of 'this barbarous nation, arrogant in proportion to their ignorance ...'.[2] But when, on 8 March 1835, the Canton governor and the *hoppo*, acting with imperial approval, sent yet another order to restate the old regulations in even more stringent form, the new Superintendent continued to be 'quiet'. Robinson, too, left the scene at the end of 1836.

But the country merchants were not content with 'quiet'. The end of the East India Company monopoly made their problems worse. As trade increased and more traders came to Canton, the existing system seemed more inadequate than ever. On the Chinese side, various difficulties, including growing competition among tea suppliers, weakened the Hong group. Some members even went broke. At the same time, the foreigners found themselves paying higher prices. The old East India Company monopoly had had a bargaining clout which, together with foreign credit devices, kept the price of Chinese goods down. Now that independent foreigners faced the Hong monopoly, prices rose. There may have been increases of 25 per cent for silk and 55 per cent for tea.[3] At the same time American manufactures, especially in textiles, were undercutting British sales, so increasing even further the importance of opium trading. There were new security worries too, as the Chinese started to build more forts along the river and the coast.

Furthermore, for the country traders especially, not only were markets kept closed by the Cohong system, and not only were they still subject to the whims of corrupt Chinese officials, but patriotism had been affronted: Napier and the British flag had been insulted. They made a good deal of that in London. In December 1834, 64 merchants headed by James Matheson and William Jardine signed a memorial to King William IV asking for stronger action. It had been unwise, they said, to leave Napier without power to negotiate, or to have submitted quietly to China's 'arrogant assumption of superiority'. Because 'the most unsafe of all courses that can be followed in treating with the Chinese government, or any of its functionaries, is that of quiet submission to insult, or such unresisting endurance of contemptuous or wrongful treatment, as may compromise the honour, or bring into question, the power of our country.'[4] London should send out an experienced diplomat to negotiate directly with Beijing. He should arrive with, at least, a couple of Royal Navy frigates, and explain to the Chinese how easy it would be to put a stop to China's entire coastal trade. Such a display, said the memorial, far from being likely to lead to conflict, would be the surest way of avoiding it. The envoy should also demand an end to the Cohong monopoly, an extension of Chinese trading facilities to other ports, and reparation for the insults offered to Napier. Davis was contemptuous of this document from a 'vulgar rabble of free traders' and, just before he resigned, wrote to Palmerston, by now back at the Foreign Office, to condemn it.

Not that there was much alternative to being 'quiet'. For one thing, while the government was interested in free trade principles, it cared little about the details and specifics of trade, or the fate of individual firms, let alone about giving priority to commercial matters over state relations. For another, the superintendents and their deputies still had neither permission to negotiate with the Chinese nor, as Palmerston kept reminding them, authority over British subjects in China.[5] They could certainly not expel or deport British subjects from the empire.[6] Indeed, on 22 July 1836 Palmerston went further, writing that the superintendents should

> exercise great caution in interfering ... with the undertakings of British merchants. In the present state of our relations with China, it is especially incumbent upon you, while you do all that lies in your power to avoid giving just cause of offence to the Chinese authorities, to be at the same time very careful not to assume a greater degree of authority over British subjects in China than that which you in reality possess.[7]

Coincidentally, five days later Captain Elliot wrote a prescient note to the Foreign Office about the lack of control over British merchants, and especially over the opium traffic. '... [A]t last,' he wrote, 'some gross insult will be perpetrated, that the Chinese authorities will be constrained to resent; they will be terrified and irritated, and will probably commit some act of violence that will make any choice but armed interference, impossible to our own government.'

Yet the freedom of movement allowed to the Superintendent and, for that matter, to the Governor-General, was critical, since any twenty-first-century 'fine tuning' of policy would have been quite impossible. Even within China, a dispatch from Canton to Beijing, moving by horse relays, took some twenty days, so that an answer to a question might be to hand in six weeks. But before the invention of steamships, or the creation of the Suez canal, the time between sending a dispatch by sail between London and Canton, and the arrival of a reply, could be up to seven to ten months. So when Palmerston wrote on 7 June 1836 to dismiss Robinson, the Superintendent did not hand over to Elliot until December.

Charles Elliot was round-faced, courageous and intelligent. He also had a lovely, dark-haired French wife from the West Indies, named Clara, who was witty, well-educated and evidently quite charming. Charles was the son of a former Governor of Madras, and well connected in London, especially to his first cousin, the Earl of Minto, whose family had once warmly received the teenage Palmerston after his father's death. Another cousin was Lord Auckland, Governor-General of India and another, more distant, relative was the Earl of Malmesbury. Before coming to China, Elliot had had a decent career in the Navy and with the Colonial Service – in Navy attempts to stop the Atlantic slave trade, and as 'Protector' of not-yet-freed slaves in British Guiana. But there may have been questions about him. Given his connections, one might have expected him to go further and faster. Perhaps he was kept back by a combination of natural acuity with a certain undiplomatic bumptious-ness and, not least, a tendency to know better than his superiors. He was clearly aggrieved at finding that his first China appointment was as mere Master Attendant, and wrote that he only accepted from a sense of duty. In fact, he badly needed the money. And while serving under Robinson, his private letters made clear his resentment at serving 'under men, my inferiors in rank, and my juniors in age' whom he had to prop up.[8] That he was appointed to the top post now was surely due, at least in part, to Davis' high opinion of him. Nevertheless, while in charge at Canton, he would repeatedly make it clear that he knew better than the people giv-ing him instructions, especially Palmerston. The fact that his despatches were distinctly long-winded can't have helped either.

On the larger question, Elliot had long before put sensibly moderate views in his private correspondence with senior people in the Foreign Office.[9] He thought that Napier had failed because of his own pretensions to exalted official rank. He thought, as Wellington had done, that existing trading conditions were quite tolerable and that in matters of protocol Chinese rules should be accepted until a better *modus vivendi* emerged. 'Practically speaking, the aggregate of our trade with China is less bur-dened than it is in any other country with which we have commerce to an analogous extent.' Conciliation would achieve everything needed. Britain should not send out a high official, or make a demonstration of force, unless some specific cause arose. Nor would a formal treaty be much use, since the Chinese were very good at interpreting any text as might suit them. For example, if some specific article of imports attracted exces-sive duties, the officials would just list the shipment as being something else. It would be silly to disturb a most prosperous commerce just to let some of the English merchants 'try their hands at the social, commercial, political and religious regeneration of this Empire.'

Once Elliot took charge, he promptly reported – correctly enough – that London's conciliatory policy, which he himself supported, was extremely unpopular among the merchants at Canton.[10] But, like his predecessors, he found himself between the upper millstone of the Celestial Empire's determination not to recognize any other state as an equal, and the lower one of British resolve to maintain equality and refuse to accept the protocol of a tributary state. Nevertheless, Elliot wrote in proper form to the new viceroy Deng Tingzhen – Lu having died the previous September – giving notice of his appointment and asking for a passport to go to Canton. Beijing duly agreed, and he stayed for some three weeks from mid-April 1837. Five days after his arrival, he wrote privately to his sister, emphasizing that his views differed from those of the government in London but '[my] own judgment in such matters is as likely to be a reasonable judgment, as my Lord Palmerston's. I think of what I am about: he neither knows nor thinks any thing about the matter…'. Presumably it was just as well that the letter was confidential. With the Chinese, though, Elliot's conciliatory tactics produced some progress: the Governor began to indicate that he would receive communications from Elliot under unofficial cover, and allowed Elliot to move freely between Macao and Canton.

But Palmerston was distinctly unamused. He insisted, repeatedly, that the Superintendent should communicate directly with the Governor, that messages were on no account to be sent through the Hong merchants or in the form of petitions. He was quite unambiguous and emphasized the point repeatedly between 1836 and 1839.[11] The first of these letters reached Elliot on 21 November 1836, when he was at Canton again. It clearly meant that he could make no further concessions to Chinese protocol. Nor did Beijing give its own Governor more room for manoeuvre. So Elliot, unable to find a way of communicating which would satisfy both Palmerston and the Chinese, withdrew to Macao. But he also suggested that Palmerston should send a letter directly to Beijing and have a warship of the Royal Navy carry it north, to the mouth of the Bei He (Peiho) river that gave easy access to the capital.

By this time China was experiencing a relentless increase in opium demand, probably fuelled by general social unrest. Between 1830 and 1836 imports multiplied to perhaps 30,000 chests per annum. One result was a fundamental policy debate about opium, trade and currency matters. As we have seen, back in 1828 the Canton governor had issued a proclamation denouncing opium smoking and ordering a more rigorous enforcement of the laws against it. One response by the opium traders at Canton was to leave anything smacking of local bribery and smuggling to the Chinese buyers. Another was to get opium finance and transport even more inextricably mixed up with the financing of China's legal imports, which also came via the East India Company through the estuary to Whampoa.[12] For opium trading spread from the Lintin base to the east and north coasts. That, in turn, had two important results. One was greatly to increase total Chinese demand for opium. Another was that the trade was done not for goods but for cash and bullion. Although this was promptly used, back at Canton, to buy tea or other Chinese exports, not only did the trade seem to be spreading opium smoking everywhere but to entail, as well, a seriously distortion of the Chinese economy through a growing outflow of bulk silver. The inflow of opium was therefore a serious economic danger as well as a moral poison and a solvent of social relations. It was nothing less than a facet of barbarian aggression. Yet the entire Chinese administrative system, as well as the great merchant houses, seemed more or less involved. Growing numbers of imperial officials were not just permitting the drug traffic, but promoting and exploiting it. By the later 1820s the patrol fleet established to stop coastal opium smuggling routinely let smugglers pass for a fee of 36,000 *taels* a month.[13] The admiral in charge, Admiral Han, himself transported opium for a cut of the profits.

Later, once ships arriving at Canton had to certify that they were opium-free, shipments were simply unloaded into receiving ships anchored outside the harbour and beyond the Pearl River. Men like William Jardine and James Matheson took to operating largely from Lintin island which, though technically Chinese, was in practice beyond the empire's control. So Chinese wholesalers could buy, in Canton, certificates from the traders which could be exchanged for opium at these fortified hulks at Lintin. The opium chests could then be taken on by fast armed boats, built and operated by Chinese smugglers, who fought or bribed their way to inlets or up the river systems to distribution points run by gangsters. From there it was distributed, often under the protection of anti-Manchu secret societies. These Chinese shippers and distributors were often financed by major Chinese banking houses, which could use opium trading profits to make official loans to the Chinese government. Often, indeed, the boats delivering opium were themselves mandarin boats meant to stop the smuggling. One method of transporting opium to the more northern regions of China was said to be by the annual dispatch of imperial junks carrying presents from Canton for the Emperor. By 1835 some foreign estimates suggested that every single officer of the Canton government was involved in the trade.[14] Moreover, since the smugglers paid off the revenue authorities with tax-like regularity, they helped the controller of customs to carry out his unofficial duty to supply large quantities of money to the Emperor's private funds. The imperial household itself therefore profited handsomely. No wonder the foreigners thought Chinese official protestations were only for show.

By 1836 it was clear that the opium prohibitions had become quite ineffective and the Emperor asked for a serious discussion of policy options on what might be done about foreign trade, opium smuggling, currency difficulties and how to manage all that with the available but limited administrative means. Senior officials understood that, as the Napier episode had shown, pressure on trade could force the British to stay within the rules at Canton. But that would neither stop opium smuggling nor resolve currency problems. There were no effective mechanisms for on-shore policing, let alone for effective action against native smugglers. Since there was no independent police force, officials had to depend on civil informants, who might just be rival smugglers wanting to put competitors out of business. Nor could the military be relied on,[15] partly because they were themselves aiding and abetting the opium distribution and partly because they were anyway greatly weakened by opium consumption. That had important social effects, for instance leaving southern China open to insurrection.[16] Already in 1832 imperial troops had been notably ineffective in dealing with rebellious Yao aborigines on the Hunan-Guangdong border. Because the shocking truth was, as an investigating imperial clansman discovered, that the troops were themselves stoned on opium. Even if there had been an effective force, the Napier episode had shown all too clearly that China lacked the means to drive away well-armed foreign ships. And Guangdong was by no means the only problem, since opium use was even greater elsewhere. By the early 1830s as many as 40 per cent of the half million people in Souzhou (Soochow) may have been on opium.[17]

In any event, by 1836 the chief divisions of opinion on what might be done were very much those of the agonized drug policy debates in the Western world during the 1980s and 1990s: legalizers versus prohibitionists. The debate opened in June 1836 with a memorial to the Emperor from the Vice-President of the Sacrificial Court, a former judge. It recommended legalization. Opium had long been known, had medicinal value and had, in the previous century, been included in the official customs tariff. Since then, penalties had been gradually increased to long terms of imprisonment, even death, but there were more smokers than ever, together with a serious export of silver. Trying to stop the whole trade would be futile. Smuggling could not really be halted. The prohibitions, being futile, should be repealed. Opium should be legalized as a medicine, duty paid on imports, and opium sold only to the Hong merchants, though a ban on smoking might be continued for soldiers, scholars and officials. In fact, domestic production should be allowed, too, and that would in time drive the foreign traders out of business. Support came from other quarters including, influentially, a Grand Councillor and one of the foremost scholars of his generation, Ruan Yuan. Clearly, legalization would end corruption and crime.

The Emperor asked the Governor-General, Governor and *hoppo* at Canton to comment. They, in turn, asked the Hong merchants, who – despite the fact that Viceroy Deng was himself pocketing regular payments on illegal opium imports[18] – also supported legalization. Indeed, they said, a state monopoly on opium could be established, with foreigners duly taxed and traders licensed by the *hoppo*. So the official reply to the Emperor in September 1836 agreed that the various edicts against importing or smoking opium had failed, and that the evils of the vice had increased. Opium should be legalized as a dutiable import, under strict regulation. Not surprisingly, everyone became so confident that this would happen that some people started speculative buying.

In the meantime, the moralists' response to the Emperor – from three senior officials, the Vice-President of the Board of Ceremonies, the Censor for the Kiangnan circuit and, most importantly, the Supervising Censor of the Board of War[19] – came in October 1836. They argued that evil should be removed, not tolerated; and crime was no reason for legalization. If opium was legalized, everyone would use it and China's already large domestic opium production would even be encouraged. As it was, half a dozen provinces had already sent memorials asking for tougher prohibitions, not looser ones. Opium was causing serious economic distortions but, even so, the chief objection to it was not economic but the way in which it corrupted and weakened the people. That was, in fact, why the English had introduced it to China, following the precedent of the Dutch who had conquered Java by such methods. Only total prohibition would save the army from ruin through opium, or officials and scholars, who were suffering equally. The only logical alternative to legalization was moral reform and strict punishment of the opium merchants.

The Emperor asked the Canton authorities to reconsider. But in late 1836 he sided with the prohibitionists. He may well have been influenced by last-minute revelations that some of the legalizers were involved in illegal currency dealings[20] as well as by broader fears of rebellion. In any event, he ordered a more energetic enforcement of the laws against smugglers and dealers, as well as the ban on the export of uncoined silver[21] to pay for the drug. At Canton, Deng duly clamped down. At the end of that month, a number of prominent foreign merchants were charged in connection with the opium trade and on 23 November they were expelled. Not that the expulsion was enforced; and during the opening months of 1837 Elliot and the Canton merchants continued to think that the opium trade would soon be legalized. In fact, during late 1836 and early 1837 Elliot, who was well aware that Deng was taking a cut from opium smuggling,[22] repeatedly advised London that legalization was likely.

But by this time views at home were hardening both on principles and particulars. As far as London could see, the Chinese had arbitrarily withdrawn established merchant privileges. It was up to the imperial government, not the British, to redress such grievances. In any case, as far as the Victorians were concerned, the ambition to open up China to trade was wholly admirable. Even that strongest of mid-century critics of British imperial expansion, the radical Richard Cobden, was in favour of opening up. In a modern world of investment and trade, China and Japan could not possibly be allowed to remain isolated; and, in any case, free trade was the blood-brother of international peace, welfare and virtue, even of Christian advancement. The specifics of the current situation pointed in the same direction. A stream of pamphlets had explained the defenceless position of British merchants at Canton and argued that the government must intervene to restructure the entire system of commercial relations with China. Some had spoken frankly about threats of force. Matheson promoted these ideas personally in England from the moment he got back in 1835. He was not alone. The government was receiving representations from the mill-owners and merchants in Manchester and elsewhere. By 1836 Palmerston was reading memorials from the Manchester Chamber of Commerce, from Liverpool, from Glasgow, stressing the importance to Britain's economic welfare of the China trade, let alone of its huge potential for expansion. It was not even just a matter of British exports. Canton was an outlet for some £3 million per annum (tv: over £130 million) of Indian goods and those sales gave to India a greatly increased ability to buy British manufactures. So that Britain, and British subjects, faced a possible loss of some £5 million per annum (tv: some £220 million) quite apart from the dangers facing the unprotected British merchants at Canton, or problems created by the whims of the local mandarins or Hong merchants.

For instance, Palmerston received a letter from a Mr H. Hamilton Lindsay, a former East India Company official,[23] which emphasized that while the East India Company monopoly on the China trade had been abolished, the Chinese monopoly on Canton trade had not. Not only that, but the Chinese were heaping insults and humiliations on the people who dealt with them. Only two kinds of remedy were feasible: a forcible demand for redress, or the withdrawal of all British Commissioners and an end to all political relations with China.

> I am in no way prepared to dispute the general principle, that if a stranger goes to reside in a foreign country he is bound to obey its laws and conform to its regulations; but ... it always presupposes that

your intercourse is with a civilised nation, that the laws and regulations to which your compliance is required are clear and defined, and
that they give reasonable protection to life and property. Now in
China this is not the case ...[24]

Moreover, the Chinese were determinedly arrogant and insulting:
'...terms are premeditatedly used by the Chinese in the most insulting
sense, and with no object but the deeply rooted one of persuading themselves that all foreigners are beings morally degraded and inferior to
Chinese ...'.

As to what should be done, Mr Lindsay went on: 'we have on so many
occasions used threats and then retracted them, that I cannot doubt the
Chinese will refuse all concessions to mere negociation [sic], and thus
render an appeal to arms necessary.' Britain should send a small naval
force to interdict coastal shipping. Even then, '... our entire demands
should be no more than a commercial treaty on terms of equality.' That
should address such things as Chinese customs duties, which were quite
inadequately defined, with the result that actual demands for payment
could be up to ten times what they were supposed to be. But the British
should take no land, not even some tiny island. They should also avoid
irritating the general population, which was remarkably non-
nationalist. Britain's attitude should be that '... our only wish is to cultivate friendly intercourse with the Chinese; that, however, is rendered
impossible by the oppressive acts of ... government.' Britain should
make clear that it wanted to liberate trade, not rob the Chinese, nor seize
territory. When a force was sent, all provisions should be punctually
paid for. Moreover, if such an operation were mounted, the French and
Americans would also be glad of it.

The Chinese should, Lindsay went on, discontinue insults and offensive assertions of their national superiority. That was of particular
importance for general British public opinion which, so far as the China
merchants were concerned, was altogether too complacent and supine.
James Matheson – to be sure, not an unbiased witness – complained
privately that 'The good people of England think of nothing connected
with China but tea and the revenue derived from it, and to obtain these
quietly will submit to any degradation ...'. But in 1836 he published a
pamphlet that became widely read. It was entitled 'The Present Position
and Future Prospects of the China Trade'[25] and argued that China could
become a vast market for British cotton goods. But current policy there
was due to the 'marvellous degree of imbecility and avarice, conceit and
obstinacy' of the Chinese, who were '... uniformly overbearing and

insulting to all those who happen to be in their power, but cringing and abject to those who exhibit a determination to resist them.'[26]

For most of London, however, there were still quite other things to worry about. Like the destruction of the House of Commons by fire in 1834 (an event dramatically and marvellously depicted in a painting by Turner). Or the way in which London was growing into a great urban metropolis. Or the death of William IV in mid-1837. Or the accession of the 18-year old Queen Victoria who, for all her reliance on her Prime Minister, the 'dear, wise, witty Lord Melbourne', or the advice dinned into her ear by her uncle Leopold, now King of the Belgians, turned out quite quickly to be a 'little queen with a mind of her own.' Or social problems or Poor Law reform or, as ever, Ireland. Anyway, in the same year of 1837 came that general election in which Palmerston went to some trouble to make friendly journalists comfortable in Devon. And the public giggled when one voter told a Tory candidate at Canterbury 'Sir, I would as soon vote for the devil.' Only to be asked: 'But Sir, if your friend should not stand, may I hope for your support?' Some months later, in 1838, there was even the excitement of an insurrection in Canada. So, as late as 1837 another China merchant was writing, from London, to Jardine in Canton: 'The fact is ... the people appear to be so comfortable in this magnificent country, so entirely satisfied in all their desires, that so long as domestic affairs, including markets, go right, they cannot really be brought to think of us outlanders ...'[27]

Still, for official London as well as the merchants, the truculence and arrogance with which the Chinese authorities treated foreigners were increasingly irritating. And while the British public cared nothing about Chinese 'conceit and obstinacy', let alone about diplomatic protocol, gross insults to the British flag and press stories about the imprisonment of Englishmen in Canton, even threats to their families, were another matter entirely. No doubt some of this merely had the intellectual voltage of the coffee houses. Nevertheless, as one writer put it:

All that presented itself to the mind of average man was the fact that Englishmen were in danger in a foreign country; that they were harshly treated and recklessly imprisoned; that their lives were in jeopardy, and that the flag of England was insulted. There was a general notion, too, that the Chinese were a barbarous and ridiculous people, who had no alphabet, and thought themselves much better than anyone else, even the English, and that, on the whole, it would be a good thing to take the conceit out of them.[28]

Chinese complaints about opium, too, were just hypocrisy. The pro-merchant lobby argued consistently that it was not the English merchants but corrupt Chinese officials who were to blame for the evil consequences of opium smoking. The mandarins themselves were hand in glove with the smugglers. In fact, seeing what the profits were, the official import bans had much less to do with efforts to end consumption of the stuff, than with protecting China's domestic opium production and profits.

It would have been impossible for Palmerston to ignore this volume of views and advice, even if he had wanted to. Not that he did want to, since much of it tallied with his own patriotic instincts. So, in the midst of his larger concerns about Belgium or the security of India, or the Atlantic slave trade, he had some five items on his Chinese agenda. The first, as always, was insistence on state equality and the honour of the British flag. The second was security and fair treatment for British subjects in China. A third was the complex issue of the mounting debts owed by Chinese to British traders. The fourth was the general issue of trade and its expansion into China. And the last was the matter of opium.

The temperature at Canton was also rising. The authorities began to clamp down and succeeded in breaking one smuggling ring. They even destroyed a number of Chinese-operated galleys onshore in the Bay of Canton. But too many vessels were operating along the coast and some merchants started to send armed boats under the British flag all the way up the Pearl river. There were armed clashes between mandarin junks and boats carrying contraband, but the traffic was not halted. In fact, the prices of smuggled goods dropped, suggesting an increase in supply. In August/September Elliot received several Chinese 'orders' to stop the traffic and remove the receiving ships anchored at various places like Lintin. 'Foreign countries would not endure contraventions of their laws; how much more must the government of this empire punish the contumacious disobedience of barbarians.'[29] On 4 August 1837 a new command arrived, by express order of the Emperor, calling 'on the English superintendent to send away all the receiving ships' within ten days; and on 17 August a fresh document arrived, asking him to explain why the various earlier orders had not been obeyed.[30] A month later, on 18 September, the Governor-General was even more explicit, writing that the King of England 'has sent the Superintendent Elliot to Canton to hold offenders in check' and he should now send the storage ships away. On the following day Elliot was ordered to stop the opium traffic on China's east coast as well.

The trouble was, of course, that Elliot still had no authority to do any-thing of the kind, even to British merchants, let alone the American, French, Dutch, Danish and Spanish ships operating there. He could hardly ignore Palmerston's warning that he should not assume greater authority over British subjects than he had, in fact, been given. However, the Chinese were now assuming that Elliot indeed had proper authority both over British subjects and over trade. So Elliot replied that he could not tell what might be the nationality of ships outside the port, and anyway he had no authority over non-British ships. This produced another salvo from the Canton prefect, on 29 September. It was sent directly to Elliot, in the form of an order to an inferior. To which Elliot responded that his authority extended only to regular trade with China, that is, not to irregular or smuggling trade.

On 19 November Elliot wrote to Palmerston to say that this state of affairs was threatening the entire China trade. He urged London to send out a special commissioner to somewhere other than Canton, perhaps to the island of Zhoushan (Chusan), near the estuary of the Yangzi. He should be escorted by two or three ships. This envoy should explain to Beijing directly how impossible it was for Britain to do what China wanted, since over half of China's opium imports came from non-British areas and the British naturally had no authority to intervene in foreign nations' trade. Even opium grown in Bengal could easily reach China via somewhere else.

It has to be emphasized that at no point were the British authorities in favour of opium smuggling, even though most people thought that opium was no worse than gin or whisky. Three successive superintend-ents, Davis, Robinson and Elliot, all disliked the trade. Sections of British public opinion, especially Nonconformists, Evangelicals, High Church Tories and those associated with missionaries, were increasingly uneasy about the opium business. Throughout the decade Palmerston himself had no trouble in acknowledging China's right to stop opium imports, or with the notion that 'any losses would have to be suffered by the par-ties' doing the trading. True, the opium trade was of great importance to Indian finances and to purchases of China tea. One observer thought that by the 1830s the opium trade may have been the largest commerce of the time in any single commodity.[31] Even so, London was less worried about a prospective end to the opium trade than about time to develop alternative ways of paying for tea and silks. The idea that it might be ended by Chinese action was fine. So was the idea that China might legalize opium, even though it was clear that, if that was done, sooner rather than later Chinese production would drive out imports. What was not fine was the idea that Britain might try to police China's coasts. Nor was there any point in trying to stop Indian supplies at source, for Chinese demand would only be filled by opium from Turkey, Persia or the Malay archipelago while any ban on British-owned shipping would only give the trade to the eager Americans and to flags of convenience. As some people in London argued: '... with one or two exceptions, every American [commercial] house in China was engaged in the trade... in fact, both in the act which originated the dispute [of 1839] and the insults and outrages consequent thereon, our transatlantic brethren have had their full share...'[32]

Beyond all that, the core issue, which was never satisfactorily resolved, was jurisdiction, with its clear implications for state sovereignty. That foreigners should largely govern themselves was, as we have seen, not new. As early as the ninth century China had granted such privileges to Arabs who built a mosque at Canton. Then and later, foreigners were also allowed to govern themselves by their own laws and deal with foreigner-to-foreigner suits, crimes or breaches of the peace, although the Chinese maintained a right of intervention in serious cases. Such extra-territorial jurisdiction was informal and not intended as a surrender of Chinese sovereignty. But the system also rested on the traditional Chinese concept of group responsibility, so that chiefs, such as ships' captains, could be held responsible for crimes by those under their command. Chinese practice also made the group responsible for an individual's offence if the offender was not delivered to justice. Someone had to be punished for a crime, even if he turned out to be a scapegoat. That had created problems in the past. In 1773 the Portuguese at Macao tried an Englishman for allegedly killing a Chinese. He was found not guilty, but Qing officials insisted on re-trying and executing him. In 1780 a Frenchman killed a Portuguese in a fight. The Chinese forced him out of his refuge with the French consul and had him unceremonially strangled. In 1784 a salute fired by the *Lady Hughes* had accidentally killed a Chinese onlooker. A sailor was eventually turned over and unceremoniously strangled. Similar things happened to the English again in 1807 and once more in 1821 to an Italian sailor aboard an American ship, the *Emily*.

So by European standards, many Chinese judicial decisions seemed profoundly unjust. For the British (and the Americans), it was fundamental that their citizens could not be subjected to such an arbitrary, unreliable, corrupt and altogether unacceptable Chinese judicial system;[33] or, indeed, surrendered to local Chinese authorities unless they had been found guilty by their own people. But in that case, who should have authority to deal with smugglers, with drunken sailors, with merchants who broke Chinese laws, with Chinese who had grievances against Englishmen? London, in making the 1833 changes, had provided for the creation of some British courts but that had been sidelined by Palmerston. Wellington, at the Foreign Office in 1835, had immediately seen that the English 'officer must have great powers to enable him to control and keep in order the King's subjects'.[34] In the same year Robinson had made similar arguments about civil cases. Elliot sent repeated pleas, continuing to believe that the Canton superintendent had to be given powers to deal with British smugglers who were '... men whose rash conduct cannot be left to the operation of Chinese laws without utmost inconvenience and risk, and whose impunity ... is dangerous to British interests ...'.[35] Or, again, that 'We want police regulations to which Chinese could resort.'[36]

Still nothing happened. In November 1836 Palmerston did ask the Treasury for a draft Bill to create a British Court in China. But this immediately ran into difficulties. In Parliament, the Opposition worried about giving the Superintendent power to expel British subjects from China, or even civil jurisdiction in cases between British subjects. Some, like the East India and China Association in London, objected to giving the Canton superintendent sweeping power to determine offences. Others worried that no non-Englishman would have to submit to such a British court. Anyway, and especially since Palmerston did not seem to get very far in trying to get Chinese agreement to such a court, setting it up would lead to dispute with the imperial government. In fact the Chinese, given their long tradition of leaving foreigners to deal with foreigners, would probably have been quite happy with most of the proposed British arrangements, but the objections in London proved decisive. Various lesser expedients were suggested from time to time, but none ever came to anything. The upshot was that the government stuck to its refusal either to engage British power in policing China's coasts, or to set up its own machinery to control British subjects there.

There were other civil and commercial problems, too, including the increasing debts owed by Hong merchants to foreign traders. They stemmed from commerce, or foreign loans, or even from the customs duties payable by Hong merchants on behalf of foreigners. Since the 1770s a number of Chinese firms had been bankrupted in such ways, in spite of official prohibitions against incurring debts to foreigners or borrowing money from them.[37] Even worse, the Hong merchants' money, which should have gone to settle each season's accounts with foreign traders, could be unexpectedly used up to meet demands from various mandarins. These might range from contributions to flood relief, or birthday presents to the Emperor, to straight gifts to various local and regional officials themselves. Not surprisingly, interest rates on loans were high: creditors could ask for rates ranging from 12 to 20 per cent per annum. The sums involved were substantial and the grievances of the British traders were essentially two: first, that major reasons for the debts were the official and unofficial exactions of China's own mandarins; and second, that discussions about these debts often dragged on for years.

Even more important, though, than opium, debts or jurisdictional problems, was the physical protection of English people and property. On this, perhaps a naval display would help. Wellington had, some years earlier, suggested sending a 'stout frigate' and some other vessel of war, to police British subjects and protect British interests. Not to mention the need to police waters notoriously swarming with pirates. Palmerston made a similar request to the Admiralty in March 1836 and again in September of the next year. In February 1837 Elliot, too, wrote again to ask for a naval force to be sent to protect British interests in China and 'for the relief of the whole trade from the embarrassment into which it is thrown by the restrictive spirit of the local govern-ment'.[38] His dispatches, written at the start of February and again at the end of April 1837, reached London in mid-July and early October respectively. This time Palmerston reacted more strongly to Elliot's hints about possible trouble. He suggested to the Admiralty that a warship or two should visit China, to protect British interests, back Elliot's repre-sentations to the Chinese and help maintain order among British sailors at Canton. It was a demonstration, meant to focus Beijing's attention on the need for a more predictable system at Canton, not a move to change Chinese methods of controlling either smugglers or commerce. The new commander-in-chief of the Royal Navy's East India station, Rear-Admiral Sir Frederick Maitland, duly arrived on the China coast in mid-July 1838 in his flag-ship, the 72-gun *Wellesley* – massively more powerful than any collection of Chinese junks – accompanied by a corvette and a brig. He was under orders to avoid any use of force except in 'extreme necessity'. On 15 July the Governor-General was informed, and promptly began to strengthen his forts and maritime defences. The Admiral carefully announced his arrival to the Chinese, via Elliot, explaining that he was merely carrying out his government's obligation to see that British ships and subjects were 'duly protected from injury and insult, as is the case in all other portions of the globe.' Elliot went to Canton at the end of July, and wrote, asking the Governor-General to

send officers to communicate with the Admiral. Once again, the letter
was returned, to rising British irritation, for not being marked 'petition'.
Other kinds of friction were increasing, too. Chinese warning shots were
fired at a small British civilian vessel at the Bogue. She was boarded to
see whether the Admiral, or soldiers, sailors, or women were on board,
in which case she would not be allowed to move upstream. A few days
later, at the start of August, the Admiral moved three warships up to
Chuenbi (Chuenpi) and demanded an explanation. He had no wish, he
explained, to violate any Chinese customs or prejudices, but would not
tolerate any insult to his flag.[39] Maitland was met by the local Chinese
naval commander, Admiral Guan and, after an exchange of courtesies,
withdrew his ships.

By October, Maitland left again for India, leaving the corvette *Larne*
behind on station. Both Elliot and the Chinese thought they had made
their respective points. The British traders, on the other hand, were confirmed in their view that as long as the China trade was not interrupted,
London would not consider a war, though without that, the larger
Chinese market would remain closed. So no immediate solution was in
sight. From London's point of view, there still seemed to be only three
kinds of broad policy options. The low-key one, complying with
Chinese demands on Chinese terms, was thought increasingly intolerable by a growing number of merchants and manufacturers. A second was
to abandon the China trade. That was impractical and anyway unthink-
able, whether on grounds of prestige, or those of pragmatic economic
and trading interests, including the welfare of India, or even because of
the general, including moral, compulsions of the drive towards free
trade. A third remained a resort to the threat of force.

Most of 1838 was therefore a period of confusion, with continued
smuggling, and Chinese prohibitions alternating with inaction or even
rumours of impending legalization. In London, in July, Palmerston
again brought forward a Bill to give the Superintendent power to set up
a court at Canton and deport any British subject convicted of contravening Chinese law. But it was introduced late in the parliamentary
session and opposition once again forced the government to withdraw
the idea.[40]

Meanwhile, given poor Chinese controls, widespread official corruption,
and enthusiastic smuggling by outsiders, opium supply had risen
sharply in response to growing demand. The local English-language
press had throughout continued, quite regularly, to report on the
arrival of opium cargoes, to whom they were consigned and opium
prices. It has been estimated that total shipments to China, from all

sources, rose from around 11,100 chests in 1827/28 to 40,200 chests in 1838/39.[41] By the later 1830s, therefore, as supplies increased, the price dropped and the number of smokers had greatly increased. At Canton the American medical missionary, Dr Peter Parker, thought there were tens of thousands of them. Some villagers fought small battles with soldiers sent to confiscate the drug. Senior imperial officials insisted that at least 1 per cent of the entire population was involved – which would mean 3.5 to 4 million people; but some foreigners thought there might be 12 million of them. The social consequences were thought to be most damaging. As the censor Yuan Yu-lin had explained back in 1836, if the addiction continued 'Fathers would no longer be able to admonish their wives, masters would no longer be able to restrain their servants, and teachers would no longer be able to train their pupils...'[42]

Early in 1838, even larger numbers of English opium boats appeared, and some of them clashed with government junks. So now, in June, came a famous memorial to the Chinese throne from Huang Chueh-tzu, of the Court of State Ceremonial, on how to deal with the problem. It said that embargoing trade would be useless, since it would not wean the British away from profitable smuggling. Nor would a campaign against Chinese opium dealers help. But one could strike at Chinese opium consumers and addicts, with strict penalties including death. Although most of the mandarinate refused to support executions, the anti-opium campaign intensified. In the Canton region some 2000 people were arrested and some quickly strangled. Mandarins and soldiers would bring the man to the place of execution, tie him to a wooden cross, with a cord around his neck which was then twisted tight. It was all quite public. At one point the Governor-General even threatened to stop all foreign trade again; and Elliot proposed co-operation in chasing smugglers from the Canton river. On 12 December the authorities tried to have an opium dealer strangled – again *pour encourager les autres* – right in front of the factories, in fact directly under the windows of the United States Consul, Peter Snow, and under the American flag. A number of foreign merchants rallied round to prevent this. That led to a riot but achieved nothing, since the culprit was simply taken away and executed elsewhere. Palmerston was seriously displeased by this attempt to interfere with a foreign sovereign authority. But the tough new Chinese measures had their effect. It became almost impossible to sell opium at Canton because the dealers were too frightened. William Jardine noted that Deng 'has been seizing, trying and strangling the poor devils without mercy – the prisons are full.'[43] Around the start of the new year Elliot wrote to Palmerston that 'There seems ... no longer any room to doubt that the court has firmly determined to suppress, or, more probably, most extensively to check the opium trade'.

On 18 December Elliot served notice on the smugglers that if they did not withdraw beyond the Bogue he would, since he had no legal powers, denounce them to the provincial government. Shortly afterwards he informed Deng that he would not assist any English boat caught inside the Bogue carrying opium. By 31 December, he issued a notice to the British at Canton and Whampoa, pointing out yet again that the opium trade 'in its general effects [is] intensely mischievous to every branch of the trade; and that it [is] rapidly staining the British character with deep disgrace; and, finally, that it [exposes] the vast public and private interest involved in the peaceful maintenance of our regular commercial intercourse with their empire, to imminent jeopardy.'[44] Also, the British government would not interfere if the Chinese seized ships and contraband. And if any British subject caused the death of a native, he would himself be liable to the death penalty. Still, at the end of January Jardine, at a farewell dinner before he sailed for London, insisted that the foreigners were not smugglers at all. It was the Chinese government and its officers who were doing that.[45]

Elliot went on to order all British opium boats to leave the river. Normal trading, which the Chinese had suspended, resumed the following day. The Governor-General underlined his success by arranging, in February 1839, to have another opium dealer executed by strangulation immediately in front of the foreign factories. By that time, throughout China, and along the coast, not just sellers but smokers were being seized. Early in 1839 Beijing, in the face of growing domestic political pressures, began to crack down even more forcibly. A still more severe edict appeared, threatening condign punishment for everyone involved in the opium trade. Chinese addicts were to be given 18 months to seek a cure. For the first time, even foreign opium dealers would become liable to have their heads cut off, and their Chinese associates would be strangled. In spite of all that, domestic Chinese opium production continued. So did bootlegging. So did much official profiteering.

Some months earlier, in July 1838, the Governor-General of Hunan and Hubei, Lin Zexu, had joined the Chinese policy debate with a markedly detailed and thorough memorial of his own, offering a comprehensive view of all aspects of the opium problem. He strongly supported the Huang memorandum, arguing that drug takers might be breaking the law, but should not be executed because, in fact, they were morally ill. Death might be too harsh a punishment for smokers, yet it was true that the drug was an extraordinary danger for society. Capital punishment could therefore be used just to frighten drug-takers into giving up the habit. Someone could be sentenced to death, but put into a sanatorium for a year pending execution. The year would be then divided into quarters with increasingly sharp penalties each quarter for those who did not quit. At the same time, the campaign against traffickers and pushers should be intensified; and foreign smugglers treated like native ones. As he wrote to the Emperor in September 1839: 'Opium must be fully suppressed, while risks should be avoided which might give rise to hostilities on this frontier.'[46] It was a shrewd strategy from a man who was probably playing foreign policy issues, at least in part, for longer-term domestic bureaucratic and political prizes.[47]

In October the Emperor ordered a joint session of the Grand Secretariat and the Grand Council to plan a comprehensive anti-opium strategy for the empire. At the end of the month he summoned Lin, who was received in no less than 19 imperial audiences. The Emperor, with tears in his eyes, said that he could not, after his own death, meet his august father and grandfather unless the great evil of opium was removed. He gave Lin special honours, such as being allowed to ride a horse within Beijing's Forbidden City; then conferred plenipotentiary powers on him as imperial commissioner and sent him to Canton to see what he could do.

4
The British and
Commissioner Lin 1839

The new commissioner was that most admirable type of official: one who combines deep ethical convictions with great energy and a sense of public duty. In person, he was an imposing man: thick-set, with strong eyebrows and long moustaches merging into a long beard. To be sent to Canton at the relatively tender age of 54 was evidence enough that, in a society which attached special importance to age and seniority, he was regarded as exceptional. He was known as a can-do administrator: energetic, incorruptible and devoted to the welfare of the people. His nickname was 'Blue Sky': meaning that his reputation was as clear and clean as the wide heavens. A native of Fujian, by the time he went to Canton he had a highly distinguished career behind him, not only as a legal administrator and financial controller, but also in scholarship and learning. He wrote poetry and was a noted calligrapher. Indeed, like other senior personages in China before or since – including, a century later, Mao Zedong – he saw himself not only as an administrator and governor but as a literary figure. A man of sharp intelligence, with an enquiring, perceptive and subtle mind, he was quite clearly a senior member of the official elite and very much the highly educated Chinese gentleman and scholar-intellectual.

His views were not simple, nor were his interests narrow or merely personal. He was interested in Western thought and while at Canton much concerned with the education and examination of future generations of public officials. One English resident wrote home admiringly in July, to say that 'The commissioner Lin is a very remarkable man ... He has frequently sent to me for information upon subjects of history, geography, coins, medals, the steam engine etc etc'.[1] Lin might be unrelenting in his desire to suppress opium, but he thought as much of education as of punishment and even, at some points, sought the views of Western medical missionaries. Even his two-month journey from Beijing to Canton, by land or river-boat, was carefully considered and controlled. He travelled in a sedan chair, with a very small personal staff: 12 bearers, a mere six servants, three cooks and an orderly. He brought no clerks or junior officials. And he paid personally for his bearers, drivers and carriers, as well as for any boats and crews needed for river travel. All supplies for his train or his people had to be punctually paid for, and no-one was allowed to accept tips or gratuities. He also sent notices ahead to each stop, asking that he and his people be given only ordinary food and that no one should go to the trouble and expense of banquets. In this fashion he managed to cover the 1200 miles from Beijing to Canton in just 60 days, or an average of 20 miles a day.

The mere notice of his coming, which reached Canton on 21 January, began to affect the locals and the opium trade. In fact, Governor-General Deng is said to have fainted away when he heard of Lin's appointment. There were signs of increased determination by the Canton authorities, too, including that decision by the Viceroy to have another opium dealer formally strangled on 26 February in front of the factories. Many local Chinese promptly took fright. A few of the foreign merchants simply stopped trading opium and many of them quickly moved their goods beyond the Bogue and therefore beyond Lin's effective control. But the Commissioner was convinced that Canton was a complete cesspool of corruption, and he would have to begin by taking much stronger measures within the Chinese community itself to stamp out drug use. So, two weeks before he even reached Canton, he drafted secret orders for the arrest of several of the more notorious of the corrupt officials and Chinese smugglers and traders.[2]

He reached the city on 10 March 1839, and was duly welcomed by its high officials. The Emperor had given him extraordinary powers, as Imperial High Commissioner and Imperial Commissioner for Frontier Defence and of the water forces of Guangdong. He was the vice-regent of the Emperor and, within the limits of his commission and jurisdiction, could override the authority of everyone else, including that of the Governor of Canton. But he promptly announced that he was only concerned with import and export issues, not with any other sort of current business. Indeed, throughout his anti-opium campaign at Canton, Lin virtually equated opium with foreign imports, quite ignoring the substantial supply of domestically grown opium, which was qualitatively somewhat inferior.

He spent a week studying the local situation and then made it very clear that he was in earnest. He mobilized the Confucian gentry and sought detailed information. For instance, he summoned some 600 students, candidates for the examinations, and asked them to identify opium distributors. There seem to have been at least four death sentences and it is said that by May there were 1600 arrests.

Unfortunately for all concerned, while he claimed to have 'an intimate acquaintance with all the arts and shifts of the outer barbarians',[3] he quite misunderstood the people he had to deal with. And both then and later, misunderstandings must have been made more acute on both sides by poor translators and translations. Indeed, on the British side good judges thought that '... nothing could be more wretched, till very lately, than our translation of the state papers and official edicts published in the Gazette of Pekin'.[4] Whatever the cause, Lin still thought tea and rhubarb were essential to Western health, that he should be suspicious of all foreign trade, that the foreigners should be more closely controlled and there were too many of them anyway. He also assumed that British traders were under the ultimate control of their government, that opium was banned in England, and that British ships, licensed by their government, were violating their own licences in carrying opium. Nor did he at all appreciate the political and exchange problems caused by the requirement for silver to buy tea. So Lin held a meeting with senior officials to discuss drafting a letter to Queen Victoria, asking that the traffic be stopped. The idea of sending such a message had been raised in memorials to the throne as early as 1830 and again in 1835 and 1836. Now, a letter to the Queen from Lin and the Governor of Canton was, in fact, written, dated 15 March 1839, made public and the text circulated among the people. According to a letter of 8 July, sent home by a private citizen in Macao, it was couched in terms of equality with the Queen, so Elliot refused to forward it. Later, Lin asked some American merchants how it might best be delivered but it seems never actually to have been dispatched. It was, however, said to be a 'very good and sensible letter', though its reception also suffered from mistranslations. For instance, the reference to 'barbarian Queen' should more properly have read 'foreign Queen'.

Lin therefore laboured under several mistaken assumptions. He could see, correctly enough, that the opium traders had no support from their home government, but was quite wrong in believing that opium was a prohibited import in Britain. Furthermore, he assumed, also quite wrongly, that Elliot represented the opium merchants. He even told Beijing that 'it is common knowledge that Elliot is not an English official but a renegade merchant'.[5] In fact, of course, Elliot did not represent the traders, lacked authority over them and had no legal standing to interfere with their activities. At the beginning of January 1839 he was still writing somewhat plaintively to London, emphasizing the danger and shame of the illicit trade which would endanger so much else.[6] But since he had no judicial powers and could hardly hand over Englishmen to the Chinese, British smugglers were in effect free of *both* British and Chinese law. A year later he was still making that point. He continued to regard the opium trade as 'a traffic which every friend to humanity must deplore'. He could even see that, given the difficulties facing the Chinese authorities in distinguishing clearly between legal and illegal trade, '[t]he Chinese government had just grounds for harsh measures towards the lawful trade.' Still, by March–April 1839, when push was indeed coming to shove, he simply assumed authority over the traders as an emergency measure, to protect the safety and welfare of British subjects. So, whatever Elliot's protestations, Lin must have thought his assumptions well justified.

In any case, on 18 March, a mere week after his arrival, Lin summoned the Hong merchants. On their knees before him, they were berated for having connived at the opium traffic, co-operated in exporting silver and entirely failed to keep the foreigners under control. If they did not get all opium stocks surrendered within three days, he, Lin, would ask the Emperor for permission to execute one or two of them and to confiscate all the Hong merchants' possessions.[7] They were to transmit another order to the foreign merchants themselves. It made the point that it was only by Chinese grace and favour that they were allowed to trade at Canton at all. China was, after all, entirely self-supporting, while the foreigners badly needed Chinese tea and rhubarb. It was in any case wrong for them to make a profit from harming others. The laws against opium had now been strengthened, Lin said, and the death penalty was about to be introduced for smoking as well as trading in the drug.[8] He went on: 'Let the Barbarians deliver to me every particle of opium on board their store ships. There must not be the smallest atom concealed or withheld. And at the same time let the Barbarians enter into a bond never hereafter to bring opium in their ships' or else to submit to the extreme penalties of the law[9] to which they were, under Manchu rules and regulations, subject as much as the Chinese themselves. They were given three days to comply. The following day came another edict, this time from the *hoppo*, forbidding any foreigner to leave Canton. The effect of this was to confine the foreigners within the grounds of the factories. They were also cut off from communication with their shipping, since ships' boats were allowed to come to Canton but not then to return to Whampoa. Moreover, all business came to a standstill when the customs office was shut down. The British, accustomed to Chinese vacillations and talk of opium legalization, were astonished.

Chinese troops were mustered in the Canton suburbs and on 21 March, the day on which Lin's three-day grace expired, armed junks halted all normal communications with Whampoa and appeared on the river in front of the factories, while armed men assembled on the landward side. In effect, the entire foreign community found itself a prisoner at large within the factory and grounds. Clearly, Lin thought that the way to go – remembering Napier – was to frighten the foreigners into compliance. He had, after all, been given a degree of freedom of action which arguably allowed him to use force against the English – whom the court regarded as mere rebels, to be properly managed.

The Hong merchants, trapped between the upper and nether millstones of the assertive foreigners and the Commissioner, appealed to the foreigners' Chamber of Commerce, arguing that two of them might actually lose their heads if the foreigners did not comply. The Chamber held a meeting, that same day of 21 March, which discussed the problem. They could hardly allow their Hong colleagues to be executed, or ships to be refused permission to sail. On the other hand, for most of the opium they were merely agents, not owners, and could hardly give away other people's property. The upshot was that they stated a general intention to rid themselves of any connection with opium. And some members, though not the Chamber as a body, agreed to surrender 1037 chests of it. Lin treated this as mere prevarication and declared the offer entirely inadequate. At the same time he sent an invitation – amounting to an order – to Mr Lancelot Dent to come to see him, Dent's firm being suspected, quite correctly, of being the biggest opium trader after Jardine Matheson.[10] But the traders feared he might be arrested and taken hostage, even executed, as a few other Westerners had been in earlier years. Accordingly, Dent refused to go. He kept saying that he would not resist if he were taken by force but, while Lin threatened to do that, he did not want to force an open break with the British. All this, amid appeals from the Hong merchants, took up the next day, 23 March.

Throughout this fortnight Elliot was at Macao, having previously assumed that the new imperial commissioner would make his headquarters there. Copies of Lin's orders of 18 March reached him on the 22nd. He at once sent copies to London, telling Palmerston that he intended to take firm measures to check the 'rash spirit' of the Chinese. He also told all British ships at the outer anchorages to 'proceed forthwith to Hongkong, and, hoisting their national colours, be prepared to resist every act of aggression upon the part of the Chinese government' and to place themselves under the protection of the Royal Navy.[11] At the same time he wrote to the Governor, protesting against the threatening Chinese military moves, the marshalling of troops, ships and fire vessels and the holding of an execution in front of the factories. He asked, 'in the name of the sovereign of [the British] nation' what might be the purpose of making war upon the British residing in the Chinese empire. Simultaneously he wrote a note to Palmerston saying that his firm attitude would surely bring the Chinese to see sense.

On the following day, 23 March, he wrote a note to the British at Canton telling them to prepare to leave, before putting on his full naval uniform and leaving Macao for Canton in his cutter, the *Louisa*. At Whampoa, finding that all communication with Canton had been cut, he transferred, apparently with four Royal Navy ratings, to a small boat and went on. As he travelled, he found himself passing a number of Chinese vessels in various stages of preparation for action. Not surprisingly, within days the Elliots sent two of their children back to England.[12] He landed at the British factory on 24 March and promptly raised the flag. One American saw him striding around 'sword in hand' and immediately becoming the chief actor on the stage.[13] As the senior person on the spot, he immediately assumed the authority over the British which his government had steadfastly refused to give him. In particular, he at once set about dealing with the affair of Mr Dent, escorting him personally from his house to the comparative safety of the factory.

That evening, he addressed the traders. He explained that Chinese threats and the appearance of Chinese soldiers made staying at Canton dangerous. He therefore advised all the British to move their property out of the river and said he would try to get passports for anyone who wanted to leave. If that were refused, it would be tantamount to British people being taken hostage, with possible injury to them or their Hong merchant colleagues. He thought that two American frigates that happened to be visiting, the *Columbia* and the *John Adams*,[14] could surely be relied upon for support. He was sure that the British and Americans must stand together.[15] In fact, by this time the Canton Americans were writing to Congress asking that a US Navy squadron be sent into Chinese waters and an ambassador dispatched to Beijing. There was, though, very little support in Washington for anything of the kind, opinion remaining deeply suspicious about any kind of co-operation with the British.

On the same day Lin accentuated the Napier precedents still further. He ordered the *hoppo* to stop all trade and withdrew the servants and *compradors* of the foreigners. Houseboys, cooks and other servants disappeared. The traders woke up to find boats with soldiers lining the waterfront. The ring of armed troops was tightened with coolie militia armed with sticks and even pikes, and the factories effectively walled up, with gongs beating at night to deprive the 350 foreign inhabitants of sleep. Barriers were placed across the river to prevent the approach of boats from Whampoa. Even letters could not pass. In effect, Lin imposed a blockade – indeed a siege – of the factories as well as of the ships at Whampoa that was to last for 47 days. Not only that, and not only were the British cut off from communication with the outside world, deprived of servants, and surrounded by Chinese troops, but they were officially deprived of food and drinking water.

Yet the reality of their 'imprisonment' was nothing like as harsh as they later made out, or as the British public was led to believe. It is true that the traders had to cook, clean and generally fend for themselves. But food, water and firewood were smuggled to them by friendly Chinese merchants.[16] They may have suffered from humiliation, monotony and the hot weather – and some deplorable sanitary conditions – but they played cricket in the square. The surrounding soldiers were friendly. Some of their officers would come in for a glass of beer and a chat and the 'prisoners' were shown great good will by the translators and their assistants, who even helped with domestic chores. As Matheson himself later commented: 'They suffered more from an absence of exercise and from overfeeding than from any actual want of the necessities of life.' Though their servants were taken away, they themselves, having no business to attend to, '...cheerfully turned their attention to the various domestic departments, and there was never a *merrier* community than that of the foreign merchants at Canton, during their imprisonment within the limits of their own houses.' As for the ships at Whampoa, though they could not move, they were not molested and were regularly supplied. Indeed, Charles Paterson, the surgeon on one of them, wrote to *The Times*, full of indignation at suggestions of Chinese maltreatment. On the contrary, he said, they had all been excellently treated. They had been given lots of food including mutton, turkey, capon and a rich variety of vegetables and fruit, not to mention Chinese supplies of clothing. They were, in fact, very kindly dealt with.[17] Still, there were other and more psychological pressures, like the silent menace of the surrounding troops, or that public strangling of a criminal in the square outside the British factory. On 27 March the *hoppo* added to pressure by ordering that no foreign ship at Whampoa should be allowed to load or unload cargo or to leave the port without official clearance.

From Elliot's point of view, not only was the British community at Canton, together with the ships at Whampoa, under some threat, but so was the whole of Britain's, and India's, Canton trade. But the chief worry, naturally enough, was for the safety of the English civilians who had no protection from the thousands of Chinese troops surrounding them. He therefore formally demanded from the Governor that passports be issued within three days to all British ships and people at Canton, failing which it would be evident that they were being detained by force. This was referred to the Imperial Commissioner who said that once his orders had been obeyed, and the opium surrendered, passports would of course be issued.[18]

By then it was becoming evident that British verbal firmness and diplomatic protest might not be enough. Nor was it good enough for Elliot to protest that he lacked legal authority once Lin very pointedly asked: if the Superintendent could not stop the merchants from bringing opium into China 'I would ask what is it that Elliot superintends?'.[19] There was obviously no answer to that, so Elliot now took two fateful decisions. He decided that he had no choice and issued a notice on the 27th requiring all British subjects to surrender their opium for delivery to the Chinese. On the same day he returned to the petitioning mode in addressing Lin, promising delivery. In the event, 20,283 chests were handed over,[20] 1540 of them by US merchants. On the morning of the 28th that message reached Lin who promptly sent the foreigners a 'present' of food, including 250 animals for meat,[21] and the British were allowed once again to exchange messages with Macao. Coincidentally, two days later Lin received a congratulatory present from the Emperor for his splendid efforts. But Elliot's petitioning form, contrary to Palmerston's instructions, inevitably reduced him once more, in Chinese eyes, to the status of a *taipan*, or the headman of the merchants. And the evidence that he could, in fact, command the surrender of the opium made nonsense of his previous protestations that he had no authority over British subjects in China.

More important still, and critical for the government in London, were the terms on which he got the merchants to surrender their opium. For Elliot ordered its surrender in the name of the British government, which would compensate the merchants, at a price to be determined later, for the value of their lost property.[22] The traders were, of course, delighted. Following the arrest of so many Chinese traffickers, they had anyway sold little for quite a while. Matheson himself noted that 'not a chest of opium has been sold at Canton for the last five months'.[23] So the traders now pledged to Elliot not just every chest of opium they could lay their hands on, but even more opium than they actually had or expected to get. Some of them, in fact, made huge profits from the confiscations. One trading house was said to have made no less than £400,000 (tv: £23.5 million).[24] As Matheson's nephew Alexander bluntly explained to the House of Commons a year later 'the opium was deposited in our hands to dispose of it, and the money of the British government was as good as any other money we could get.'[25]

Once Elliot's pledge to Lin had been received, the Chinese actually tightened the blockade, strengthening guards and bricking up the back doors of factories. But by the start of April the surrender of opium had begun and Lin, recognizing that there must inevitably be some delays in completing it, ordered that deliveries of food and water might be resumed and that some dispatches might be sent down-river to Macao. He also laid down that once the first quarter of the promised opium had been delivered, the Europeans' servants should be allowed back. After the second quarter communications with Whampoa and Macao should be reopened, after the third quarter the embargo on trade should be lifted and when everything had been delivered the *status quo ante* should be resumed. So, gradually, through April 1839, the blockade of the factories was lifted, and on the 13th Elliot wrote to Palmerston to say that the Chinese government was probably too weak domestically to carry through the various prohibitions consistently. By 2 May Lin agreed that passes for travel to Macao would now be issued. Two days later Elliot told the British not to bring any ship to Canton until he had declared the city safe for life, liberty and property. A day later again, on 5 May, the blockade was finally lifted and destruction of the surrendered opium began at the start of June.

There remained the matter of the bond – for future good behaviour – that Lin wanted the merchants to sign. Many of them were quite willing to do that but pointed out that they could not command other merchants and other nationalities. So, on 4 April, Lin proposed a form of voluntary bond, to be accepted by the Superintendent heading the merchants of all nationalities, in which everyone would undertake to abide by the laws and import prohibitions of China. If, having signed the bond, a merchant should break the law, his ship and cargo would be confiscated and it would be agreed that he should be executed. Elliot replied on 10 April. He agreed that foreigners at Canton must obey China's laws. 'But the new regulation regarding these bonds is incompatible with the laws of England.' So, if bonds were absolutely required, the English would have to leave Canton. A week later he wrote to his cousin, Lord Auckland, in India requesting the dispatch of some warships and a few days later to Palmerston to urge forceful British action and the demand of an indemnity from China.

Naturally enough, neither Elliot nor the English merchants thought they could safely stay in Canton anyway, in case Lin for some reason decided to renew the blockade. Nor was that the only danger, since Lin had asked that a special clause be added to the new Chinese opium regulations. It said that in future foreigners caught importing opium would lose their heads. So Elliot asked most of the British to leave Canton for Macao. On 18 May he wrote to Palmerston again, suggesting that a manifesto be drafted, and translated into Chinese for general circulation, instructing all officers of any proposed British expeditionary force, and all British subjects in the Chinese empire, not to molest Chinese civilians or their property or to violate local customs. Four days later he stated publicly that he could no longer have any 'confidence in the justice and moderation of the ... Imperial Commissioner', that the threats which had made it necessary to surrender property had brought 'immense public liabilities' to the British crown and that it was essential to remove British people from Canton lest new demands and risks should be inflicted on them.[26] A day later Lin and the Governor ordered the Hong merchants to see that the 16 previously named foreigners, thought to be the chief opium offenders, sign a promise that, once allowed to leave Canton, they would never come back. Under duress, they all signed.

Elliot knew that alternative instructions from London could hardly reach him before the beginning of the next year, 1840, and he wanted to keep the British, and their ships, out of danger. So, three days after the last of the opium was handed over, on 24 May, Elliot evacuated the remaining British subjects from the Canton factories. They left with all their goods, furniture, wine, ledgers and stocks. Refuge would be sought at Macao if possible, or else on ships anchored in deep water between Kowloon and the small islet of Hong Kong. By the beginning of June, the American missionary, Dr Parker, noted that only 15–20 Americans, six Englishmen and no Parsees were left at Canton.[27] In the meantime, Lin, as reward for his success, received a message in the Emperor's own vermilion pencil, promoting him to the most coveted of China's governor-generalships, that of the provinces of Kiangnan and Kiangsi (roughly, the modern Jiangxi and Jiangsu), though he was not to leave for his new post until the opium problem at Canton was resolved.

By May–June Matheson thought that Elliot's policy of general appeasement would merely encourage Chinese rigour and so might actually make conflict unavoidable. Certainly if Lin, or his master, thought the surrender of the opium or the evacuation of the English were the end of the matter, they were profoundly mistaken. Even with respect to opium, Lin learned of a most prescient criticism of his policy by the Censor Pu Chidong. Lin, said Pu, had made no proper plans for the future. The only result of having the merchants promise not to bring opium into Canton would be that the smugglers would avoid the estuary, go further up the coast, and transfer their cargoes to small ships sent out from shore. What was needed was some plan to put a truly final stop to the traffic.[28]

But there was much more. The British, having left the Pearl River, proved to be in no great hurry to resume trading for their tea and rhubarb. Elliot had said no British ship was to enter the river. On 5 June he informed the Commissioner that in future British ships would load and unload at Macao. But Lin could not allow trading at Macao, since that would undermine the entire Canton system. Nor could Macao be controlled, whether for taxation or for opium. So, on 9 June, the *hoppo* placed a ban on anything other than local trade at Macao, and ordered all foreign ships to load or unload at Whampoa but not linger there. Two days earlier, an armed British merchant vessel, the *Cambridge*, had arrived and offered to protect British ships in the estuary. There seems to have been a verbal arrangement for the British government to hire the *Cambridge* for eight months for £14,000 (tv: £550,000).[29] On 14 June Elliot appealed to the traders not to send their ships to Canton on Chinese terms, 'consenting for themselves and their countrymen to trial and condemnation by Chinese officers and forms of Chinese judicature ...'. Two days later Elliot appointed the captain of the *Cambridge*, Joseph Douglas, as commodore of the fleet, and the merchants voted to treat Elliot's request not to enter the river as a positive order from the London government. Chinese expostulations were met on 21 June, with Elliot issuing a kind of manifesto, outlining the British grievances. He mentioned the close imprisonment for over seven weeks of innocent people, as well as guilty ones, and pointed out that 'the traffic in opium has been chiefly encouraged and protected by the highest officers in the empire, and that no portion of the foreign trade to China has paid its fees to the officers with so much regularity as this of opium.' British ships and traders would not go to Canton 'because there is no safety for a handful of defenceless men in the grasp of the government at Canton; [and] because it would be derogatory from the dignity of their sovereign and nation to forget all the insults and wrongs which have been perpetrated, till full justice be done ...'.[30]

More serious, from a Chinese point of view, was the fact that a head of steam for retaliatory action was beginning to build up on the British side. After all, as far as the British were concerned, Lin had changed the whole issue from the opium traffic, about which much of London sympathized with China, to the very different matter of British citizens being taken hostage. Elliot could be fairly sure that having urged 'powerful intervention' on Palmerston, London would not sit quietly by while British property was forcibly seized and British civilians threatened. 'This man,' he wrote of Commissioner Lin 'is hastening on in a career of violence, which will react upon this empire in a terrible manner.'[31] The traders, too, were writing to Palmerston, asking for payment of the promised compensation for their losses and urging strong action. So were industrialists and merchants from London to Manchester.

In the meantime, Lin's destruction of the surrendered opium was treated as a social occasion and public spectacle. On 17 June a group of foreigners, headed by an American trader, C.W. King, and including several ladies, came to watch the process which involved dissolving the opium in water and running it into the sea. Fortunately we have an English-language account of Lin's interview (via an interpreter) with these foreigners. 'Lin was bland and vivacious,' we are told,[32] 'without a trace of the fanatic's sternness with which he was credited. He looked young for his age, was short, rather stout, with a smooth round face, a slender black beard and a keen dark eye... Once he laughed outright when Mr King, on being asked which of the Chinese guild-merchants was the most honest, found himself unable to name one.'

On 23 June the Chinese issued new and tougher regulations for foreign shipping, for the wording of the bond to be signed by foreign traders, and for the Hong merchants dealing with them. But while the British remained outside the Pearl River, the Americans and other neutrals, including the Danes and Germans, traded at Canton on Chinese terms. The Americans, in particular, were making a lot of money by trading, not just on their own account but as commission agents carrying tea from Canton to the British ships beyond the river. Elliot tried to prevent such 'unfair competition' from the Americans by persuading them to leave Canton, in the name of common interests. However, one of their leaders, Robert Bennett Forbes, answered him: '...I had not come to China for health or pleasure, and that I should remain at my post as long as I could sell a yard of goods or buy a pound of tea... We Yankees had no Queen to guarantee our losses...'.[33] So on 29 July Elliot issued a notice to say he had asked the British and Indian governments to forbid the import of tea procured in this way.[34] Since the roundabout buying continued, he wrote again to Palmerston on 8 September to oppose the practice; but later changed his mind on the grounds that it was a kind of safety valve.

In fact, Chinese policy was confused, even counter-productive. On the one hand, Lin promised drastic action against Chinese opium-smokers. At the beginning of July 1839 he gave his countrymen 18 months to kick the habit, on pain of death by strangling. On the other, just as Censor Pu had forecast and Elliot now pointed out, none of this actually stopped the opium trade, which continued to flourish. In fact, as soon as the British had left Canton, trading along the coast resumed. There were a number of reports that opium sales along the coast were continuing, from fast and heavily armed clippers operating under a variety of flags, often supported by armed Chinese boats well able to defy officialdom.[35] Elliot reported that recent events had simply made native Chinese smuggling stronger and more active. Immediately after Lin's destruction of the opium, the price per chest in Canton was said to have shot up from $500 to some $3000 (Spanish dollars), but by the end of the year it had come back, with increased supply, to a range of $700–$1200.[36]

Not only did bootlegging by traders of all nationalities continue, and Chinese officials continue to profit handsomely, but opium growing continued in China itself. And in July Elliot was again reporting that 'In several parts of Fukien (Fujian) [Commissioner Lin's measures] have already produced a formidable organisation of native smugglers, and the officers of the government do not venture to disturb them'.[37] Although he himself tried hard to keep opium away from ships seeking protection at Hong Kong, by the end of the year there were as many ships as ever involved in the trade, if not more. There were reports, too, that:

> The principal agents of this traffic are no longer resident in China, and their vessels, both large and small, are so manned and armed as to be able to put all native craft at defiance; moreover, not a few of the native smugglers are arming themselves, in order to defend themselves against the officers of their own government.[38]

There were even larger consequences. The entire China trade was brought to a standstill. For one thing, Lin still did not understand – any more than did anyone else – the detailed political economy of the exchange of tea for silver. Stopping that exchange would harm China, as well as foreigners. Furthermore, Lin's actions had undermined the old mutual confidence on which the entire Canton trading system had rested. He had also done much more than simply seize some £2.4 million (tv: almost £94 million) worth of British property. And, as had been pointed out before, the Canton merchants, whom Lin had ordered to surrender the opium, were merely agents for merchants in India. They did not actually own the opium, and therefore had no right to hand it over on demand. Moreover, since Elliot had no legal authority to interfere with the opium traffic, Palmerston could later point out to the Chinese, quite fairly, that Lin was trying to compel the representative of another power to enforce Chinese law and to do so by giving orders to people over whom that representative had no authority. Not only that but, as Palmerston added with considerable exaggeration, 'a Law... for a great length of time ... allowed to sleep as a dead letter [was] suddenly ... put into force with the utmost rigour and severity.'

Lin's demand that the merchants sign bonds raised other and even more difficult issues. The mid-nineteenth-century assumptions about protecting British subjects anywhere naturally extended to protection from a bond extorted by threats. For the Chinese, on the other hand, Chinese legal concepts and jurisdiction must, equally naturally, prevail on Chinese soil. And from a Chinese point of view, official documents, including bonds, were in some ways more important than individuals. Foreigners who signed such a bond were accepting that they were trading on China's terms, under Chinese jurisdiction. If fear of arrest and severe punishment kept the merchants from signing, that meant expulsion from Canton. But Lin fully expected that the lure of trade would soon bring them back, and they would then have to sign the bonds. As, indeed, the non-English traders, American, German, Danish and others were doing, and trading with enthusiasm.

Even more serious jurisdictional problems now arose. In early July 1839 a party of English seamen beat up some Chinese peasants in a drunken brawl ashore at Kowloon. One of the peasants, Lin Weihi, died the next day. That, even more clearly than the matter of the bonds, raised issues of jurisdiction and fundamental justice. Inevitably, it created a direct clash between Chinese views about group responsibility and the subordination of individual rights to the priority of righting wrongs, as against British views about individual guilt or innocence.

On 10 July Elliot rushed to the scene and tried to deal with the affair by offering money to Lin Weihi's family, and to the villagers, and offering a reward for evidence leading to the murderer's conviction. Two days later Commissioner Lin learned of the affair, and demanded the surrender of the murderer to Chinese justice. But investigation failed to identify anyone. A month later, on 12 and 13 August, Elliot put six sailors who had been involved in the brawl on trial. It was held on board a British ship, with himself as chief judge. Still no killer could be identified. Though Elliot found the seamen guilty of rioting and sentenced them to fines and imprisonment, it remained impossible to specify a murderer. The trial was in accordance with those arrangements back in 1833,[39] which allowed the crown to set up courts to try British subjects on the China coast, but which had never been implemented. But now, when news of the affair reached London in late 1839, opinion in Parliament was that Elliot had exceeded his powers, so even the gaol sentences on the sailors were never carried out. In the meantime, Commissioner Lin refused to believe Elliot's protestations that it was not possible to identify the actual killer. He also saw that as long as the English were at Macao, they would go on resisting, not only on this but on the bonds as well. He therefore decided that the entire British community must suffer for Elliot's evident 'incompetence'. He cut off supplies for Macao and the British there, and moved 2000 troops into an adjacent town.

Elliot was still without military or naval support of any kind, partly because the Navy was badly stretched. With France and Britain at loggerheads over the fate of the Ottoman empire, the Admiralty was expecting operations against the French in the Mediterranean. So Elliot issued a public notice on 21 August advising British subjects to leave Macao and seek refuge on board the merchant fleet off Hong Kong. In the general alarm, Chinese servants were leaving and shopkeepers started to make difficulties. On 24 August the Portuguese governor, Pinto, ordered the English to quit, and two days later the British families, escorted by Portuguese troops, retreated to the ships. In fact, they found accommodation there without much difficulty, since the end of August was the normal time of the year for the main merchant fleet to arrive, and the multi-coloured flotilla now numbered several thousand men and some 50 ships. Some were even armed with 18-pounder guns. Not only that but Matheson, for one, had prudently foreseen the evacuation and written to his agents in Manila to send over supplies, including bread, pigs and poultry, not to mention beer and 'some moderately good French claret'.[40] Even so, Lin thought he could deprive the English of supplies and communication. On 31 August he issued a proclamation urging the people along the coast to arm themselves. They should repel any foreigners trying to land, and even refuse them permission to get fresh water.

But that very day a 28-gun Royal Navy frigate, the *Volage*, did finally arrive, in response to Elliot's earlier pleas. He immediately offered British protection to the Governor of Macao if he would agree to the return of the British and their families. The Governor declined, in spite of earlier orders from Lisbon about giving sanctuary. By 2 September a notice was issued asking the local Chinese not to poison wells against the foreigners, which it had been thought they might do. The British, of course, could only be confirmed in their view that they badly needed some spot on the China coast that would be under their own control. Two days later again, on 4 September, with the flotilla by now very short of food and water, Elliot tried to remonstrate personally and in writing with the Chinese officials at Kowloon, asking in the name of 'peace and justice' for regular supplies.[41] He arrived in the cutter *Louisa* accompanied by a small, armed vessel, the *Pearl*, and a boat from *Volage*. He found himself left hanging about for six hours, lost his temper and opened fire on Chinese war-junks that were – quite properly, given their orders – refusing him permission to go ashore and buy supplies. The junks were severely damaged. Local tensions increased further when, on 12 September, the Chinese attacked and burned a Spanish ship in Macao harbour, under the quite false impression that she was a British opium trader.

There were more exchanges with the Chinese about the expulsion of ships or people involved with opium, the bonds to be signed by merchants, and the Lin Weihi business. Elliot pointed out that his authority did not extend to non-British people or ships. And he flatly refused to allow any trader or ships' captain to sign a bond which would accept, in advance and without evidence, or witnesses, or even trial, the penalties of Lin's new laws. As for the Lin Weihi killing, since no killer could be found, he was in effect being asked for a scapegoat. But it also emerged that the Chinese were so alarmed by the action against their war-junks that they allowed the people of Kowloon to supply the merchant fleet with food and water after all.

By now, though, some British merchants were becoming fretful at seeing the Americans, who had signed the bond, earn high profits. Two British ships' traders therefore decided they, too, would sign Lin's opium bond. On 13 October the *Thomas Coutts* arrived at Macao and her master, a 'bolshie' character named Warner, who had been advised beforehand in Calcutta that Elliot had no legal power to embargo trade, signed the bond and sailed to Whampoa.

Elliot was furious, since Warner's action could only strengthen Lin's hand in demanding that all British ships should follow the *Thomas Coutts'* example, or else be threatened with destruction if they did not leave altogether. In fact, of course, Lin thought that the other traders would also comply. On 25 October he sent a further order for the surrender of Lin Weihi's killer, and a fresh demand for the merchant vessels to accept the bond.[42] Obviously, that compliance by some 50–60 ships, and virtually the entire British group of men, women and children, would have been a complete victory for Chinese pressure tactics, with

large consequences for the future conduct of both sides. Lin also threatened to send warships and continued with the assembly of war-junks
and fire-rafts, and warned Elliot that naval and military forces were
assembling at Canton and would go to the Bogue to prepare for an assault.
There were even some attempts to send Chinese fire-ships among the
merchant fleet. Elliot asked *Volage's* commander, Captain Smith, to
arrange protection. Smith composed notes to Lin and the Governor, asking them to withdraw their threats to merchantmen which failed to sign
the bond, to pull back their war-junks and fire-ships and to let the
British merchants live normally ashore. He also, on 2 November,
brought *Volage* and the smaller 20-gun *Hyacinth* to Chuenbi. Smith
failed to get his letters accepted for delivery, but was unwilling to withdraw in the face of Chinese threats.

Next day, 3 November, the Chinese commander, Admiral Guan,
advanced with 29 junks and fire-ships towards the two Royal Navy vessels. At this point another merchantman, the *Royal Saxon*, tried to move
towards the river. Her captain had, like Warner of the *Thomas Coutts*,
agreed to sign Lin's bond. Neither ship, however, seems to have signed
clauses that might make their masters liable to capital punishment,
although it was later implied at Westminster that this demand was a
basic cause of dispute with China. In any case, *Volage* sent a shot across
the bows of the *Royal Saxon*, Admiral Guan moved to protect the merchantman's progress, and there was a general engagement in which four
junks were sunk, others were badly damaged and the rest dispersed. On
20 November Elliot notified all concerned that British ships would be
prevented from entering the port of Canton, by force if necessary.

Lin decided to counter by severing trade relations with Britain entirely.
On the 26th he issued orders that after 6 December no British ship would
be allowed to enter and on 5 January 1840 followed this with a proclamation barring Britain for good from trade relations with China. Even
then there were loopholes: although British goods were formally banned,
no steps were taken to prohibit British imports coming into Chinese
ports in non-British ships. Indeed, the Americans were making more
money than ever. They now 'talk with contempt,' as Joseph Coolidge Jr
wrote on 12 December, 'of the sort of business done formerly, for now a
ship can make 18,000drs freight from Lintin to Whampoa.'[43] Though
some English merchants complained about the 'fantastic' freight charges
for transshipping goods, Elliot actually thanked the Americans for keeping trade going pending the arrival of British forces.

It was clear at the time, and is even clearer in retrospect, that whatever
the rights or wrongs of Lin's views and objectives, they remained entirely

consistent. He was determined to end the import and consumption of opium, certainly by commercial or legal pressures, by force if necessary. At Canton itself he issued a proclamation, as early as 6 July 1839, warning his own Chinese people that they had 18 months' grace to kick the habit. He issued further proclamations in 1840 to emphasize that by mid-January 1841 behaviour would have to be reformed. Or else 'Death will then stand before your eyes.'[44] But he was also quite willing to try high-level persuasion. At the end of August there was another letter from Lin to Queen Victoria. He clearly continued to labour under the misapprehension that Victoria could control her merchants in China, and that China's own views must surely be reaching her in garbled form. So his letter stressed the benevolence of the Chinese emperor who only sought to bring peace and harmony to his people and had prohibited opium, because it was harmful. He also allowed exports that were helpful. '... Is there any single article from China which has done any arm to foreign countries? Take tea and rhubarb, for example; the foreign countries cannot get along for a single day without them. If China cuts off these benefits ... what can the barbarians rely upon to keep themselves alive? ...' Queen Victoria ought, on moral grounds, to co-operate in banning the opium traffic. 'Where,' the letter asked, 'is your conscience? I have heard that the smoking of opium is very strictly forbidden by your country ... Since it is not permitted to do harm to your own country, then even less should you let it be passed on to the harm of other countries – how much less to China.' How could the English benefit from doing harm to the Chinese?[45] The letter also explained the new Chinese anti-opium statutes, which included the death penalty even for foreigners importing the drug. The Emperor approved the draft of the letter in his own vermilion pencil: 'This is appropriately worded and quite comprehensive.' Lin then had the letter translated into English and showed it to the American Dr Parker. Apparently it was then entrusted to Captain Warner of the *Thomas Coutts*, who signed a receipt for it on 18 January 1840 and promised to deliver it safely. On arrival in England, Warner duly wrote to the Foreign Office on 7 June 1840, asking for an interview to deliver the letter. But Palmerston remembered the trouble Warner had caused by signing Lin's bond, and refused either to talk to him or to transmit any letters. There seems to be no further trace of Lin's document and there is no evidence that the letter reached the Queen, or even the British government, by some other route.

There is, then, every sign that for Lin the opium traffic was, throughout, the sole cause of dispute with the foreigners, and that he had no notion that they might have any other and legitimate grievances.

He was willing, in conformity with traditional Chinese doctrines, to segregate and virtually confine the entire foreign community, opium traders and others, to compel the handing over of all opium held in China, as well as to secure guarantees that further imports would stop. The opium stocks therefore became, in effect, the ransom for the release of the foreigners. Lin even secured, in the signature of the bonds by some ship's captains, their commitment to unquestioning acceptance, for themselves and their crews, owners and correspondents, of the penalties of confiscation – even of death – if the bonds were violated. Lin seems to have been well aware that in pressing matters so far the result might be conflict. But when the American missionary, Elijah Bridgman, warned that the British were likely to retaliate, Lin replied simply 'We have no fear of war.'[46] His emperor backed him. In fact, Lin expected that evidence of his own determination would have a huge effect on the barbarians. Certainly his countrymen came to regard him as an heroic figure and a century later put up statues in his memory.

At the same time, he could see that he must avoid blame for having provoked a military confrontation at all. He therefore needed to persuade everyone that going to war was not a serious risk. So he tried to belittle the British, referring to them in highly traditional terms as mere marauders and seaborne raiders, with the implication that they were not likely to fight for political or territorial objectives. He was confirmed in that by two other ideas. He thoroughly misunderstood British war finance and logistics, believing that British operations, like those of other sea raiders, would be inherently limited by reliance on whatever they could seize or steal as they went along.[47] In addition, he seriously underestimated the determination of the British, as well as their military and naval capabilities. Nor were such misconceptions peculiar to him. Here is the 1840 opinion of an unnamed Chinese mandarin: 'The English barbarians are an insignificant and detestable race, trusting entirely to their strong ships and large guns... Notwithstanding the riches of their government, the people are poor, and unable to contribute to the expenses of an army at such a distance.'[48] Even allowing for the language of official dispatches, here were surely some massive misunderstandings.

It was all entirely different from the perspective of British officials. And Lin, brought up in the world of the China-centred tribute system, quite failed to understand the modern international implications of what he had done. As Matheson perceptively wrote to Jardine as early as the beginning of May 1839, '... the Chinese have fallen into the snare of rendering themselves directly liable to the British crown.'[49] With the result that, as early as mid-October of that year, Palmerston wrote to Elliot that an expeditionary force would be coming soon and, shortly afterwards, accepted Jardine's offers of help with the forthcoming expedition. For the British, including Elliot, the opium traffic was simply not the central issue. As late as December 1839 he wrote to Palmerston that '... no man entertains a deeper detestation of the disgrace and sin of this forced traffic on the coast of China than the humble individual who signs this dispatch. I can see little to choose between it and piracy; and in my place, as a public officer, I have steadily discountenanced it by all the lawful means in my power and at the total sacrifice of my private comfort ...'.[50] But issues of the personal safety of English families, and of the pride and prowess of the country, were a different matter. As the engineer Ouchterlony put it later, after he had accompanied the expeditionary force, all that the British wanted was reciprocity in commercial intercourse. The real problem had been the 'unbearable and despotic conduct' of Commissioner Lin. The opium issue had merely been the spark 'into a mine which, during the past half century, the vindictiveness and insufferable arrogance of the Chinese government' had gradually charged.[51] Nor was anyone greatly concerned about China's armed forces. The *Canton Register* curtly dismissed the issue: 'The men employed in the army and navy of China must be the most worthless of the nation ...'.[52] By the time Ouchterlony wrote, the British ability to mount a sustained and effective campaign was indeed being thoroughly demonstrated.

5
London Debates 1839–40

From the point of view of the Cabinet in London, not to mention the British public, China was still a peripheral affair. At home, social and industrial unrest continued. In 1838 the Anti-Corn Law League was formed, committed to cheaper food by freer trade and the abolition of agricultural protection. By 1840, with poor harvests, there was real hunger, with riots in some places, including Birmingham. At Newport 3000 armed miners were on the march. Chartism, with its demand for much broader social and political reforms, was rallying thousands. In the middle of all that, in February 1840, came the brilliant wedding of Queen Victoria with her Prince Albert.

Amid such domestic concerns, foreign policy was very much Palmerston's own business. Most members of 1830s Cabinets were still not much interested in foreign affairs, ministers being rather expected to get on with the affairs of their own departments. And as for 'Pam's' own perspectives, we have a long, handwritten and much amended memorandum from him, written in October 1840, when the fight in China was already well under way. It is evidently meant to outline the whole range of England's foreign affairs interests and to set them into context. Interest in the 'oriental question', he writes, is essentially twofold. First, the maintenance of the European balance of peace. Secondly

> ...it is a standing prejudice in Europe, that England should be desirous and anxious to gain new colonies. She has shown during her whole modern history since the french revolution, that she does not long for conquests and acquisitions but for the maintenance of the Balance and security of her commercial advantages. England wants the free trafic [sic] with those colonies, which are necessary for her

prosperity and does not much care about it if the country with which she is trading is a free one or dependent on her ... England has gained in this respect great experience since the independence of the united states of America.[1]

There were, therefore, many more urgent issues. One was the 'Eastern Question': the problems posed by Mehemet Ali of Egypt to the cohesion of the Turkish empire. Mehemet wanted Syria, his ambitions sharpened by Syria's money, men and materials for naval expansion. That also affected the interests of Russia, Austria, France and Britain in the cohesion of the Turkish empire, its Balkan lands and Russian access to the Dardanelles passage from the Black Sea into the Mediterranean. France's own ambitions in Syria brought confrontation with Britain, and even danger of war. Then, too, there was Afghanistan. In early August 1839 – the very time when Elliot at Canton was trying to deal with the Lin Weihi death – a British expeditionary force marched north from India to bring an ally, Shah Shuja, back to the Afghan throne, and head off Russian threats to India's northern frontiers. Wellington's foreboding that British difficulties would begin once the military successes ended was to be cruelly fulfilled. The expedition left India with great pomp, with something under 10,000 soldiers and not far short of 40,000 camp followers. In one regiment, the officers needed two camels just to carry their Manila cigars, and the personal baggage of one brigadier needed no less than 60 camels.[2] They settled down comfortably enough in Kabul and a few of the officers married Afghan ladies.[3]

Relations with America were a problem, too, partly because the British tried to insist on a right to search ships suspected of carrying slaves, something which the Southern states would not tolerate. By May 1841 Palmerston was telling Parliament that his negotiations on slave trading were almost everywhere successful and he hoped that soon 'we shall have enlisted in this league against the slave trade every state in Christendom which has a flag that sails on the ocean, with the single exception of the United States ...'.[4] Even apart from slave trading, there were continuing difficulties about defining the border between the United States and Canada. In Europe, of course, there was the final settlement of Belgian independence. Apart from commerce, China was simply not very important.

Palmerston himself was not inclined to change his lifestyle. Quite early in Queen Victoria's reign, for instance, some members of her household at Windsor were awakened one night by panicked cries from one of the ladies-in-waiting. When they reached the scene they found she was trying to fend off the Foreign Secretary. It turned out she had a room in which Palmerston usually spent the night, but with another lady. No wonder Victoria was inclined to talk of him as 'the immoral one'. Not that such things tempered his self-confidence and good humour. At one point, when the Cabinet resigned, he was just about to give a dinner for the heir to the Russian throne, the Tsarevich. Someone suggested that the dinner might now be cancelled, but Palmerston just laughed. 'What?' he said, 'lose my place (that is, my post) and my dinner, too?' Still, in 1839 things changed considerably, as Palmerston finally married his dear mistress, Lady Cowper – rather against the advice of her prime ministerial brother, Lord Melbourne. Whereupon, under her management, Palmerston's house became one of the most influential social and political centres of London.

For all that focus on England's affairs, or Palmerston's domestic ones, at the end of September 1839 political attention did shift, quite suddenly and for a while, to China. On the 21st news of the confinement of the British at Canton reached London for the first time, with the arrival of Elliot's dispatches up to the previous 29 May. There was an immediate outcry about the dangers and sufferings of British civilians and the insults to the British flag and its representative, against the background of China's arrogant and provocative assertions of superiority. Further pressures came from commercial groups, especially Midland and Northern textile firms keen, as always, to expand their sales into the allegedly limitless Chinese market. Also in September, 39 Manchester cotton firms sent a memorial saying they had goods worth £1 million (tv: £39 million) stored at Canton and the people in charge were in imminent danger. They had suffered damage and wanted reparations. They also wanted a just trading arrangement with China for the future. At the start of October, 96 London firms made similar appeals, as did firms from Leeds and Liverpool. In the months that followed a series of other memorials reached the government, from the Chambers of Commerce of Blackburn, Bristol, Glasgow, Leeds, Liverpool and London, as well as from the East India and China Association, all urging strong action.[5] The Canton merchants were even more vocal. Matheson, who had urged their case in previous years, had by 1840 returned to China. But Jardine, perhaps the richest of the Canton traders, had set sail in January 1839 to press London for more positive policies, including a threat to use force. He launched an energetic and sophisticated publicity campaign, encouraging pro-merchant pamphlets like 'The Opium Question', a shrewd defence of the trade by the barrister Samuel Warren. He allied himself with some of the textile firms and made efforts to see the Foreign Secretary.

Palmerston began to think about more decisive action. The timing of his reactions makes it abundantly clear that what moved him was not mere commercial interest – those voices had been heard for several years – still less the opium trade, but the business of national honour and the security of English people. A week after the Canton dispatches arrived, on 27 September, Palmerston finally called Jardine in. The visitor brought along a former commodore of the Jardine & Matheson clipper fleet, as well as maps and charts of the China coast, which Palmerston kept. They discussed, in detail, what ships, troops and arms would be needed to deal with the Chinese. Jardine seems also to have offered Palmerston the services of the Jardine–Matheson fleet as naval auxiliaries. The advice was warmly welcomed and throughout the campaign Palmerston looked to Jardine's London offices for intelligence about China. Information directly from Canton could not, of course, get to London quickly and anyway the Jardine–Matheson people were bound to have the best intelligence on local waters and conditions ashore.

Three weeks after that first meeting, on 18 October, Palmerston wrote to Elliot that an expeditionary force from India would reach Canton around March 1840 and should blockade Canton as well as the Bei He river below Beijing. On 26 October Palmerston received Jardine once more to get his assessment of Britain's, and the merchants', longer-term needs: a fair treaty of commerce, a blockade of Chinese ports to obtain reparations, the occupation of several islands like Hong Kong and the opening of four new ports to commerce. And at the end of November Palmerston wrote more fully to Elliot to outline the terms of future diplomatic negotiations with the Chinese.

Between 2 and 9 December 1839, London received further dispatches from China about the surrender of the opium and Elliot's pledges of compensation to the merchants. It was at once clear that China's suppression of the opium traffic, with which much of London sympathized, was now entirely subordinate to the issue of British subjects, even innocents, being held hostage, and of some £2 million (tv: £78 million) of British property that had been forcibly confiscated. Palmerston reacted immediately. As early as 14 December Jardine was writing to Matheson that Cabinet had made up its mind to demand reparations from the Chinese. Coincidentally, the American merchants at Canton were sending a memorial to Washington also calling for a joint blockade of the China coast by the British, French and Americans. That would obtain a satisfactory treaty of commerce, perhaps without any need for bloodshed at all.

Simultaneously, Jardine sent a memorandum to Palmerston with further suggestions. Britain should send two ships of the line, two frigates and two river steamers, together with transports sufficent for seven thousand men. They should blockade the Bei He river leading to Beijing and demand an apology for the insults suffered by the British and payment for the 20,000-odd chests of opium. In addition, there should be a treaty on free trade through ports like Shanghai, Xiamen (Amoy), Fuzhou (Foochow) and Ningbo. If those demands were not met, Britain should seize certain coastal islands until the Chinese accepted them. Jardine also wanted the opium traffic reorganized on a safer and more regular basis. Other advice suggested that forces be sent to the junction of the Yangzi and the Grand Canal, so threatening Beijing's own communications, including food supplies, from the South.

It is worth noting that much later, after the conflict, Palmerston privately acknowledged the importance of the advice and help he had received from Jardine and his London agent, Abel Smith. It was to this 'so handsomely afforded us [that] it was mainly owing that we were able to give our affairs naval, military and diplomatic, in China those detailed instructions which have led to these satisfactory results [i.e. the 1842 Treaty of Nanking] ... There is no doubt that this event ... will form an epoch in the progress of the civilization of the human race ... ' He also thought how remarkable it was that this information and help 'which was embodied in the instructions which we gave in February 1840, was so accurate and complete that it appears that our successors [e.g. the Peel administration that took office in 1841] have not found reason to make any alterations in them'.[6]

Given the views of later generations on the opium issue, it is worth noting that as long ago as 1831 – even before the abolition of the East India Company monopoly – a Company dispatch laid before Parliament had said '... if it were possible [the Company] would gladly prevent the use of the drug altogether, but that was absolutely impracticable'.[7] And the Committee of the London East India and China Association submitted the following thought to Palmerston in November 1839:

> When we find the growth of opium within the territories of the East India Company is a strict monopoly, yielding a large revenue; that the drug is sold by the Government of India in public sales; and that its destination is so well known that in 1837 the East India Company's Government actually directed by a public notice a large sum of money to be given as a bonus to shippers to China of the season; when we observe that the Committees of the House of Lords and Commons have enquired minutely into the subject of the growth of opium; the amount it contributed to the Indian revenue; and with

a full knowledge of the place of its ultimate destination have arrived without any hesitation at the conclusion 'that it did not appear advisable to abandon so important a source of revenue'; when we look at the persons composing these Committees, and those examined before them, consisting of Ministers, Directors of the East India Company, former Governors of India etc, etc; men of all parties and of the highest moral character; when we know, moreover, that the India Board, over which a Cabinet Minister presides, has an effective control over the East India Company and might prevent what it did not approve – we must confess that it does seem most unjust to throw any blame or odium attaching to the opium trade upon the merchants, who engaged in a business thus directly and indirectly sanctioned by the highest authorities.[8]

Jardine pushed the same line from the moment he got back to England. He organized pressure in ways rather new to British politics and stressed, not morals, but the role of the government itself in encouraging opium-growing in India, quite specifically for the Chinese market. The traders would have been quite willing to sell other things. As even one American observer, Elijah Bridgman, admitted, the opium problem at Canton was largely one of China's constraints on other trade. 'Ninetenths if not every one of (the traders) would abandon (the trade) at once and forever, provided it was disowned and disapproved of by their government, and a well-regulated and honourable commerce in all other articles opened and ratified with the Chinese.'[9]

On 9 January 1840 the Foreign Office received further reports from Canton on the Lin Weihi affair and the expulsion of British families from Macao. It was bad enough for British men to have been imprisoned and threatened, but it was now clear that even women and children had been under threat, both at Macao and on the ships. But for Victorian England, womanhood, pure, unsullied and idealized, stood on a pedestal, long before the late twentieth century reduced her to mere equality. If there was one thing likely to make the average Englishman incandescent, it was the notion that innocent English women, and babies, were being exposed to dark and nameless insults and dangers at the hands of dirty Chinese ruffians. These were not matters on which London was able or willing to compromise. Jardine himself, who was to win a seat in the Commons next year and hold it until his death in 1843, saw Palmerston again on 6 February 1840. By that time, indignation in London had become seriously heated although, even then, not everyone wanted an armed response. On 12 February, for instance,

Prime Minister Melbourne sent Palmerston a note to say that both he and Lord John Russell wanted to have a 'man of station' sent out to conduct negotiations with China on the security of trade in the future.[10] There were suggestions that a Select Committee of Parliament should look further into the opium question. But the dice had fallen. Nine days later, on 21 February, the Foreign Secretary wrote to the government of India to start military preparations. Sixteen warships with 540 guns were to be got ready. That should include three of the biggest ships of the line, accompanied by four armed steamers and transports for 4000 troops. The naval command should be given to Admiral George Elliot, Charles Elliot's cousin, and the two Elliots should be joint plenipotentiaries in pressing British demands upon China. That fleet should arrive at the Pearl River estuary by the end of June. Canton, Ningbo and the mouths of the Yangzi and Yellow rivers should be blockaded and China threatened with a total paralysis of her foreign trade. That accomplished, the force should sail on to Bei He, the gateway to Beijing, and put its demands.

These were laid down in three documents of 20 February.[11] One was a letter from Palmerston to 'The Minister of the Emperor of China'. The vagueness of address was dictated by the fact that London was entirely ignorant of the structure and *modus operandi* of the Chinese government and empire. The other two were instructions to the two Elliots. Between them, the documents detailed British grievances, demands for redress and instructions to the Elliots about the strategies to be pursued and the settlement to be sought.

From London's point of view, there were now some five broad issues to be settled with the Chinese, by the threat of force and, if necessary, its use. First and foremost, there was the arbitrary imprisonment of British men, women and children. Second, there was the Chinese affront to the British crown, government and flag, not only in its treatment of the British at Canton but in the assertions of Chinese superiority and Britain's 'subordinate' status. Third, there was the matter of compensation to the merchants whose goods had been forcibly seized. Fourth, there was the future arrangement of China's trade with the outside world. And fifth, in the background, there was also the question of controlling China's coasts and borders, which Britain consistently refused to be involved in, as distinct from offering advice to the Chinese.

The first issue was self-explanatory and accepted by the great majority. Even on the second, there was little public dispute about China's unacceptable 'insults' to the British crown, or to the honour of the flag; or about the apologies now due. It was also widely agreed that trading arrangements needed reform. The difficulties of channelling foreign trade solely through a single Chinese merchant monopoly in a single port could not be allowed to continue. Trading arrangements would have to be opened up, the Hong monopoly abolished and Chinese customs duties regularized.

Honouring Elliot's promise of compensation to the merchants for the lost opium was an altogether more sensitive business. It was clear to Cabinet that Elliot, having given the pledges in the name of the British government, could not decently be repudiated. Yet his promise meant that the government should accept a huge financial and budgetary burden in order to pay vast sums to opium dealers. It was true that Elliot had given the pledge only in response to Chinese *force majeure*, and to fend off dangers to life and limb of unprotected British subjects. But how could an administration already in deficit find the money? Ministers would have to ask Parliament – and a Whig parliament at that – for around £2 million (tv: £78 million) to compensate admitted opium smugglers. It was not to be thought of. Asking China to pay for property extorted as ransom was an altogether more plausible proposition.

Plausible or not, was it wise, or just, or legitimate, to try to settle these matters by force? Was it justifiable even if all that the government seemed to envisage was limited reprisals and armed demonstrations leading to Chinese reparations, not a serious resort to war? Especially armed action against a ramshackle but essentially peaceable empire which had never invited the intrusion of British trade, let alone British power, yet which had every right to make and enforce its own arrangements for the behaviour of foreigners on its own territory.

Policy debate varied from sophisticated discussion of Chinese affairs or trade by people with long experience in the East, all the way to mere jingoism and clouds of indignation about China's behaviour. What it did not include was any widespread agitation about opium. It is true that the churches, and especially the increasingly influential evangelical groups and missionaries made themselves felt, but majority opinion was more relaxed and in Britain itself opium, and other drugs, remained freely available, quite uncontrolled. And not just in Britain. By the 1840s marijuana (which probably reached Europe after a French army got used to it after being marooned in Egypt by Horatio Nelson's victory in the Battle of the Nile in 1798) had become fashionable in both France and America. Opium itself had, after all, been known since ancient times and used in Western medicine at least since the sixteenth century. In England, by the mid-seventeenth century Thomas

Sydenham had argued that 'among the remedies which it has pleased Almighty God to give man to relieve his sufferings, none is so universal and efficacious as opium'.[12] By the later eighteenth century it was in fairly widespread use, mostly in the form of laudanum, or in cordials or syrups, used as a remedy for laryngitis or coughs. In fact, consumption was rising and the East India Company shipped a good deal of it to Britain. One House of Commons report pointed out that for 1839 British opium imports amounted to some 95,800 lbs of the stuff. For 1840 the figure was 196,200.

So that, although by the nineteenth century opium was often socially rather frowned upon, the English were quite unconvinced that they had an opium 'problem'. No-one thought that Thomas de Quincey's famous 'Confessions of an English Opium-Eater', published in 1821, was evidence of anything remotely criminal. Many others, including the poet Samuel Taylor Coleridge and the anti-slavery activist William Wilberforce, were opium users, even addicts. Florence Nightingale found that it helped her greatly. Morphia, derived from opium, was isolated in 1805 and seems to have come into use in the 1820s (with morphine itself coming into medical use shortly after the invention of the hypodermic needle in 1853).[13] Victorian babies were kept quiet with Godfrey's cordial, containing opium, while remedies for the common cold were apt to contain cocaine. Packets of laudanum were widely available in every manufacturing town. Temperance societies found that their philippics against gin, while somewhat reducing gin consumption, made people turn to opium instead. It was widely held, therefore, that the evils of opium were greatly exaggerated; a lot of people used it in moderation with no ill effects and it could actually be highly benefi-cial.[14] In China itself there was known to be widespread poppy growing. Opium was widely, even universally, used in Turkey, also in Persia, Arabia and the entire Malay archipelago as well as India.

The facts behind the opium trade in the East were also well under-stood and publicly acknowledged. Opium was being produced not only by the East India Company or by those parts of India which were under British rule. It was also produced by independent Indian princes, by Persia and Turkey. London perfectly understood the general trading profits from it, the special importance of the trade to Indian revenue and the cash that the Treasury earned from tea imports which were themselves partly financed by opium sales. As we have seen, the opium traders repeatedly complained that attacks on them and their trade were quite unfair given Parliament's explicit approval of what they were doing. If production, trade and revenue patterns were disrupted, there would be great damage to the public as well as private interest. Anyway, in areas beyond British control, production would continue, especially within China itself. Nor would control of shipping interrupt the opium traffic, even if such controls were desirable and legal. Stopping the traffic between India and China would, at minimum, require the deployment of serious naval forces; and even if that were done, the trade would merely be diverted to other flag-carriers.

In any event, the British were by no means alone in trading opium. According to a new pamphlet by the same Mr Lindsay who had written to Palmerston in 1836, almost all the American trading houses at Canton were also taking part in it. They even had their own depot ship at Lintin.[15] Hundreds of Chinese merchants and officials were involved as well. According to Mr Lindsay, the Chinese admiral who was supposed to stop smuggling took such a regular 'tax' from the smugglers that he actually requested the British, as a special favour, to allow him to have these payments collected on board the foreign depot ships at Lintin, lest his smuggling compatriots should cheat him. *Blackwood's Magazine* agreed that talk about opium was to raise a false issue. It was no worse than tobacco or gin. Stopping Chinese imports would in any case not stop consumption. And given the profits the Chinese themselves made from the traffic, indignation about it was 'humanity-mongering hypocrisy'.[16]

It was, however, widely agreed that Commissioner Lin's actions against English civilians, putting them in fear of their lives, were beyond the pale. For the *Quarterly Review*,

> ... above all, the brutality of the Imperial Commissioner in expelling [that is, even after the surrender of the opium], *en masse*, our countrymen, who had neither offended him nor the laws of China, from Macao ... forcing men, women and children, at twelve hours' notice, to flee to the ships already crowded, depriving them of all provisions, and preventing them by armed vessels from taking off those they had purchased from the willing natives ...

was an 'unquestionable atrocity' and made 'the interposition of the English crown inevitable.' Altogether, the *Quarterly Review* thought, China was '... full of insolence, full of error, needing to be enlightened ...'.[17] So the general feeling in the country, as well as the government, seemed to be for war. *Blackwood's Magazine* also thought that Commissioner Lin had been guilty of 'overt aggression', aggravated by 'injuries so atrocious', including the murder of British seamen and threats to Elliot's life, that there was no way to avoid conflict.

Even so, Parliamentary support for the government was by no means guaranteed. The government had already moved to head off some criticisms. Back on 11 November the Treasury had announced, ominously, that it had no money to pay the compensation that Elliot had promised to the merchants; and the government did not intend to ask Parliament for the funds. At the same time, the administration made no attempt, then or later, to defend the opium trade. Nor did it question, in any forum, China's right to regulate imports and exports, or the way in which it dealt with smuggling on its coasts.

Rumours about the use of force started to fly around London as early as the end of 1839. When Parliament opened in January 1840, the Queen's speech only said, cautiously, that the government would soon have to attend to Chinese affairs; though there seemed little doubt that it had indeed been decided to support the officials and merchants on the spot. In late January, and now under some pressure, the government promised to table papers, in the form of six years' worth of correspondence on China. It was becoming known that preparations for action were going forward at Calcutta and on 18 February, Sir James Graham, for the Opposition, asked pointedly in the House of Commons when the papers might actually be tabled. Three days later Lord Ellenborough in the Lords asked whether papers would be accompanied by a government policy statement. The Prime Minister answered blandly that there would be no message from the crown. By March *The Times* was reporting 'War declared on China.' As domestic politics began to focus on all this, the way that the government presented its case in Parliament naturally became more important. Palmerston himself continued to pay close attention to public opinion and worked to manipulate various editors and newspapers, even if they had, by modern standards, tiny circulations.[18] He constantly supplied friendly newspapers with comment and exclusive information, as usual tending to favour the *Globe* rather than *The Times*, which often got special treatment from the other side of the political fence.[19] He went on taking care to cultivate his image as the nation's favourite Englishman and to use support outside Westminster to fend off challenges not just from the opposition but from political colleagues, and even from within the royal family.[20]

Papers dealing with the March 1839 events at Canton reached the Commons on 5 March 1840 and the next day Sir James Graham was on his feet again, asking why they did not deal with the November naval fight at Chuenbi, news of which had reached him privately. Lord John Russell, as Secretary for War and the Colonies, correctly explained that no official report on this action had yet been received. Six days later another member of the Opposition, Mr Mackinnon, asked bluntly whether it was true, as was widely believed, that war against China had been declared. Russell was delphic, saying there was no official intelligence to say that, though some instructions had been sent to India to be ready for eventualities. The Leader of the Opposition, the great Sir Robert Peel, then asked whether, if there were to be a war, it would be an imperial war, or simply an armed demonstration by the government of India. Palmerston agreed that any communication with the government of China would be in the name of the Queen.[21]

The Opposition was not satisfied. Even less so the churchmen and other groups strongly opposed to opium. On 19 March the Peelites demanded more information since the newspapers were full of unconfirmed reports, and urgent preparations were clearly being made in India. In reply, Russell now admitted that the aims of the expedition were:

> In the first place, ... to obtain reparation for the Insults and Injuries offered to Her Majesty's Superintendent and Her Majesty's subjects by the Chinese Government; and, in the second place, they were to obtain for the merchants trading with China an indemnification for the loss of their property, incurred by threats of violence offered by persons under the direction of the Chinese Government; and, in the last place, they were to obtain security that the persons and property of those trading with China should in future be protected from insult and injury.[22]

Various people made clear that none of this meant support for the opium trade; others that any war against China would be entirely unjustified.[23]

On 7 April Peel and his colleagues moved a vote of censure,[24] setting off a full-dress, three-day debate in the Commons. The debate was oddly limited. What the Opposition did *not* criticize was the government's intention to fight a war. Nor did it suggest disbanding the proposed military expedition. The Tories, at a prior meeting at Peel's house, had decided that making the war the central issue would merely divide their own party. They were almost equally constrained in talking about opium, even though the topic could hardly be avoided. The Opposition's senior members had themselves helped to protect it, by accepting the recommendations of the 1832 Parliamentary Committee. Nor had they since then shown much interest either in opium or in reforming the trade. They were bound to find it hard suddenly to develop a high moral line, the more so as the government had consistently made clear that it did not support the trade, as distinct from protecting opium production within India. But the government found the topic awkward, too. It had the problem of India's production of the drug and the profits which both British and Indian revenue made from it. It was even more embarrassing to talk about the money involved in compensating the traders.

Even given such limitations, the debate was notably serious and well-informed, with several people taking part who had long experience of China and the East. Though there were moments of passion, there was no slanging match. The cases for the two sides were essentially these. The Opposition, given its need not to attack the forthcoming war, attacked government bungling in allowing matters to come to such a pass. The government might not have been knowingly wicked. But it had been indolent, had neglected its duties and, in the words of the Anglican prayer-book (though no-one actually quoted it) had 'done those things which it ought not to have done and left undone those things which it ought to have done.' In particular, while the trouble at Canton had been almost wholly caused by the behaviour of private British merchants, various superintendents, and especially Elliot, had time after time been refused the judicial and other powers to do anything about it. Indeed, Palmerston had repeatedly reminded Elliot that he had no power to control or discipline the British merchants. The government had also failed to establish sensible lines of communication with the Chinese authorities; and ignored repeated Chinese requests and warnings about smuggling. Yet it would have been easy to try to help. It would have been entirely feasible to do something about opium production in India and to close down opium exports at Indian ports. It was the Chinese who now had right on their side.

Ministers, however, pointed out that Britain had no right to police parts of China and wholly lacked the means and resources to control smuggling on that distant coast. While smuggling and breaking China's laws could not be excused, Chinese dealings with the British had been entirely unacceptable. They had threatened both innocent and guilty with starvation, even death. Similarly, there had been confiscation, on pain of death, of very large quantities of British property. Equally unacceptable was the insult to the British flag and to the British Sovereign, in the person of her representative Charles Elliot. It was only fitting that reparation should now be sought, preferably by negotiation but at the point of the gun if necessary.

The debate was opened by Sir James Graham. In his three-hour speech there was only brief mention of '... the growing evils connected with the contraband traffic in opium ...'. After all, Graham had himself served (as First Lord) in the 1830 Grey ministry, which had abolished the East India Company's monopoly of trade with China in 1833. So he had been personally associated with the policies he now condemned. Since the Opposition also accepted that war was now necessary, Graham concentrated on the government's 'want of foresight' and its incompetence. It had failed to give adequate instructions and powers to the superintendents on the spot. Its policies had been incoherent in allowing the situation to deteriorate to this point, given the overall importance of the China trade and the clearly peaceable instructions which had been given to Lord Napier a few years earlier. Indeed, Graham said, Britain's own revenue earned no less than some £4.2 million (tv: £164 million) from the total China trade. He also emphasized the vast importance and strength of China, with her 350 million people, her unity and national pride, but also her extreme suspicion of strangers. That meant refusing a right of residence to the foreigners and any direct communication between them and China's own authorities. It was a great mistake to try to intimidate the Chinese, rather than pay attention to their laws.[25] Yet Napier's very first communication to them had asserted that he had political and judicial functions; and the great Duke of Wellington had already commented on the folly of that approach. Palmerston himself had been repeatedly warned, for instance by Elliot's dispatch of 19 November 1837, that unless the illicit trade in opium was put down, legitimate trade would be in danger.

The response came in a powerful speech by Thomas Babington Macaulay, who was by now not just a brilliant and famous essayist and historian but the Secretary of State for War.[26] He was highly indignant. Why had no powers been sent to Elliot? Because, as late as May 1838 there had been good reasons to think that the Chinese government would legalize the opium trade. In any case, whatever powers the British government might have given to the superintendent at Canton, the opium trade could never have been stopped except by the action of the Chinese themselves. In Britain, with no less than 6000 customs officers, there was a lot of smuggling – for instance some 600,000 gallons of brandy a year were brought into the British isles. Why should a mere piece of paper stop that kind of thing? Did anyone think it feasible that Britain could pay for a preventive service for the whole of China? There was also the absurd idea that the British government was in favour of opium or of contraband. Members '… had seen it asserted, over and over again, that the government was advocating the cause of contraband trade, in order to force an opium war on the public; but he thought it was impossible to be conceived that a thought so absurd and so atrocious should have ever entered the minds of the British Ministry.' In fact, Britain's course was clear.

They might doubt whether it was wise policy for the Government of China to exclude from that country a drug which, if judiciously administered, was powerful in assuaging pain, and in promoting health, because it was occasionally used to excess by intemperate men – they might doubt whether it was wise policy on the part of that government to attempt to stop the efflux of precious metals from the country in the due course of trade. They learned from history – and almost every country afforded proof, which was strengthened by existing circumstances in England... – that no machinery, however powerful, had been sufficient to keep out of any country those luxuries which the people enjoyed, or were able to purchase, or to prevent the efflux of precious metals, when it was demanded by the course of trade. What Great Britain could not effect with the finest marine, and the most trustworthy preventive service in the world, was not likely to be effected by the feeble efforts of the mandarins of China. But whatever their opinions on these points might be, the Governor of China alone, it must be remembered, was competent to decide; that government had a right to keep out opium, to keep in silver, and to enforce their prohibitory laws by whatever means which they might possess... and if, after having given fair notice of their intention, to seize all contraband goods introduced into their dominions, they seized our opium, we had no right to complain; but when the government... resorted to measures unjust and unlawful, confined our innocent countrymen, and insulted the Sovereign in the person of her representative, then... the time had arrived when it was fit that we should interfere...[27]

Macaulay went into a sunburst of rhetoric. British subjects imprisoned in China would naturally

look with confidence on the victorious flag which was hoisted over them, which reminded them that they belonged to a country unaccustomed to defeat, to submission or to shame... to a country which had made the farthest ends of the earth ring with the fame of her exploits in redressing the wrongs of her children... they had not degenerated since her Great Protector[28] ... vowed that he would make the name of Englishman as much respected as ever had been the name of Roman citizen. They knew that, surrounded as they were by enemies, and separated by great oceans and continents from all help, not a hair of their heads would be harmed with impunity....[29]

All of which went down extremely well with the government's supporters.

One member with personal experience of the East, Sir W. Follett, summed up a main pillar of the Opposition's case by harping on the 'deficiency of powers possessed by the Superintendent ... every captain of a British vessel had full power to do as he pleased at Canton'.[30] Palmerston had told Elliot that Britain 'cannot interfere for the purpose of enabling British subjects to violate the laws of the country with which they trade. Any loss, therefore, which such persons may suffer ... must be borne by the parties who have brought that loss on themselves ...'[31] But by what authority were the merchants to be disciplined? According to Elliot, the Chinese would only interfere with the British in case of 'extreme emergency', for they did not understand, and knew that they did not understand, British customs and laws. That being so, they could see that it would be unjust to apply to the British rules devised for people of different habits and disciplines, like the people of China. Equally, Elliot had said that he would 'resist to the last, the seizure and punishment of a British subject by the Chinese law, be his crime what it might.' By the same token, Follett asked, why should European international law be applied to a country like China? Although the British were violating Chinese laws all the time, it was now being said that the violation of international law by the Chinese justified going to war.

He was answered by another man with personal experience of the region, Sir G. Thomas Staunton, who thought that before Lin's arrival at Canton 'there was no law ... in China by which the hair of the head of any European could have been touched for smuggling.' In fact, the Chinese were behaving towards the English as if to a 'refractory village' in their own country.[32] Yet Parliament should remember that the entire British Empire was founded on prestige. If they submitted to insults from China, British political ascendancy would collapse. As for opium, it was indeed bad for a great trade to depend on some prohibited traffic. Britain should have gradually shifted Indian production away from opium. But it was unreasonable to expect a sudden shift from the great levels which opium imports had, by 1837/38, reached as a proportion of China's total trade.

Some younger members were more passionate. Sidney Herbert, for the Opposition, said baldly that Britain was 'contending with an enemy whose cause of quarrel is better than our own.' In this dispute with China, Britain had shown herself to be the less civilized of the two. Britain was engaged in 'a war without just cause', a war to 'maintain a trade resting on unsound principles, and to justify proceedings which are a disgrace to the British flag.' In response, someone pointed out that even ending the contraband trade at Canton would not stop the trade in opium, given the amount of smuggling elsewhere along the coast. And Britain could hardly provide China with a coastal protection service.

A still more powerful philippic came from young W.E. Gladstone, destined to become one of Britain's most remarkable Prime Ministers and already a man of magisterial presence, evangelical fervour and exhausting fluency. He was also a politician well able to use his face and body-language as part of his argument. Also a man who regularly used laudanum when preparing for a major presentation in Parliament. He now recalled what Wellington had written to Napier years earlier: 'It is not by force or violence that His Majesty intends to establish a commercial intercourse between his subjects and China; but by the other conciliatory measures so strongly inculcated in all the instructions which you have received.' Elliot should certainly have been given greater powers and British courts should have been established to deal with British subjects at Canton. But Palmerston had been unwilling to do that and Elliot had consequently been ordered to make bricks without straw. It had been deceptive of Elliot to say to the Chinese: 'His Government had no knowledge of the existence of any but the legal trade, and that over any illegal trade he could exercise no power.'[33] The Chinese had given repeated warnings that the British trade would be stopped if the opium receiving ships at Lintin were not sent away. They had shown 'exemplary patience', but found themselves treated with contempt in a situation where, actually, the British community almost to a man was involved in the illegal traffic.

Even if it had been beyond Britain's power to put down the opium trade, some co-operation might have been given to the Chinese, for instance by refusing to give the receiving ships the protection of the British flag. But in fact, it was nonsense to say that opium smuggling into China could only be stopped by the Chinese themselves. Did the Minister not know '...that the opium smuggled into China comes exclusively from British ports, that it is from Bengal and through Bombay? If that is a fact – and I defy the right honourable gentleman to gainsay it – then we require no preventive service to put down this illegal traffic. We have only to stop the sailings of the smuggling vessels....'

In sum, though Gladstone made no call for the war plans to be altered or cancelled, he condemned what he called an iniquitous war, which would leave an indelible mark on the conscience of Britain.[34] It was the obstinacy of the government itself in continuing with the 'infamous and atrocious' opium trade which had produced this trouble with China and it was difficult to see how the withholding of food from British people living in China but refusing to obey China's laws could be regarded as a crime. He indicated, to the shock and horror of the government benches, that 'the Chinese had a right to poison the wells, to keep away the English'.[35] Altogether, 'A war more unjust in its origins, a war more calculated in its progress to cover this country with permanent disgrace, I do not know and I have not read of.' Although 'the Chinese are undoubtedly guilty of much absurd phraseology, and of no little ostentatious pride and of some excess, justice in my opinion is with them, and whilst they the pagans and semi-civilized barbarians have it, we, the enlightened and civilized Christians, are pursuing objects at variance with both justice and with religion.'

The issue continued to weigh on his mind. A few weeks after the debate he noted in his diary: 'I am in dread of the judgements of God upon England for our national iniquity towards China.'[36]

After further discussion, the Opposition's case was summed up by Peel himself.[37] He was careful to make his critique narrow and specific. He was deeply concerned about the prospect of conflict with so large a country as China. But he made it clear that he was offering no views on either the opium trade or on the justice or otherwise of the conflict: only on the deplorable conduct of the government in allowing – even if war were now necessary – things to get to this point. Napier and, after him, Elliot had been sent out with inadequate instructions, or powers, and even without the moral backing of some naval force. He, too, therefore thought that Britain's representatives had been given the semblance without the reality of power. As early as 27 December 1835 Elliot had warned of the dangers of allowing the British to ignore Chinese orders regarding traffic on the river. It had always been very likely that the Chinese would 'resort to some general measure in assertion of their power and independence as a government, involving the interruption of trade, till some required concession shall be made. No government can afford ... to be reduced to utter contempt in the sight of its own people by a handful of foreigners ... .' There were therefore serious dangers stemming from attention to the '... gains of a few individuals, unquestionably founding their conduct upon the belief that they were exempt from the operation of all law, British or Chinese.'

Yet in 1833 the government had explicitly been given the power to allow the Superintendent to make regulations and establish courts for British subjects in China.[38] In spite of that, the only response to the

Superintendent's pleas had been a note from Palmerston to say that British regulations and police powers for British subjects 'would be an interference with the absolute right of sovereignty enjoyed by independent states...' even though Elliot had said he was sure the Chinese provincial authorities themselves would favour the establishment of British courts.

As things now stood, it was true that outrages had been committed against British subjects and war might well be necessary. Even then, however, it was necessary to remember the 'forbearance of the Chinese under great irritation and exasperation' and that it was of the utmost importance to restore amiable relations with the Chinese once the fighting was over. Before the present troubles had started Elliot himself had said that in no part of the world was life and property as secure as in Canton, and that the Chinese were in many ways 'the most moderate and reasonable people on the face of earth.' Even if there had to be a war, the measures taken should be temperate and the damage done should be minimal.

Palmerston's reply was calm and detailed.[39] No less important for its impact on a House of Commons audience, it was assured, self-confident and full of cheerful good sense. He clearly did not think it necessary to repeat, yet again, that China was obviously entitled to prohibit any import it wished and to enforce that prohibition. Britain could not interfere in that. Instead, he pointed out that, until very recently, intercourse with China had been prosperous, successful and friendly. He was no more in favour of the opium trade than anyone else, and had been 'desirous, even under present circumstances, of discouraging on the part of our agents any extension of the cultivation of the poppy.' Elliot had 'from the first to the last ... endeavoured to discountenance the traffic to the utmost of his powers.' But it had been said that the government should also have given him the power on his own authority to expel from China every ship and man engaged in the opium trade. But that would have been 'a momentous and arbitrary power, a power open to great abuse.' As it was, criminal and admiralty jurisdiction in China had actually been established under the 1833 Act and the instructions issued back in 1837 had been just those given to any consul or officer sent abroad. But they were not intended to allow him to expel from China anyone he thought involved in the opium trade. Beyond that he, Palmerston, had himself brought forward a China Courts Bill in 1837 and again in 1838 to extend the previous powers. At that time Peel as Leader of the Opposition had personally objected on the grounds that one could not establish a court in the territory of an independent sovereign without his consent; and that the courts, far from being expanded, should on the contrary be withdrawn.

It was also true that Napier had insisted on personal and direct communication with the Chinese authorities. But both of his successors, Robinson and Davis, had entirely approved. 'Unless,' Davis had written in August 1834 'we can have direct access to the Government officers, we can do nothing.'

In fact, Palmerston was elaborating on a situation in which no nineteenth-century British government had an ability, remotely akin to that of the later twentieth, to direct and control the overseas mercantile activities of its citizens. He protested at the suggestion

> that to put down the opium trade by acts of arbitrary authority against British merchants – a course totally at variance with British law, totally at variance with international law, a course of the most arbitrary kind, and liable to every possible objection – was a fitting course for the British Government to pursue … Any Government would have been greatly to blame which, without taking the sense of Parliament, would upon its own responsibility, have invested a consular officer, at 15,000 miles distance, with powers so arbitrary … He was perfectly sure that, if he had made such a proposal, it would not have been agreed to … .

Even if such a power had been granted, would it have been obeyed? There would have had to be a system of punishment for violation. The Superintendent would have had to be able to use force. But the idea of putting armed men under his orders would hardly have appealed to the Chinese.

Anyway, if the Chinese were so keen on banning opium why had they not banned its production in China? Their real motive had to do with bullion exports and the protection of their own agriculture. And in a situation where Britain was not even able to stop smuggling at home, he 'wondered what the House would have said to … Ministers, if they had come down to it with a large naval estimate for a number of revenue cruisers to be employed in the preventive service from the river at Canton to the Yellow Sea for the purpose of preserving the morals of the Chinese people, who were disposed to buy what other people were disposed to sell to them?' Even if such an attempt had been made, it would have taken time. Yet as late as April 1839 Elliot had written that he expected the confiscations to end up with the legalization of an opium monopoly in the hands of the Chinese government itself. Even that left aside the obvious consideration that if the British stopped, the trade could carry on under the American flag. And if the supply from India was reduced, supplies from Turkey, Persia and elsewhere would fill the gap.

Palmerston concluded with two points. One was to quote a memorandum written shortly before, on 24 January, by the American merchants at Canton to their own government. It sought the co-operation of the United States government with the British in establishing safe commerce with China, and did so in terms remarkably similar to those which Palmerston also had in mind. The American government, these merchants wrote, should seek Chinese permission for envoys to reside at Canton. There should be fixed duties and tariffs on exports and imports. Bonding warehouses should be established. Trade should be extended to other ports. The Chinese should pay compensation for the losses caused by the stoppage of all legal trade at Canton and the detention of property and ships. And until such time as Chinese laws clearly laid down punishments, the punishment of wrongs committed against Chinese should not be greater than those which would be imposed under British or American laws. The actions of the Chinese Commissioner had been 'unjust and no better than robbery'. A joint British, American and French naval force should be stationed on the Chinese coast to look after Western interests. Palmerston added that though a military force was being sent to China, it would probably not have to be used. A military demonstration would probably prove enough to have British grievances met.

It was a highly effective speech and won general praise,[40] perhaps even more for its style than for its content. 'He did not argue much ... but ... He was so gallant and confident, and claimed the support of all on our side ... with so much gay assurance, that he completely succeeded in his appeal, and sat down amid thunders of applause, which lasted some time ... .'[41] Palmerston won his vote by 271 to 261.

Nor did the Opposition do any better in the Lords. There, Lord Stanhope tried to repeat the kinds of moral argument Gladstone had used in the Commons. The answer came from Melbourne himself who said quietly that opium was probably less harmful than gin and anyway it was the Chinese who insisted on smoking it. While no one used the language of modern economics, the obvious point – which Commissioner Lin would have largely agreed with – was that unless one reduced demand, there was no point in trying to strangle only one of several sources of supply. The discomfiture of the Tories was complete when the Duke of Wellington himself declared that in half a century of public service he had seen no insults and injuries as bad as those visited on the British at Canton. Elliot deserved all praise and the Chinese deserved to be punished. On 10 April, Melbourne confirmed, in answer to Lord Aberdeen, that the government meant to ask China for reparations. Otherwise, action would be taken against China's trade and courts would have to be set up to authorize the sale of ships and goods that might be seized.

American opinion was not so divided. It is hardly surprising that, a mere thirty years after the Anglo-American war of 1812 and only half a century after the War of Independence, popular opinion leapt to the conclusion that Britain was the sole villain of the piece while America's China traders had been entirely law-abiding. In fact, they had been responsible for some 10 per cent of the opium trade.

6
Fighting and Talking: Elliot 1840–41

By the start of 1840 the military and political manoeuvres were gathering pace. The British had left the factories, the river, and even Macao. They were living on ships off Hong Kong, awaiting troops from India and orders from London. Elliot was busy keeping up morale and dealing with Chinese attempts to send fire-ships against his merchantmen.

In March, Palmerston's instructions for the China expeditionary force reached India and the outlines of his strategies became clearer there. The Governor-General in Calcutta, Lord Auckland, who was directly responsible for the expedition, ordered it to assemble at Singapore, which Stamford Raffles had acquired for Britain back in 1819. Arrivals were erratic, many ships being delayed or damaged by wind and weather, not to mention the difficulties of assembling and moving troops, their Indian servants, supplies of water and food, ammunition and stores. Which left a lot of officers free to socialize at Singapore while marines practised landings. The interim commander was Commodore Sir James Gordon Bremer, pending the arrival of Maitland's successor as Commander-in-Chief East Asian station, Rear-Admiral Sir George Elliot. The bulk of the force left Singapore at the end of May and straggled to China, with the flagship, the 74-gun *Wellesley*, reaching Macao Roads on 24 June. In the meantime, there were more fire-ship attacks on the merchantmen at Hong Kong,[1] and once Bremer arrived he ordered an immediate blockade of the estuary. Shortly afterwards Admiral Elliot also arrived. He brought three of the ships from the Cape of Good Hope, where some officers had promised their girlfriends to bring back a few Chinese pigtails as souvenirs. The command now included 16 warships with 540 guns, four armed steamers and 28 troop-ships and transports with 4000 troops, from British units as well as Indian regiments with British officers, in the service of the East India Company. The Indian soldiers, or sepoys, were of course also regulars, generally drawn from the military castes for whom it was an honour to serve under arms.

Even some missionaries were pleased. As the American, Elijah Coleman Bridgman, cheerfully noted 'A force has entered that cannot be expelled and will not pay homage.'[2]

But what, exactly, was the force supposed to do? Its instructions were set out in the three Palmerston documents of 20 February. First, the formal letter to the Chinese government noted earlier and, given London's ignorance of the structure of Chinese government, addressed simply to 'The Chinese Minister'. Three copies of it were included with the other two letters, both addressed to the Elliots. All of them make it abundantly clear that whatever else the British may have sought, no one was thinking of anything like forcing opium on the Chinese, still less of territorial conquest. That would have been impossible anyway, since even if London had not been seriously worried about expanding overseas responsibilities, the force was manifestly inadequate for anything of the kind. Instead, these documents suggest a quite limited expedition, to force a particular kind of agreement on the acknowledgement of status, reparation for injury done and a removal of restrictions on trade.

The letter to the Chinese Court detailed British grievances and demanded redress. Chinese officials had committed 'violent outrages' against peaceful British residents at Canton. Of course, when British folk went abroad, they should obey local laws, including the Chinese prohibitions against opium imports. The British government did not wish to protect them 'from the just consequences of any offences'. But violence, injustice and insult were something else. And it was unjust that general laws – like the anti-opium edicts – should be enforced only against foreigners and not against Chinese. (It is not entirely clear whether Palmerston understood that he was wrong about that.) Nor was it reasonable to let a law become a dead letter and then, without warning, enforce it 'with the utmost rigour and severity.' Anyway, it was notorious that officials at Canton had for years connived at the opium trade and earned large bribes to allow the drug imports. Even mandarin boats had been busy doing it. Yet Chinese officials had remained unpunished, while violence was used against foreigners who had been 'led into transgression by the encouragement and protection' of Chinese officials.

There would have been no complaint, the document went on, if the Chinese government, after due notice, had started to enforce its laws and confiscate all the opium. Instead, it had tried to 'punish the innocent for the guilty, and to make the sufferings of the former, as the means of compulsion upon the latter'. It had tried to use an officer of the British crown as an instrument of the Chinese authorities for enforcing Chinese laws. Peaceful British merchants had been imprisoned in their houses and threatened with death by starvation – which was hardly true, either – so as to force other people, over whom these merchants had no power, to surrender opium which the Chinese themselves had neither found nor managed to seize.

The British would therefore demand the restoration of the 'ransom which was exacted as the price for the lives' of the British merchants, as well as restitution of the value of the goods seized. Britain would also demand satisfaction for the insult to the British crown by the treatment of its officer, the Superintendent, and the establishment of normal official communications between his successor and Chinese authorities. The security of British people trading in China must also in future be guaranteed. An island off the coast should therefore be handed to the British, for residence and commerce. In addition, the debts owed by the Hong merchants to British creditors should be paid. Palmerston added that it had been necessary to send a British military and naval force to China to support these demands. It had been told to blockade the principal Chinese ports and then to move north to the coast off Tianjin (Tientsin) and the mouth of the Bei He. It would then be close to Beijing, and so could communicate easily with the Chinese government. Naturally, the Chinese should also reimburse Britain for costs of the expedition. Palmerston's advisers, like James Matheson, probably knew that many of the substantive demands (except for money) were quite similar to the concessions Beijing had made some years earlier in Central Asian border regions. Even the idea of treaty ports was a replay of old Chinese ideas about frontiers: the naming of specific places designated for trade.

The letters to the Elliots[3] told them to put pressure on China's trade, starting with a blockade of Canton, whose governor should be given one copy of the letter to 'The Chinese Minister', together with a translation into Chinese, asking him to forward the documents to Beijing. They were then to occupy Chusan (Zoushan) Island, 100 or so miles south of Shanghai and just off the Hangchow (Hangzhou) estuary. Another copy of the letter to the Chinese should be sent ashore from there. The force should blockade that estuary, as well as the mouths of the Yangzi and the Yellow River. The Elliots should then move to the mouth of the Peiho and send the third copy ashore, also for forwarding to Beijing, together with their own request for a reply. (In a further instruction of 4 March they were rather quaintly told to distribute handbills as they sailed along the coast, to reassure the population about British intentions.)

If there was no satisfactory response, they should carry on with military action, but stand ready to negotiate at any time. If Chinese plenipotentiaries appeared, they should be accorded equality with the two Britons. The document also mentioned the British demands outlined in the letter to Beijing: reparations for the affronts to the British crown, the Superintendent and the British subjects. Furthermore, either the British should occupy one or more offshore islands as surety for the future, or else the Chinese should, in a formal treaty, grant personal security and freedom of commerce to British subjects in China.

The treaty should give security to British persons and property, give freedom of residence at China's main ports and open the chief ports along the coast, that is Canton, Xiamen (Amoy), Shanghai, Ningbo and Fuzhou. It should also give the British freedom to trade with anyone in China and set import and export duties at fixed and published levels, to replace the old ad hoc imposts. It should allow China to confiscate illegal or smuggled imports, but without molestation of British people. It must also agree to the presence of British consuls-general and consuls, ranking with mandarins, and to official communication between them and Chinese local and central governments; and accept the right of the British consul-general, or superintendent, to make regulations, and establish courts to deal with British subjects in China. The British occupation of Zoushan should continue until all these demands had been met. Finally, the new trading arrangements should be extended to all foreign powers, since Britain did not seek special or exclusive privileges.

Furthermore, the Elliots were told to use minimum force to bring the Chinese to reasonable terms. Perhaps a mere blockade of the China coast would be enough. But they were also firmly told to stick to the government's demands. In fact, Palmerston seems to have had his doubts whether Charles Elliot could be relied on to follow orders. In a dispatch of 3 February 1840 – that is, three weeks before he even issued formal instructions to the two cousins – he told Charles that none of the government's demands were to be treated as negotiable. And on 4 March he wrote again to say that if, by the time his instructions of 20 February arrived, Charles had concluded any agreement that did not entirely meet these demands, the Chinese should at once be told that it had been concluded without authority and would not be recognized by London.[4]

So it was going to be an odd kind of war, with a British campaign that was fitful, at times even hesitant. It was also bound to be slow, given the transport facilities of the day. Even twenty years later, when the British navy had to carry a much larger invasion force of 20,000 men to China, it did so in 173 ships, mostly ancient sailing vessels, moving at maybe five knots. This sort of thing gave everyone plenty of time for relaxation. When Major-General Lord Saltoun set off for the 1842 campaign, he was careful to bring along a staff officer, Captain Hope Grant of the 9th Lancers, who could accompany Saltoun's violin on his cello. In fact, Hope Grant brought his piano along as well (and when, some years later, he was posted to Simla, up in the Himalayas, it took 93 servants to carry his gear).[5]

Furthermore, while the fighting might be done by military professionals and specialists, the campaign relied heavily on local civilian and commercial support. The merchants, and their colleagues in London, had helped Palmerston to design aims and strategy in the first place. Those in China waters now gave material help. They leased their ships, including opium vessels, or lent their captains as pilots. They provided translators, too, and helped with hospitality, advice and the latest local intelligence. The merchants' silver reserves, including earnings from opium, were exchanged for bills on London or Calcutta and the bullion itself made available, together with the merchants' local money, to meet the expedition's local costs. Matheson himself understood very well that the Elliots had no way of raising money for local expenses except through the silver earned by the opium trade.[6] That alone – and quite apart from the political influence that the local British might have in London – made for friendly relations between the expedition and the traders. Opium clippers became good neighbours with the Navy, for all the anti-opium philippics of some British and American missionaries – or of the French Catholic fathers. Indeed, in the summer of 1840 the opium traffic remained much what it had been. By the autumn, the chief operators, still Jardine–Matheson, thought that of the 6500 chests on the coast just then, 3700 were in ships connected to their firm.[7]

Nor was that kind of relationship peculiar to this time and place. Such support for the forces has always been normal. Leasing merchant vessels to the Navy or the government had long been, and remained, regular practice. Merchant seamen and captains helped, or served in, many a war; while to have local civilians, persons in good standing with Parliament and the government at home, offering hospitality to the Navy remains customary. Similarly, that local British people should offer locally usable money to British forces has happened in every war and campaign before and since. Moreover, throughout the campaign no one, not even the Chinese themselves, had anything like reliable maps. At Canton, and along the coast, no one except the merchants and their people had close local knowledge and the expedition had few other ways of collecting intelligence. Certainly neither Palmerston nor Auckland had alternative ways of getting adequate information about China's needs or vulnerabilities, or even its topography.

Even with such help, though, Palmerston's orders were one thing. How to fit them to local conditions was something else entirely. It was all very well to tell the Elliots to blockade Canton, seize Zoushan, deliver a letter addressed to the Chinese Emperor's minister and go north to the mouth of the Bei He to sign a treaty with a Chinese government representative. Or to give the cousins a draft of the intended treaty, together with their orders. But how to do all that? Who would accept letters, and on what terms? Would the documents be delivered to the Court, and if they were, what might the reaction be? Or again, as Charles Elliot well understood, a comprehensive blockade of Canton, even if it had been possible, would have badly damaged Britain's own interests, since it would have cut off China's exports of the tea that Britain wanted, not to mention all other legal trade. But in fact, a proper blockade was a non-starter. Trade at Canton was bound to continue throughout the war, whatever Lin, or the British fleet, might say or do. Trade on British account simply continued through neutral shipping and with goods transferred at Hong Kong into ships sailing under Swedish or Prussian or Danish colours. Or English goods could be taken to Manila, get fresh bills of lading there, and sail unmolested into the estuary. The Americans especially, also being neutral, continued to do business on commission or trans-shipping. The fleet would anyway have to tread softly with the local British people on whom, in so many respects, it would have to rely. That certainly applied to the opium merchants. In fact, throughout the war, opium ships were able to follow the flag. When British troops occupied points on the coast, opium clippers invariably sailed in their wake, to Xiamen, Zoushan and the Shanghai region. When Canton surrendered, even the opium receiving ships went back up the Pearl river from Hong Kong to Whampoa.

Or again, it was all very well for London to issue an Order in Council in April 1840 for the Royal Navy to seize Chinese ships and cargoes. But the China coast had local commercial junks numbered in their hundreds or even thousands. It was quite impossible for the Navy to seize them all, let alone find enough prize crews. And if it had been possible to seize them, what could be done with them anyway? In any case, what was the point of orders to blockade Canton or to seize ships? Beijing would care neither for China's exports nor for the junks. The imperial government was quite indifferent to hardship for ordinary Chinese. Indeed, Chinese governments, before and since, have often been ruthless with their own citizens. When fourteenth- and fifteenth-century emperors wanted ships built, they simply had hundreds of artisans and their families dumped at the ports. It was clear that if attempts were now made to carry out the order, it would only serve to alienate the very coastal population with whom the British wanted to extend trade.

So Charles Elliot had an entirely different perspective on the war from that of Lord Palmerston. Elliot saw the affair as a pragmatically minimal form of pressure-plus-persuasion to get the Chinese to continue, safe-guard and expand British commerce. While Palmerston was much less interested in the commercial well-being of a particular set of Canton merchants, but very interested indeed in Britain's power, prestige and standing – as well, of course, as getting the Chinese to meet costs that Parliament at home would certainly not stomach. These differences caused friction almost immediately.

In the meantime, with the turn of the year, Lin had begun to shift the emphasis of his anti-opium campaign even further from attacking sup-ply to attacking demand. He set about seizing drugs, organizing searches and gaoling users and addicts. In January, he also issued his new edict, listing British crimes and banning their traders from doing business in China ever again, though everyone else's merchants could trade as usual. No product from Britain, or any British territory, would be allowed into any Chinese port. None of this, though, had much effect. The ships at Hong Kong continued to supply opium to smugglers and peddlers of all shapes and sizes, while the Americans were even happier to earn money from the British for shipping tea from Canton out to Hong Kong or to international waters.

In February, placards began to appear at Macao to say that soldiers were coming to expel the red-haired devils. Elliot was delighted to get Palmerston's dispatch of the previous October, saying that a British expe-dition was on its way, and sent his wife and small son off to Singapore. On the 12th the Emperor confirmed the decision to embargo British trade and put Lin in personal charge of Canton, in addition to continuing as Imperial Commissioner. Now trade became, even for neutrals, more difficult. And Lin – who had flatly disbelieved reports that a fleet was on its way from India – issued proclamations which amounted, in time-honoured Chinese tradition, to a declaration of war. He had spent six months making his preparations. The Napier affair had already shown how vulnerable China was on water, and the Emperor now approved his view that it was not wise for China to fight off-shore. It would be better to opt for defence and wait on land, with fresh troops, to deal with an enemy who would be tired and worn out by the time he came on. Lin now offered rewards for the capture or destruction of English people or ships.[8]

Capturing a warship would earn a man its entire contents, except arms and any opium, plus a sum of money depending on the size and value of the vessel. An 80-gun man-of-war, for instance, could earn the captor 20,000 Spanish dollars in cash. By early 1841 the price for a British ship of the line had gone up to $100,000. The skipper of a Royal Navy warship was worth $5000, with $100 offered for a live ordinary sailor or soldier. Charles Elliot, though, was worth $50,000 alive, his head alone just $30,000. Quite similar proclamations, and cash offers to the Chinese soldiery, were issued against the French in 1884 and against the Japanese ten years later, in 1894. Around the end of the century one old-fashioned Chinese official remarked to a Western observer: 'You know the Chinese soldier, and how impossible it is to make him fight, except by special inducements, and, besides, it is our immemorial custom.'[9]

The British ignored this kind of thing and moved on, leaving behind a detachment to demonstrate their command of the Pearl River and its estuary. The expedition sailed towards Zoushan, a 25-mile long island around 800 miles up the cost and 100 miles below the mouth of the Yangzi. The first stop was Xiamen (Amoy), where the Elliots planned to deliver Palmerston's letter to the Chinese authorities. However, boats trying to land were shot at and it proved impossible to deliver anything. The force arrived at Zoushan on 4 July, to Beijing's complete surprise, since Lin had given no warning that other parts of the Chinese coast might be assaulted. The ships arrived at Dinghai harbour – the opium skippers knew the waters well – the following day, to find the locals arguing loudly that if the British had complaints about Canton, they should go and fight the Cantonese, not make Zoushan suffer.[10]

Bremer and the local Chinese commander exchanged courtesies, but next day the British drew closer. A landing force from the 26th Regiment (Cameronians), and the grenadier company of the 18th (Royal Irish), together with some marines and artillery, was readied, waiting for a Chinese surrender. When it did not come, the Navy's guns hammered the defences for 8–9 minutes – using round shot instead of canister, so as to minimize Chinese casualties – and the landing parties went in, with detachments moving towards the town, which turned out to be a mean and dirty place, whose people had largely fled, leaving behind stores of rice and an arsenal of quaintly antique weapons. Charles Elliot, when he saw the place, thought the massive naval and military assault had been quite unnecessary.

The local magistrate committed suicide, as many Chinese officials and soldiers were to do in the face of defeat by foreign devils. Few of the British understood that a war, which to them was an honourable but limited way of settling differences, was for the Chinese nothing less than the defence of civilization against barbarism. Little wonder that defeat meant disgrace and despair. The invaders appointed a new civil magistrate, in the person of a captain of the Cameronians (very much foreshadowing the civil controls imposed in 1945 by the British and Americans in occupied Germany). There were inadequate attempts to stop 'looting' by the local population (loot originally being the Bengali word for plunder),[11] of whom one interpreter remarked that 'A more subtle, lying and thievish race it never was my luck to live amongst'.[12] (Did he really expect the invaders to be received with open arms?)

However, if occupying Dinghai was easy, staying there proved exceedingly painful, largely because of poor command and the sheer incompetence of British supply arrangements. Once the town's magistrate was dead, and most of the locals had gone, there were no local supplies or labour for the British. European troops would not eat rice, but the flour they brought was foul after months of storage in ships at sea, and the biscuits, salt beef and pork were equally unfit for human consumption. By the end of July, too, foraging parties found they could no longer buy fresh food. Water was drawn from muddy fields or, worse still, from canals alive with sewage. Also, to spare the town, and avoid further native hostility, the troops were put into more out-of-the-way places. The Cameronians got a bare hill inside the town. The Bengal Volunteers were even put into tents in low-lying, sodden paddy fields. In the stifling heat of summer, and with awful food and water, the men fell ill by the dozens and hundreds.[13] Dysentery, diarrhoea, heat exhaustion and, of course, malaria and food poisoning, were soon rife. As early as the end of September, some 150 were dead and 1300 were sick. By the end of the year things were much worse. Of the 3300 men who had gone ashore only 1900 remained and many of those were sick. One regiment, which had left India with 28 officers and 902 British other ranks had lost 240 dead, hundreds sick and had only 110 men fit for duty. Quite similar supply and medical horrors would occur in the Crimean War of 1853/54 and the Burma campaigns later in the 1850s. It was all very different from Wellington's efficient logistics in Spain and Belgium thirty years before. On the other hand, medical missionaries established a hospital at Dinghai that dealt with some 1600 Chinese in the last four months of 1840.[14]

There was also the question of what to do about British people captured or kidnapped by the Chinese and gaoled on the mainland. For instance, a small British vessel, the *Kite*, foundered off the coast. The captain was drowned, but his pregnant wife, Ann Noble, and three crew members managed to reach land. They were beaten, put in irons and placed in small bamboo cages – hers was a yard high and three-quarters of a yard wide – to be paraded through the streets, enduring whatever insults or filth the rabble could throw at them. When they reached Ningbo they found themselves in small and dirty cells. English gentlemen were apt to be infuriated by such public maltreatment of an Englishwoman, rather as people in London had been when reading about the Canton crisis in 1839.

At the end of July 1840, the Elliots sailed further north with ten of the naval ships. At Chinhai, at the entrance to Ningbo, they tried to leave another copy of Palmerston's letter to the Chinese, but it was returned, unopened. So two ships were left to blockade Ningbo and two more to seal the mouth of the Yangzi. The others, as foreshadowed in Palmerston's correspondence back in 1839,[15] sailed north towards the Bei He and Beijing. Once again the Chinese court was totally unprepared, since Lin had given no warning of a possible British northward thrust. Not only were they unprepared, they were wholly ignorant of what they were up against. Even the governor of Jiangsu (Kiangsu) province, Yukien, who had been closer to the British expedition, thought nothing of its capabilities. British soldiers wore uniforms, he reported to the Emperor, whose '... waists are stiff and their legs straight. The latter, further bound with cloth, can scarcely stretch at will. Once fallen down, they cannot again stand up ...'.[16]

By 10 August the *Wellesley* anchored off the Bei He. But she found the anchorage difficult. For fear of running aground she had to stay so far off-shore that, even from her mainmast, all that could be seen was water. Charles Elliot took a pinnace, found the channel through the mud-flats and made contact with Qishan (Kishen), the Governor-General of Chihli province (now Hebei). He agreed to send Palmerston's letter on to Beijing and sent gifts of meat and fresh vegetables to the British. Without effective Chinese defences in place, the expedition was now close enough to Beijing to cause serious anxiety, so the imperial court began to be more cautious and accommodating. In court circles, the Palmerston letter was interpreted as a complaint against Commissioner Lin, so maybe the British would be satisfied by having him punished? The British move to Bei He therefore triggered Lin's fall. He later claimed that the British had only gone north because he had blocked them at Canton; but it did him no good. At the end of September, the cases of Lin and Deng were referred to the Board of Punishment.

At the end of August, Beijing had made up its mind and Qishan invited Elliot for talks. They met for a six-hour session, which produced no agreement on any major point of substance. On the issue of opium, Elliot managed to embarrass the Chinese with a highly Confucian argument. He pointed out that over half of China's opium imports came from areas beyond British rule. Anyway, one could not make people virtuous by legislation, and if Chinese were determined to smoke opium, they would not be stopped by violence. What was needed was persuasion and good example. On the matter of Chinese territory, especially Zoushan, Elliot agreed that it would be evacuated once a settlement had been reached. But on Britain's claims for cash, there was no meeting of minds. Qishan was simply astonished that it should be seriously suggested that the Emperor would pay a king's ransom in silver to people who trafficked in drugs and did great harm to the empire. He did, however, agree that the British at Canton had been treated with undue violence. Lin would therefore be dealt with. A new commissioner, surely Qishan himself, would conduct further negotiations, but talks would be far better held at Canton, where the real trouble was, rather than close to Beijing.

The Elliots felt they had little choice. Their ships were stationed amid shoals and sandbanks, with bad weather sure to make the already poor communications between ship and shore much worse, and sandbanks making effective naval support for any landing impossible. In any case, too few troops were now fit for duty. They therefore brought the fleet back to Zoushan, *en route* to Canton.

Meanwhile, with the Elliots in the North, and with the bulk of the British away from Canton waters, the Chinese thought of dealing with the remaining foreign devils at Macao. One or two people were kidnapped and more and more soldiers and junks seen at Macao's barriers and near its waters. So, on 18 August, some British marines, seamen and 400 sepoys attacked the forts at Macao's borders, or barriers, spiked guns, burned equipment, and withdrew. They suffered four wounded. Chinese reports said the English had been driven off with heavy losses and damaged ships, but Macao was not threatened again for the rest of the war.

By the time the Elliots and the fleet returned to Zoushan at the end of September, much had changed. The British had begun to firm up control of the island, to the point where people were returning to Dinghai. The troops started to move to more sensible quarters and food and vegetables from the locals once more became mysteriously available. The arrival of the fleet helped, too, since the Elliots brought flour and bullocks from the North, while one ship was dispatched to a small island off Korea to capture another 60 cattle. With the arrival of colder weather, and Christmas, malaria cases fell away and officers could go out into the countryside and shoot woodcock and duck. And Charles Elliot went over to the mainland to try once more to do something about the running sore of those British captives held at Ningbo. However, his discussions with the elderly and genial Yilibu (Ilipu), the Governor-General of Kiangsu, Kiangsi and Anhui (Anhwei), got nowhere. Yilibu made it clear that he would not release anyone. On 6 November Elliot had to accept that release was not on the agenda. The only bargain he could strike was that in return for having the prisoners made more comfortable, the British would refrain from seizing more merchant junks or blockading more ports.

The Elliots left Zoushan and arrived back in Canton waters on 20 November. Admiral Elliot resigned on health grounds on 1 December, and sailed home a week later. Charles Elliot, left to handle things alone, now learned that Lin was in disgrace. In fact, in mid-November Lin had sent the Emperor a plea to continue with the existing strategy. The Emperor dismissed this as 'completely useless', and accused Lin of having neither stopped opium consumption nor driven away the outlaws. At the end of November Lin, for all that he had been very popular with his people, was further 'degraded' and ordered to report to Beijing. In the middle of the following year he was sent into exile.

The Elliot–Qishan talks would therefore now be conducted without either negotiator having a partner or anyone looking closely over his shoulder. Negotiations were, for much of the time, conducted by correspondence, since Elliot stayed on board the *Wellesley*. But both men immediately moved well beyond the Palmerstonian framework, since both knew that neither government would accept the other's stated terms. Qishan understood China's military and naval weakness well enough. But he also knew that the Emperor would not even consider London's demands. On the British side, too, as early as 29 September dispatches to London warned that the original demands would be hard to secure without a much longer and more intensive war, whereas a more limited and temporary settlement, including compensation for the destroyed opium, would be easier to get. Fresh instructions were needed. (When Palmerston received that suggestion in February 1841, he flatly refused.) But in the meantime Elliot felt free to make major policy decisions on the spot. On 13 December we find him writing to Auckland in Calcutta saying that he expected an agreement shortly. It would stop 'far short of the government … [but it will have] sown the seeds of rapid improvement without the inconvenience of indefinitely interrupted trade; and we shall have avoided the protraction of hostilities, with its certain consequences of deep hatred.'[17]

At the end of the year the talks were clearly going nowhere and broke off. More ominously, Elliot learned that the pro-war party was once again dominant at Beijing, since a resumption of fighting looked more promising as soon as the British moved away from the neighbourhood of the capital. At the same time, too – though Elliot could not know it yet – both London and Calcutta were seriously disappointed with the way the campaign was being run. Auckland thought it had all been a waste of time, money and quite a lot of men. Palmerston was even more critical of Charles Elliot's hesitations. He sent two more warning letters. One, on 9 January 1841,[18] severely criticized the shift of negotiations to Canton and the Elliots' failure to object to the Chinese Commissioner's continued tone of superiority. There had been phrases about the 'dutiful reverence' of the British, about 'entreating the Imperial Favour' or 'principles of deference and respect' and the desire that the Admiral should 'respectfully obey the declared Imperial pleasure', all of which Palmerston thought entirely unacceptable. Three weeks later, on February 3, he wrote to warn again that London's original demands must be maintained.[19] The forces now available should be quite enough to compel Chinese compliance. Indeed, the negotiators should check carefully that Chinese compensation payments really did come from imperial resources, and were not extracted from the British themselves by increased duties on future British commerce. He also took the opportunity of commenting once more on the opium trade. 'It is evident,' he wrote at the end of February

> that no exertion of the Chinese authorities can put down the opium trade on the Chinese coast, because the temptation both to the buyers and to the sellers is stronger than can be counteracted by any fear of detection and punishment. It is equally clear that it is wholly out of the power of the British Government to prevent opium from being carried to China, because even if none were grown in any part of the British territories, plenty of it would be produced in other countries, and would thence be sent to China by adventurous men....

On the Chinese side, the Canton elites were even keener on renewing war than Beijing. Lin and his supporters in the bureaucracy worked hard to undercut Qishan with the Emperor and to end any moves for peace. They succeeded in persuading the monarch to move to destroy the foreign threat altogether, and Qishan was told to drag out negotiations until the forces needed to crush the foreign devils were assembled. In preparing themselves, Chinese commanders studied writings about lessons to be drawn from earlier border defence in the empire's West and North. Which proved not to be very useful in dealing with modern Western troops, and especially navies. On 6 January 1841, the British discovered a Chinese edict calling for the destruction of all British ships and people. Action was clearly called for and the soldiers and sailors on the spot were anyway keen to get on with the war. An advanced naval weapon had become available, too, with the arrival of an entirely new kind of ship. She was the new iron paddle-steamer *Nemesis*. A ship of some 660 tons, she was not only built of iron but had a flat bottom and a very shallow draft of only six feet, which made her ideal for action in estuaries and other close waters. She carried two 32-pounders and several 6-pounders and, though technically a private vessel and not part of the Royal Navy, was treated as a warship by everybody.

She went into action immediately, when some 1400 British and Indian troops attacked the Chinese outer forts at the Bogue. They fell on 7 January, after a naval bombardment and occupation by landing parties, largely of marines and sepoys of the 37th Madras Native Infantry, which took the forts from the rear. *Nemesis* was able to come in below the angle of depression of the Chinese fort artillery and to pour in grape and canister, so the British suffered no casualties. Many of the Manchu regulars, on the other hand, fought almost to the last man. One American observer spoke of Chinese soldiers rushing 'upon the bayonets of the marines and soldiers and [being] slaughtered like sheep.'[20] Anyway, the British were taking few prisoners. As Colonel Armine Mountain commented 'The slaughter of fugitives is unpleasant but we are such a handful in the face of so wide a country and so large a force that we should be swept away if we did not read the enemy a sharp lesson whenever we came into contact.'[21] Elliot thought some 700 Chinese had died. On the same day, a squadron of Chinese war junks was destroyed in a naval engagement, rockets fired by the *Nemesis* alone accounting for 11 of them. The superiority of British weapons, training and discipline was strikingly demonstrated, even though the troops were not particularly well armed by the standards of the day. Most regiments still had the old smooth-bore flintlocks instead of the newer percussion-lock weapons.

A day later, by 8 January, Elliot thought he had done enough, withdrew his forces and approached the Chinese commander, Admiral Guan, for a ceasefire. He wanted the tea exports to be able to leave the estuary peacefully. Beyond that, he wanted a resumption of fruitful trade and took no pleasure in the large Chinese casualties. Indeed, it was pointed out to the Admiral that under Western military usage, if the forts surrendered, they and their people would be protected. The trouble was that the British withdrawal produced Chinese reports to Beijing claiming a signal victory. That lent weight to the efforts of the Han political elite at Canton to persuade the wider imperial political class that the war in the Pearl River delta was by no means lost. Any setbacks had merely been the fault of the Manchu commissioner, Qishan. Nevertheless, on 20 January 1841 Elliot reached a preliminary agreement with the Chinese, the Convention of Chuenbi. It said that Hong Kong would be ceded to Britain, China would pay an indemnity of $6 million, direct official intercourse between Britain and China would be established on the basis of equality, and trade at Canton would be reopened. In addition, Elliot proclaimed an 'open door' policy for Western trade with China, once again making it clear to all and sundry that Britain was not after conquest, or selfish advantage, but meant what it said about seeking free trade. Britain, he said 'sought for no privilege in China exclusively for the advantage of British subjects and merchants.'[22] Here was, it seemed, a settlement. The following day the forts were handed back to the Chinese and a week later Qishan gave a banquet, lavish with official civilities, for a large British party.

The trouble was that both governments promptly repudiated the agreement. On the British side, Lord Auckland immediately objected to the evacuation of Zoushan in return for the acquisition of Hong Kong. He thought the indemnity entirely inadequate, while Elliot had made things even worse by agreeing to have it paid off at the rate of $1 million per annum, which would allow the Chinese to pay it off from British customs duties, just as Palmerston had feared. Altogether, Auckland wrote, the terms of the convention 'fall very far short of the expectations with which this powerful expedition was fitted out'. Elliot had been weak and the government's instructions had been 'feebly and imperfectly' carried through. Palmerston was even angrier when the details of the Chuenpi Convention reached London in mid-March. The entire campaign had yielded nothing but $6 million and a small island that was barren, without ports or towns. England could not even claim sovereignty over this Hong Kong, since that would require the Emperor's signature. As for the money, it was nowhere near enough to meet the China-related obligations of a government already short of funds. Palmerston was not alone. Auckland's sister, Emily Eden, said simply 'the Chinese have bamboozled us.'[23] On 10 April Palmerston wrote to the 22-year-old Queen Victoria: 'Captain Elliot seems to have wholly disregarded the instructions which had been sent to him, and even when, by the entire success of the operations of the fleet, he was in a condition to dictate his own terms, he seems to have agreed to very inadequate conditions.'[24] The Chinese operations, he said, were not finished. Naturally the queen also blamed Elliot and wrote to her uncle and confidant, King Leopold of the Belgians, of 'the unaccountably strange conduct of Charles Elliot...who completely disobeyed his instructions and *tried* to get the *lowest* terms he could'. Palmerston, she said, was 'deeply mortified'. Lord Minto, another of Elliot's cousins, thought he had lost his head and become more Chinese than English.

Not everyone agreed. The Prime Minister, Melbourne, thought Britain could live with the agreement, though he also wrote to Palmerston that 'Elliot is not equal to the situation' and 'our people [are] too low in their language and their demands.' To the Colonial Secretary, Lord John Russell (who, incidentally, married Minto's daughter, Fanny Elliot, three months later), he said that 'the Treaty as it stands saves our honour and produces all the necessary moral effect. To renew the war would keep the whole thing alive, which it is of the utmost importance to close.'

The China merchants were divided, too. Many of them were furious with Charles Elliot and thought the convention was simply deceptive. But Matheson, with whom Elliot had maintained quite cordial personal relations, understood the growing power of newspapers in English politics. He wrote in late January to Jardine in London, urging him to find a lawyer who would defend Elliot in the newspapers, and to pay the man handsomely.[25]

The Palmerstonian views prevailed. The Cabinet would have nothing to do with any treaty based on the convention, and decided to replace Elliot. On 21 April Palmerston wrote cuttingly to dismiss him.[26] 'I gave you specific demands and furnished you with the means for obtaining them ...' The force available would have been quite adequate but had been used hesitatingly. Elliot had made a principle of insubordination and accepted terms far short of the British government's demands. In fact 'throughout the whole course of your proceedings, you seem to have considered that my instructions were waste paper, which you might treat with entire disregard, and that you were fully at liberty to deal with the interests of your country according to your own fancy.' Elliot had accepted an indemnity that was not only absurdly small but so spread out that the Chinese could recoup the sum from future taxes on British trade; had made no arrangements to get the Hong merchants' debts settled; had given up Zoushan without waiting for the payment of the indemnity; and, while he had accepted the barren island of

Hong Kong, had failed to secure trade openings at ports further north. None of the major Sino-British problems had been resolved. What he had agreed to, Palmerston concluded, could only have been justified by serious military reverses. Elliot would have to go.

On the Chinese side, the Emperor was equally furious. He was especially indignant at the surrender of Chinese land and citizens: of Hong Kong, with its handful of Chinese farmers and fishermen. Almost as bad was the proposal to resume trade at Canton. In fact, once Qishan became aware of the Emperor's anger, he tried to undo the Hong Kong surrender by offering Elliot a collection of Chinese curios and a gorgeous Chinese mistress. But Elliot would have none of it, and by the middle of February learned that Qishan had followed Lin into disgrace and fighting would soon resume. In addition to his other sins, Qishan had even sent an unpardonably honest memorial to Beijing, detailing the weakness of Canton's defences and the cowardice and corruption of its defenders. A month later he was taken off to Beijing in chains, condemned to death and had his property confiscated. However, instead of execution, he later became Imperial Commissioner to Tibet and Governor-General of a couple of provinces. At Canton he was succeeded by a triumvirate. In overall command was a prince of the blood, Yishan (Ishan), his two colleagues being Yungwen and Yang Fang, a professional soldier.

None of which prevented other arrangements from going forward. At the end of February the British prisoners at Ningbo, including Mrs Ann Noble, were brought over to Dinghai and the British duly evacuated Zoushan. Hong Kong was occupied on 26 January 1841, as agreed, to be a commercial storage centre and military and missionary base. Elliot issued a proclamation making Hong Kong inhabitants subjects of the British crown. However, any Chinese there 'shall be governed according to the laws and customs of China, every description of torture excepted', while the British and other non-Chinese would be governed according to British law.[27] Interestingly, Elliot even seems to have told Matheson that he saw no objection to storing opium on the island.

With Qishan no longer in real and effective charge on the Chinese side, it became clear that there would soon be more fighting. Chinese military preparations were obviously under way. On 25 February Elliot, who could see that the Chinese would soon move, struck first. British warships from Hong Kong attacked, and landing parties captured some of the inner Bogue forts, Charles Elliot himself landing with the storming parties. More forts were seized next day and a flotilla of 40 war junks sent scurrying to safety. Admiral Guan was discovered among the dead, with a bayonet thrust in his chest. He had earned such respect for his courage that one British ship fired a salute in his honour. The forts were demolished, the river barriers removed and Elliot sent his ships further up the river before pausing once more. But when the Chinese launched fire-rafts, he moved up towards the city, from which crowds of Chinese promptly fled. In mid-March came a general assault to secure the Canton river front, with seamen and marines landing on the factory square. Two days later Elliot raised the Union Jack, announced a suspension of hostilities and a resumption of trade. Fresh armistice negotiations followed. Elliot's repeated fight-and-talk tactics – what the American missionary S. Wells Williams called his 'ill-timed mercies' – gave Qishan, who had not yet actually left, a chance to report repeated victories to Beijing, even while his rivals at court condemned him.

On the British side, it had by now become very clear that more senior and experienced military and naval commanders were needed. So a new British general was sent out. He was Major-General Sir Hugh Gough, from the Madras army. Here was another colourful character in a campaign not short of such folk. A soldier from the age of 13, he became adjutant of his regiment of foot at 15,[28] served as a colonel under Wellington in the Peninsular War against Napoleon, and would end his career as Field-Marshal Viscount Gough. Even now, in China at the age of 61, he was wiry, energetic and as keen on strenuous exercise as another British general, Bernard Montgomery, was to be 150 years later in the Second World War. Gough arrived on 2 March 1841, bringing his son, son-in-law and nephew with him. By the time he came, a number of things had changed. Bremer had left for Calcutta, to be succeeded by Sir LeFleming Senhouse of the *Blenheim*. Opium selling had resumed all along the China coast, and in reliable ways. When Elliot suggested to Senhouse that he might stop the smaller boats carrying opium up river to Canton, Senhouse refused. Opium, he explained, was a legitimate Indian product and neither he nor Elliot had authority to restrict it.

The day after Gough arrived he started fresh operations against the Chinese defences. On 6 March his troops occupied one of the forts overlooking Canton proper, and by the 20th Yishan's deputy, Yang Fang, agreed to an armistice. The Chinese also agreed to a resumption of trade,[29] in spite of instructions from the Emperor that 'if any of you have the two words "reopen trade" still in mind, then you are completely betraying the purpose of your mission to Canton'. Not only did trade indeed resume, and some of the China merchants return to Canton, but by mid-April, almost forty British, American and French ships, all properly licensed, were riding at anchor on the Pearl River.

Trade, Gough concluded, was the only thing the Superintendent was really interested in.

Elliot visited Canton in early April. Although in public he declared himself satisfied with Chinese assurances of good faith, he could hardly doubt that in fact they were once more just playing for time. Canton's defences were visibly being strengthened, a large Chinese encampment was being prepared beyond the city and Chinese troop reinforcements were reported to be on their way south. In fact, the Emperor had decided on nothing less than a war of annihilation. Seventeen thousand troops were dispatched to Guangdong (to be maintained at local expense). Together with that came local forces, led by civilians and under the command of the provincial governor, Chi Kung.

On 11 May Elliot went up to Canton again on the *Nemesis* and noticed masked batteries of guns being constructed on the waterfront. (On the same day Auckland was writing from India to approve the March armistice.) Shortly afterwards Elliot brought up further military and naval forces. On 20 May the Chinese prefect made a point of assuring all foreigners that things were peaceful. But the very next day Elliot, now expecting a Chinese assault, advised all British and Americans to leave by sunset. They did, except for two Americans. On the evening of that 21 May, the Chinese did attack. They opened fire on British ships and sent fire-rafts against them, unsuccessfully. There was a general engagement in which 71 Chinese junks were destroyed. The Chinese occupied the factories, later sacking them. They promptly imprisoned the two Americans, who were pathetically grateful when a detachment of Cameronians under Major Pratt freed them two days later. 'I cannot tell you,' wrote one of them, Joseph Coolidge, 'with what feelings of good-will we looked upon every one of those red-coats.'[30]

In any event, on 23 May the Navy found that *Nemesis*, with her shallow draft, could actually move further upstream, beyond Canton. So Gough could start a flanking manoeuvre against Canton, aiming for the heights overlooking and commanding the city. He now commanded a mixed force of regular British infantry – the Cameronians, the 18th Royal Irish and some elements of the 49th – some Royal Marines, British and Madras artillery, a Naval Brigade, Madras Native Infantry, Bengal Volunteers and some sappers and miners. A day or so later, he put 1500 British and Indian infantry ashore behind Canton, though the landing was blind, since no one had any clear idea of the numbers or disposition of the Chinese forces. From that landing, the British marched east, across paddy fields, and captured some forts on the heights overlooking Canton. By 25/26 May Gough had placed his entire force of 3500 soldiers, sailors and marines on these hills, between Canton's half million or more inhabitants, and a force swelling to 45,000 Chinese troops massing beyond. He could now threaten the city itself. His orders for the Canton assault, as for his other operations, showed Gough to be an old-fashioned, even chivalrous, soldier who insisted that his troops should behave themselves and try not to harm civilians. 'Britain,' he said, 'has gained as much of fame by her mercy and forbearance, as by the gallantry of her troops. An enemy in arms is always a legitimate foe, but the unarmed, or the supplicant for mercy... a true British soldier will always spare.'[31]

However, at the very last moment Elliot yet again insisted on a pause, partly to give the Chinese time to accept his terms and avoid a full-scale assault – which would surely lead to fire, ruination and the sacking of the city by its own rabble – as well as to avoid immersing British troops in the narrow streets and teeming masses of Canton. He had other objectives as well. As he told Gough '... the protection of the people of Canton, and the encouragement of their goodwill towards us, are our chief political duties in this country.'[32] He mentioned to Auckland later – possibly in self-defence against criticisms in London – that he had also wanted to keep his force intact for the move northwards which, before the latest Canton flare-up, had been the next strategic move. His basic aim had been to destroy the forts, scatter the Chinese forces, drive Yishan and his colleagues away and so clear the way for the expedition to move to the Yangzi. In pursuit of such aims, he set terms for saving Canton from assault: that Yishan, and his two senior colleagues, should leave Canton within six days, that during this time the Chinese should pay $6 million (about £1.4 million) to the British government, and that there should be compensation for the damage the Chinese had done to the factories. Furthermore, the imperial troops would be withdrawn to not less than 60 miles from the city. Elliot's own troops would stay in position until the payments were duly made. There was no mention of opium or of Hong Kong, and no Chinese admission that they had been beaten.

The Chinese accepted, and British operations were halted in their tracks. Gough and Senhouse were incandescent. Once again the tough professionalism of the soldiers and sailors clashed with Elliot's much more sinuous political sense. The general was tired of Elliot's continual shilly-shallying about attacking Canton. The man, he wrote 'is as whimsical as a shuttle-cock.'[33] Not only did he and his officers agree that the Chinese were 'a treacherous, deceitful and arrogant people', who needed to be put in their place, but the British victory was turning out to be highly incomplete. Staying in position while standing the troops down was downright dangerous. Here Gough was, with a hostile country behind him and enemy reinforcements coming closer, a strongly held and garrisoned city in front and with lines of communication to the fleet which were, at best, uncertain and vulnerable. His officers, too, complained loudly that the force could be harassed and its communications threatened. Gough saw more distant dangers as well, having made his own calm assessment of the Chinese. As a military nation, he wrote 'they are very contemptible, but they are neither wanting in courage nor bodily strength' and had the capability of becoming 'very formidable'. At the same time, while they had no discipline 'they have cunning and artifice.'[34]

Meanwhile, at Canton there was something like panic and both the agreed silver payment to Elliot, and the removal of Chinese forces from the city, were hastily done. However, if the Cantonese panicked in the face of defeat, there followed an incident that changed their minds. It was an apparently insignificant affair. The British, given the hazards of their position, naturally sent out patrols. Local peasants, always xenophobic and distrustful of strangers, were enraged when an officer of the Madras Native Infantry desecrated tombs. It was even worse when, on 29 September, the very day when Yang Fang marched his regular 'bannermen' out of Canton, a few Indian sepoys – whose dark skins the Chinese found especially offensive – attacked some local women. It was normal for local gentry to form village militias in bad times. So now, thousands of peasants and 'braves' rose in wrath and armed themselves to march, not for 'China' but for their own villages. On the 30th, numbers of them approached the British positions and Gough sent troops to disperse them. Still larger masses appeared. Another British probe ran into a sudden violent thunderstorm. One detachment of the 37th Madras Native Infantry was soaked when sheets of rain made its fire-lock muskets unusable, while hordes of Chinese harassed and ambushed them. Eventually they formed a square and had to be rescued by marines with more modern percussion muskets. The British came away with slight losses: one dead and a dozen wounded. But word went round the villages that the foreign devils had fled, and thousands of fresh volunteers flocked to the Chinese black flags. By the 31st there were seriously large masses visible on the hills at Gough's rear. Eventually the Prefect of Canton and some other local worthies had to come and tell the crowds to disperse. Later that same day the entire British force withdrew, in accordance with Elliot's conditions and after the $6 million were paid (two thirds of the silver being shipped to Calcutta and one third to London). Once withdrawn from their positions, they left

Canton altogether, in accordance with the Elliot–Yishan agreement, and moved to Hong Kong. By 7 June, Elliot was auctioning small parcels of land on the island and urging merchants to move their businesses there. But it was also clear that the troops were sick with dysentery, various fevers and malaria and that, after the Canton effort, everyone was simply dead tired. At one point, some 1100 were on the sick lists. Senhouse died, it is said from frustration, and was buried at Macao, like Napier. As if that were not enough, towards the end of July there came two typhoons bringing a lot of damage to ships and stores. So any move to the Yangzi would simply have to wait. Though the war was obviously not finished, a period of repairs and recuperation was imperative.

In the meantime, however, the peasant rising behind Canton, and the pushing back of the British patrols, followed by the pull-out of Gough's entire force, had a huge political impact. For the Chinese, it was a great people's victory to be celebrated in poem and song. Among the Cantonese, and not least the villagers watching the pull-out, a legend of Chinese heroism and invincibility ballooned. The common people had risen in their wrath, killed many of the British and driven the rest away. They would, indeed, have killed them all if the weak-kneed mandarins had not saved them. The heroic tale became a national legend, still celebrated by the communist authorities a century and a half later. It was a taste of 'people's power' that was to have long echoes. Even in the short term, it fuelled a general sense that China could beat these foreigners, and a lasting anti-foreign mood. It also hardened accusations of treachery against any official who might be moderate in his dealings with the barbarians.[35] In addition, the figure of $6 million caused confusion. The English thought of it as ransom for Canton, a payment in lieu of prize money for its would-be British occupiers. But the Chinese thought they were paying, as Palmerston had demanded, for the originally confiscated opium. That impression was not corrected in the later peace talks.[36]

In any event, on the China coast the chorus of British disapproval of Charles Elliot grew louder. He remained personally quite popular with the expedition. But resentment at his military moderation, and infuriating failure to exploit success, continued to fester. So that few people on the coast regretted his departure. One of his critics, the surgeon McPherson, said the majority of the foreign residents in China were glad to be rid of him. He had unusual talents but 'wanted the decision and dignity of the diplomat.'[37]

Once he was back in England, however, Elliot defended himself with spirit against his critics, including Palmerston. His bearing was assured and self-confident. On 25 January 1842 he wrote to Lord Aberdeen – by then the new Foreign Secretary – giving his considered reasons for acting as he had done. It had been a very strange kind of war, so far away and in such odd conditions that it had been unavoidable for him to use his own judgement. Circumstances on the spot had made it necessary to diverge from his instructions. 'It is clear,' he wrote, 'that we have all been instructing ourselves, Lord Palmerston, the Governor-General of India, and myself, in this expedition of experiences so heavily visited by sickness and accident and storm.' Also, since trade had been his overriding concern, he had thought making practical arrangements at Canton and Hong Kong more important than signing a treaty with the imperial court. As for not storming Canton the year before, if he had attacked, the local mandarins and police would have fled. The city would have been sacked by the local mob. There would probably have been large fires. And there would have been subsequent guerrilla activity. Yet the British needed to sustain Chinese good will. After all, one wanted, basically, to trade, not to kill people. He also argued later that

> Between the 24th of March 1839, when I was made a prisoner at Canton by the Chinese government, and the 18th of August 1841, when I was removed by my own, we have turned a trade amounting to upwards of ten millions sterling, despatched more than fifty thousand tons of British shipping, sent to England as much produce as would pour into H.M. Treasury upwards of eight millions sterling, recovered from the Chinese treasury about 150 tons of hard silver, warded off from H.M. government pressing appeals from foreign governments at particularly uneasy moments and on very delicate subjects, triumphantly manifested the prowess of the Queen's arms, and still more signally and with more enduring advantage established the character and extent of British magnanimity.[38]

For all the criticism in London, Charles Elliot, being determined and well-connected, was not harshly dealt with. Before the end of August 1842 – in fact, while the Treaty of Nanjing was still being finalized – he arrived as British *chargé d'affaires* and consul-general in the new republic of Texas. True, *The Times* still thought he was 'unfit to manage a respectable applestall'.[39] True, too, that he thought Texas a 'den of villains, misery, murder and musquitoes [sic]'.[40] But he went on to be Governor of Bermuda 1846–54, Governor and Commander-in-Chief, Trinidad 1854–56, Governor of St Helena 1863–69, and ended his career as Rear-Admiral Sir Charles Elliot.

Meanwhile new men were about to bring new measures to the British campaign.

7
The Yangzi Campaign: Pottinger 1841–42

Elliot's replacement as sole plenipotentiary and Chief Superintendent arrived at Macao on 9 August 1841 in the new steam-frigate *Sesostris*. Sir Henry Pottinger was a very different character from his predecessor. An active, burly figure with a splendidly upturned moustache, he was energetic, shrewd, determined and notably tough. Born in Belfast, he had spent his entire career with the East India Company. He had had an adventurous time of it, including intelligence work on the Afghan borders and service in the Mahratta wars. After that, he spent much of his time as British political agent at the court of Indian princes. He rose to be senior political officer in the strategically vital province of Sind, covering the mouth of the Indus River, the frontier region of Western India with close links to neighbouring Persia and Afghanistan. His work there earned him a baronetcy. He retired back to England in 1840, at the relatively young age of 50, with a prospect of boredom. So he was glad to be offered the China appointment, especially since it came with a salary of £6000 (tv: £234.400), or double that of Elliot.

Before this new posting he may have missed by a whisker becoming the senior political officer of the Afghanistan expedition that marched to disaster at Kabul. But in China, where people were fed up with Elliot's half-hearted efforts, he was welcomed with a sigh of relief. As one letter to the *Canton Press* put it 'I really congratulate you, for he [Pottinger] is up to all the tricks and Chicanery of the native courts, and rely on it will not allow himself to be humbugged.' And Auckland's sister Emily Eden, Elliot's own cousin, put it even more bluntly. She thought that the army and navy people 'seem to be in ecstasies at having somebody who will not stop all their fighting, and I should not be surprised if [he] finished it all in six months by merely making war in a common straightforward manner.' It was not just the English, either. The American missionary

Bridgman noted, with considerable satisfaction, that 'The English now *make war*.'[1]

The new naval commander, Rear-Admiral Sir William Parker, arrived together with Pottinger. He was another veteran of Napoleon's wars, having seen service under Nelson, as Gough had under Wellington. Fighting apart, he could, like other naval commanders in this period, reasonably hope to make his fortune on the China station, from carrying bullion and destroying pirates. Even, perhaps, from some legitimate private trading.

The British chain of command was now oddly complex. Pottinger had been appointed and given his instructions by Palmerston, but it was still Auckland at Calcutta who was responsible for the China war, and it was his decisions that Pottinger had to carry out. But Parker reported directly to the Admiralty in London, his orders being merely to 'consult and co-operate' with Pottinger and Auckland. The surprise is that these arrangements worked very well in practice, perhaps partly because the three commanders, Pottinger, Gough and Parker, made a practice of dining together frequently during their whole China campaign. Pottinger would explain Auckland's general principles to Parker and Gough, who were left to decide how to carry them out in what a later century would call 'combined operations.' Wellington himself later told Parliament that the campaign was 'without parallel as the joint work of a fleet and an army.' The operation had been a 'revelation of amphibious power.'

Not that the pattern of fighting-while-talking was entirely abandoned. In some places, British and Chinese continued to fight each other, but formal communications and even relations were maintained. Nor did war, any more than talks, prevent trade from continuing throughout the campaign. The British merchants not only went on paying the usual Chinese bribes but even the official customs dues. So when, from May 1841, Chinese export duties on tea were greatly increased, it was largely, if not entirely, from all this income that they paid the Canton 'ransom' of $6 million. The quaint result was that the British were indeed, as Palmerston had feared, effectively paying themselves for that Chinese debt. By March 1842 and well before the eventual peace treaty, even the United States and French flags were still – or again – fluttering in the Canton breeze.

Palmerston's instructions, drafted when his most recent information was only of the Chuenbi convention, told Pottinger to recapture Zoushan, which Elliot had so wantonly abandoned, and to secure those parts of the original British demands that Elliot had ignored.[2] On the other hand, Auckland, whom Pottinger knew from his days in Sind, had earlier sent him a letter which accorded with Elliot's views and strongly urged the new Superintendent to set up a permanent base at Hong Kong.[3] In addition he should, of course, insist on equality of treatment as between British and Chinese, with neither side claiming 'superiority'. Palmerston stressed, yet again, that the war was not about forcing opium on China. Pottinger should urge the Chinese to legalize that trade as a way of controlling it, but Britain made 'no demand in regard to this matter, for [we] have no right to do so. The Chinese Government is fully entitled to prohibit the importation of opium if it pleases; and British subjects who engage in a contraband trade must take the consequences of doing so.'

Pottinger politely informed the Chinese authorities as soon as he landed, formally and by letter, of his appointment. But he refused to receive the Canton prefect. It was a public statement about status. It was an equally public recognition that local arrangements at Canton were no longer – perhaps had never been – important. It was the imperial government itself that had to come to terms. Pottinger dined with the foreign trading community, where he made a good impression. But he also explained in no uncertain terms that no private or commercial interests would be allowed to interfere with 'compelling [the Chinese to] an honourable and lasting peace.' And as far as smuggling was concerned, 'that if [the traders] put either themselves or their property in the power of the Chinese authorities ... it must be clearly understood to be at their own risk and peril.' In fact, general trading at Canton had resumed a few days before his arrival. Clearly the Chinese wanted both the cash flow and the leverage over the foreigners. As a report to the Emperor had commented a month earlier, for the English, commerce was 'the very artery of life' and the Chinese ability to stop commerce at will would always give them effective negotiating leverage.[4]

Within a fortnight or so of Pottinger's arrival, everyone was preparing to get the campaign under way again. Gough, for example, thought they should get on with it, as the Chinese would only get stronger as time passed.[5] As to the strategy to be followed, he was sure that the expedition should go for the Yangzi, China's most vulnerable artery, not the Bei He estuary which, although closer to Beijing, was still full of sandbanks, making it an uncommonly difficult area for ships, and worse for an opposed landing. For the moment no choice was needed, since both strategies meant going north along the Chinese coast, the first stop being Zoushan. By now, the force had been strengthened by fresh drafts of men for Gough's three British regiments, as well as by a new fourth one, the 55th Bengal Native Infantry,[6] and a mountain of stores, ammunition, food and drink, from spirits to lime juice.

So, on 21 August 1841 the force moved. Some 1300 men, including parts of the British 49th Regiment and the 37th Madras Native Infantry, were left behind to look after Hong Kong and also Canton where, by October, large bodies of Chinese militia could be seen to organize for the defence of the city.[7] The remaining troops moved northwards. Their commanders had some 2700 men, including the 18th Royal Irish and 55th Regiments, parts of two others, together with artillery, sappers and marines. They sailed with 13 warships, including two 74-gun ships-of-the-line, the *Blenheim* and the *Wellesley*, and 23 transports. They also had *Nemesis* and another iron ship.

The first objective was Amoy which the force reached on 25 August, to find that the defences had been considerably strengthened since the Elliots had previously attempted to land. Xiamen (Amoy) itself was commanded by the – now fortified – island of Kulangsu and attacks on it began on the following day. A naval bombardment was complemented by a landing of marines and three companies of the Cameronians. Amoy itself was also subjected to a naval barrage, with infantry taking the walls by storm. The population promptly panicked and there was wholesale looting by the Chinese of their own town. In spite of Gough's orders to his men to do nothing to 'preclude future friendly intercourse' and to remember that 'the laws of God and man prohibit private plunder...', after two days of Chinese despoliation, some British troops followed suit. Gough also tried to get the local Chinese merchants to appoint four men to sort out householders from plunderers, but was refused. On 5 September the expedition moved on, leaving behind a small garrison to make use of this staging port for the rest of the campaign. Meanwhile, reports to the Emperor explained that Chinese troops, helped by supernatural forces, had destroyed a number of British ships and killed 700 British and 900 Indian 'black devils'.

On the way to Zoushan the *Nemesis* blew up some forts and junks and landing parties burned a few villages in revenge for the kidnapping of a ship's officer who had tried to buy provisions. On 1 October two regiments, the Royal Irish and the 55th, landed to the west of Dinghai's defences, which had also been refurbished. The place was taken, once again without much difficulty and at the cost of just two men killed and 27 wounded; though the Emperor was told that over 1000 of the enemy had been killed. During the action an officer of the Westmorland Regiment captured an imperial standard that eventually found its way home to Kendal church. Pottinger made it clear that 'under no circumstances will Dinghai and its dependencies be restored to the Chinese government, until the whole of the demands of England are not only complied with, but carried into full effect.' Patrols were sent out, a garrison left behind, and the expedition moved to the mainland.

They made for Chinghai, a township and fortress covering the approaches to the major trading port of Ningbo. Chinghai itself, lying on a peninsula, had at its head a great fortified rock, which commanded both the river into Ningbo and the town itself. On the opposite side of the entrance were field works and large detachments of Chinese troops. The official in charge was Yukien, formerly Governor of Kiangsu and now the fiercely determined Commissioner for the province of Zhejiang (Chekiang). In fact, the place was quickly taken. Gough once again used his well-disciplined infantry to outflank the enemy on the flat, while the two 74-gun men-of-war pounded the rock's defences into silence. Chinese losses were heavy, and included some hundreds of prisoners. Yukien killed himself by swallowing opium and Gough simply released the prisoners. What else could he do, commanding as he did an expedition on the move? By now, though, Gough was not alone in acquiring a modicum of respect for the Chinese soldiery. Colonel Mountain, of Gough's staff, commented that Chinese 'arms are bad, and they fire ill, and having stood well for a while, give way to our rush and are then shot like hares in all directions ... [but] The Chinese are robust muscular fellows, and no cowards – the Tartars desperate; but neither are well commanded nor acquainted with European warfare.'[8]

In mid-October four steamers landed troops in front of Ningbo itself. There was no resistance. They marched in and, watched by some bemused citizens, had the band of the Royal Irish play 'God Save the Queen' on its walls. Efforts were made to deliver another Palmerston letter to the Chinese, in which the Foreign Secretary explained to the Emperor that Elliot had been relieved for disobeying his instructions, a mistake that would not be repeated.

Ningbo itself offered many advantages to the expedition. It was a mere 100 miles from the major city of Hangzhou (Hangchow). Even more to the point, it was within striking distance of the mouth of the Yangzi. Gough himself thought that Ningbo would be difficult to hold and the force should therefore evacuate it. But Pottinger and Parker thought that would be interpreted as a sign of weakness by the imperial court; and anyway, the town might be a good base for winter quarters. So Gough put guards on the gate, sent patrols through the streets and had his men visibly practising drills. He personally, every evening after dinner, stalked round the five miles of the city wall. He also recruited Chinese spies to scout the countryside. At the same time, anxious to avoid Amoy-style mass looting in a city famous for its silks and embroidery, he called together some leading citizens to help organize a Chinese police unit to protect property. He did not think that inflicting harshness on the provinces would move minds in Beijing. On the contrary, he thought that 'the shortest means of attaining success in the war would be...to combine energetic measures against the Government with just and kind treatment of the people...'.[9] In fact, some documents discovered in March 1842 on the body of a dead mandarin did express serious concerns that the barbarians were getting into the good books of the population.[10]

Pottinger took a much more severe view. The war had gone on quite long enough, and must not be allowed to drag on. He meant to demonstrate to everyone that his formal demands on China were serious, and the Chinese would suffer if they were not met. In fact, even Elliot, before going home, had thought that Ningbo should be made to pay. Moreover, prize money being customary in this period, a prize court had already been set up at Singapore and officers, soldiers and sailors could reasonably expect to share in the benefits of their own efforts. So Pottinger wanted public property seized, converted into money, and money and silver sent home as spoils of war. The upshot was that the British did destroy some public property, levied a 10 per cent tax on all stored merchandise, impounded large stores of copper and lead, and took the great bell from the pagoda, Ningbo's prized possession, away to Calcutta. Even the rice from the town's granaries was sold off for the benefit of the prize fund.

By now, though, the effective British force was absurdly small. Having left garrisons behind in various places, and with alarmingly long sick rolls, only about 700 men were left fit for action. But Ningbo was not at all a bad place to be. As the weather grew cooler, it also became healthier. The soldiers had better food, including local eggs, poultry, pork and bread, and could exercise in a brisk climate. They could get beds and bedding, and devise winter covering from the amply available Chinese cotton. Meanwhile the officers could hunt game, such as pheasants or duck or woodcock, in the surrounding countryside. Moreover, many of the inhabitants were friendly enough at first. They supplied the expedition with food, warm houses and servants. Some local ladies were even kind enough to provide daughters for the comfort of British officers.[11] So the British settled in for the winter; and the force, in its turn, helped the locals to fight pirates, whom the peasants would beat to death when they could catch them. Some sailors from the *Druid* were even killed when one large pirate ship blew up as they were boarding it.[12] Perhaps the pirates were high on marijuana, as pirates often were when taking on Westerners or Western ships.

But not everything was sweetness and light. When the British occupied Ningbo, they found the house where Mrs Noble and her companions had been imprisoned and tore it down. (Captain Anstruther found the small bamboo cage in which he had been imprisoned and sent it back home to Madras.) Some British soldiers found it amusing to cut off people's pigtails – a dreadful humiliation to Chinese – or, instead of bothering to forage, to take some leading citizens hostage until supplies were brought in. In spite of patrols, it was by no means always safe for unarmed individuals to wander about in narrow alleys.

By the New Year, much had changed back home. Six months earlier the government had fallen. With the economy in difficulties, and after losing a few divisions in the House, the government had finally lost a vote of confidence and resigned. Fresh elections had brought in the second Peel administration to replace Melbourne, with Sir Robert Peel himself as Prime Minister and Lord Aberdeen as Foreign Secretary. Responsibility for the China war was transferred from the Foreign Office to the Secretary for War and the Colonies, now Lord Stanley, while Auckland was succeeded as Governor-General of India by Lord Ellenborough, who reached Calcutta only at the end of February 1842.

Both new governments, in London and India, faced grave difficulties. For Peel, Aberdeen and Stanley in London, as well as for Auckland or Ellenborough in Calcutta, there were far more urgent issues than China. Peel was above all keen to transform Britain into a land of economic growth and financial stability, with increased production, tariff reform and cheaper food to save people from starvation. Employment had to be improved, especially since very large numbers were unemployed when he came into office. In Stockport, so many working men's houses were empty that one poster in August 1842 said 'Street to let.' Factory Bills were brought in; and altogether, the people had to be protected against popular radicalism.

Abroad, the overriding issue was Afghanistan, where a venture begun with such hopes a mere 2½ years earlier had ended with a major disaster. The full scale of that became clear when, on 13 January 1842, Surgeon Bryden of the Army Medical Corps, covered with wounds, stumbled towards the mud walls of British-held Jelalabad on his exhausted pony. He was the sole survivor of an expedition of 16,000 troops and camp followers who had remained (as explained earlier, 40,000 had set out on the original march some years previously). Not only had Britain failed to install a friendly figure on the Afghan throne, but the whole exercise had been desperately mismanaged and appallingly commanded. Other Afghan centres were lost with equal incompetence as well as treachery, though Jelalabad and Kandahar had held out. It had been very much Auckland's enterprise and the news of its failure left him desolate. In both London and Calcutta the absolute first priority had to be organizing an army of retribution, to fight its way through the Khyber pass and teach the Afghans a lesson they would not easily forget. And, equally urgently, coping with the political and diplomatic fall-out in Europe, the Middle East and in India itself. Not that China could be overlooked, but during 1842 it was, for both London and Calcutta, essentially a sideshow. As late as November 1842 *The Times* in London remarked sombrely that 'It is impossible to view that contest [i.e. in China] with the same exciting interest that attaches to the terrible realities of our Afghan war.'[13]

Stanley, for the new government, gave instructions to the China expedition that did not vary greatly from Palmerston's strategic and political outlines. In any case, he needed time to get to grips with the details of the campaign. So he tended to leave things to Ellenborough and the commanders on the spot and contented himself with writing that the object of the campaign was to seek reparation for the injuries inflicted on British people and the insults to the crown, and the establishment of overall friendly Sino-British commercial relations – in that order. The strategy and tactics he left largely to the three commanders, who were confirmed in their posts, Gough and Parker being promoted as well. In the meantime, masses of silver – the 'ransom' of Canton – arrived in London, producing increased agitation by the Canton traders and their friends that the government should now pay the compensation that Elliot had promised. Since the election, moreover, two or three of the traders and their friends actually had seats in the House of Commons, including Hugh Hamilton Lindsay and, most especially, Jardine himself, sitting for a borough in Devon.

So for Ellenborough, too, when he reached Calcutta at the end of February 1842, China took second place. A former president of the East India Company Board of Control, he was a less sensitive and more resolute man than Auckland. He was as determined as anyone to see that not just the Afghans but the rest of the world should be shown that there were things one could not do to a great power without serious retribution. Given those priorities, he wrote to Pottinger to point out what was perhaps obvious: that all available funds were badly needed for Afghanistan and that the China campaign, which cost a lot, should be finished off as quickly as possible. Also, unlike Auckland who would have preferred to settle things at Canton, he agreed with the view that direct pressure on the Emperor and his advisers was needed. That being so, he and London accepted that reinforcements would have to be sent out.

But what resources could be spared? In the Mediterranean, the previous year's dangers of a clash with France over French influence in the Middle East had been dissipated, not least by Palmerston's skilful balance-of-power diplomacy. The Admiralty could therefore, in spite of its post-Waterloo economies, afford to divert some ships from the Mediterranean to help Parker in China. Not only half-a-dozen frigates and some smaller vessels, but eight of the new steamers – especially useful for moving up the Yangzi – and, most particularly, another 74-gun ship-of-the-line, the *Cornwallis*. Even though the British army command at the Horse Guards in London was always strapped for men, given the large establishments in the Western hemisphere and Africa, as well as India, Gough was reinforced, too. His European regiments were to be brought up to strength, another sent out from Britain, the 98th, and they would be joined by five regiments of Indian infantry, together with artillery and more sappers from Madras. With the reinforcements came some new and varied social connections in London. Not, this time, to London merchants. Rather, various sons or nephews of prominent London figures came to serve with the expedition, including young relatives of the Duke of Wellington and of Peel himself. But this reinforced British drive for a victorious and reasonably quick end to the campaign had to pause to deal with a Chinese push against the invaders.

If the British were to be driven away, it would not be at Canton, where Yishan (Ishan) was unhappily admitting that his irregulars no longer had the stomach to confront this enemy. On the other hand, the Chinese had begun to buy more modern small arms and cannon through Macao, where the Portuguese made minor fortunes by bringing them on foreign ships from Singapore.[14] And threats to the Yangzi were altogether more serious than Canton. So the Emperor sent another of his cousins, Yiching (Iching) to drive the British not only from Ningbo but from the Chinhai forts. Yiching had some military experience having, back in 1826, fought against Moslem rebels in Southwestern Xinjiang (Sinkiang) at Kashgar. As a special sign of imperial favour, the Emperor gave him a cornelian snuffbox as a parting present. Then Yiching, a moderate and frugal fellow, went off to Suzhou (Soochow), some 50 miles from Ningbo, to await the arrival of 12,000 regular troops, assembled from various provinces, plus 33,000 local militia. The regulars included 700 aborigines from Sichuan, many of them with tiger-skin caps that quickly became the fashion throughout the army.[15] Gough's Chinese spies told him that an imperial force was gathering, and he made little spoiling raids and attacks into Yiching's territory. But the threat grew.

Or did it? Something has to be said about the organization and capabilities of the Chinese forces. By this time the empire, as we have seen, was in a process of considerable social and administrative decay. As often as not mandarins were corrupt and diverted taxes into their own pockets. Population growth had forced up land rates, increased peasant debt, dispossessed many who had drifted into minor, or not so minor, crime. In this society, where senior civil officials also often doubled as military commanders, the imperial land forces can be divided into three almost entirely separate parts. There were the local village defence groups, militias like those who had won the 1841 'people's war' outside the walls of Canton. Of higher quality were the armies of the Green Standard. Composed of ethnic Chinese, these regulars were distributed in fairly small groups around the empire and, without a clear central command and staff structure of their own, linked to the civil administrative system. Their officers tended to be posted in rotation to various places around the empire, rather like mandarins and for similar reasons. They were therefore nothing like a coherent and flexible army. Thirdly and finally, there were the Manchu bannermen, universally referred to as 'Tartars'. They and their womenfolk were organized under 'banners' and they formed the elite, living as well as fighting separately from the Han Chinese.

Not only, therefore, was the army of extremely variable quality, with no coherent structure, let alone plan of action, but during the entire campaign the differences in organization, equipment and morale between the British and Chinese were striking. So were the differences in military outlook. To be sure, soldiers on both sides were apt to pump themselves up before action: British soldiers with alcohol, for the Chinese, some drug. Nor is it clear in any war how effective even good troops are under pressure.[16] Still, the British were generalled by men trained in warfare from their early teens. For all their occasional human misgivings, they had ample practical experience of campaigning and of the strategic, tactical and often even of the logistic expertise required. Their men were tough and rough professionals and for many of their officers soldiering was a matter of pride and honour. To be sure, they had their peculiarities. Most officers knew little and cared less about strategy or the reasons for a war. In British regiments, their colonels, who in many cases paid thousands of pounds for their colonelcies, thought they *owned* their regiments and did not care for interference, even from military superiors, while their men tended to come from the lowest social classes at home. The Indian regiments, on the other hand, had much closer relations between their professional officers and the men, who invariably came from India's military castes and for whom service was the path to honour and esteem.

The Chinese also had professional soldiers, but their superior commanders, in contrast to their opponents, often lacked practical campaigning experience. Some were just princelings or even mere literary intellectuals, calligraphers or poets, who had won prizes in national examinations, their minds filled with Confucian texts and poetic expressions. In a society of organized social equilibrium, such men had always been winners in the lottery of life and government. Power meant, in principle, mild paternal authority, not violence and battle. That entire mental and social universe, shared in essence by all segments of society, was under threat from the British military challenge and, equally, the means required to meet it. Even Chinese regular forces, for all their occasional self-sacrificing valour in battle, were in the first place the means of maintaining order within the empire and asserting the psychological ascendancy of legitimate authority. It was better to win over rebels than to crush or kill them. (It was in that context that Chinese officials used phrases about 'soothing the barbarians'.)

Many of the Chinese soldiery were trained to put on a kind of pantomime, with terrifying faces and stylized gestures so as to overawe any foolish and improper resistance to the imperial centre. The military training even of the regulars was poor by European standards, and most of their equipment was worse. They might carry rattan shields on which they painted figures to terrify the enemy. They had *gingals*, or tripod-mounted guns, manned by two or three men and firing half-pound balls. But the gunpowder for their ancient matchlocks often failed to fire and some went into battle with antique weapons like bows and arrows, spears and battle-axes, occasionally even wearing chain-mail-like linen body dresses lined with iron platelets and iron helmets.[17] The Tartars often went into battle with a sword in each hand. Moreover, the ordinary Chinese soldiery were apt to distrust their Tartar comrades. Tartars might be elite troops, but the Han Chinese feared and even despised them as foreigners. Moreover, while British logistic and intelligence arrangements often left a great deal to be desired, the Chinese ones were beneath criticism. Command-and-control arrangements were riddled with addiction to omens and portents and with corruption of every kind. Although, therefore, the Chinese were beginning by 1841–42 to imitate Western military technologies, including the technology of guns, there were huge disparities between the two sides. Not just in weapons, equipment and training but in those command and morale elements whose importance, as Napoleon put it, is to the material as three to one. In sum, the British were overwhelmingly superior in leadership, discipline, technology, weapons, tactics and morale while the Chinese, though often brave, were almost aways badly armed and incompetent.

Much of this was now illustrated in the Ningbo and Yangzi campaigns. In places they were distinctly quaint affairs. There is a narrative account of the Ningbo fighting, written in the form of classical poetry, by a young man who volunteered to be a temporary staff officer.[18] His name was Pei Ching-chao. From him we learn that Yiching, on being appointed to command, placed a wooden box outside his gate and invited anyone who might seek selection to his staff to put in a visiting card. Because he worried that the governor of Chekiang (Zhejiang) province was tampering with his mail, Yiching organized his own private postal service. Beyond that, the whole Chinese campaign was planned and conducted with astonishing incompetence. Intelligence was dreadful. Financial management was appalling. Bribery and corruption were rife. The reports which commanders received from subordinates, about everything from the movements of their own troops to the behaviour of the British, were, even by the exacting standards of Chinese prevarication, often pure fairy tales. Pei himself went to spy out Ningbo – he only found 300 British troops there – and heard tales of the British dressing themselves in the clothes of Chinese statuary gods and carrying off young men to paint their bodies with black lacquer – possibly a reference to brown-skinned Indian soldiers.

Gough's patrols had indeed reported that the Chinese were massing for an attack. But his real warning came when the British found that their Chinese boy servants had disappeared overnight. It turned out that yiching timed his attack, after prayers in the temple of the God of War, in accordance with traditional Chinese war-magic.The assault came on 10 March, that being the 28th (tiger) day of the first (tiger) month of 1842, the Chinese 'tiger' year. It was also timed for the 'tiger' hour of 3–5 a.m. The fire-raft attack at Chinhai on the British ships was hopelessly incompetent and ended in a complete fiasco. In desperation the Chinese even tried to send divers to bore holes into the bottoms of enemy ships. The city itself was attacked from inside the walls as well as from outside, by soldiers who had been infiltrated and came on disguised as civilians, as a kind of 'fifth column'. The plan had originally been to attack with some 36,000 men, but with many diversions, and whole formations held back to protect yiching himself, the attack was actually mounted only by some 5000–10,000 men, the exact number being uncertain. At one point the commander of critical Chinese reserve units, yiching's right-hand man, Chang Ying-yün, was so spaced out on opium that, instead of supporting the attacks, he finally had to stagger to his litter to be carried away to safety. Both assaults, by land and sea, therefore failed, with hundreds of Chinese casualties and no loss to the British.

After the fight young Pei, to his huge surprise, discovered a dispatch which said that he, together with some 500 Southern irregulars, had captured a British battery. At another point during this 1842 campaign, the British found another Chinese report that said, even more quaintly 'the ignorant barbarians, not knowing that guns could not be fired against an object behind them, came upon us in rear, and thus rendered all our cannon useless'.[19]

Not that defeat was the end of the matter for the Chinese. To the huge indignation of the English, the Chinese command engaged in the kidnap and murder of individual Britons or Indians. In fact, the British lost more men by booby-traps and murder than they had in battle. Some were poisoned. Others might be lone British or Indian soldiers who were inveigled into some tavern, given drink until they were unconscious and then abducted as prisoners of war. One was Sergeant Campbell, who went to Dinghai towards the end of February to buy poultry. He was lured into a side street, attacked and tied up, put into a sack, had his left ear cut off with a pair of scissors and only four days later was let out, untied and given food. He was a prisoner for a month before being handed back. The Chinese police chief of Ningbo was killed, presumably for his treason in working under the British. The occupiers, of course, responded in minor ways or by sacking houses. Many Chinese began to leave the city. Others would loot deserted houses. Ningbo became a sad place.

Even apart from such things, Pottinger and Gough decided that at Ningbo they had become strategically vulnerable, and on 7 May withdrew to concentrate at Chinhai. That move was, once again, reported to the Emperor as a great Chinese victory and a barbarian retreat. Nevertheless, Yiching was disgraced, though later reinstated, and died in 1853 while fighting rebels. In the meantime, following the Ningbo disaster, two princes of the blood were now sent to try to tame the barbarians. One was the aged and courteous Yilibu (Ilipu). He it was who had arranged the truce with Elliot back in 1840, and though his conciliatory attitude then had led to disgrace, it now seemed likely to be an asset. Yilibu was given a high military rank and sent south. Together with him the Emperor ordered the much younger Qiying (Kiying), a close personal friend of his and another Imperial Clansman as well as junior guardian of the heir apparent, to Hangzhou to explore the possibility of negotiations. Yilibu's and Qiying's instructions seem to have been to entangle the English Gulliver in endless webs of talks: conciliate, delay things, avert threats and, in general, to manage the barbarians.

While all this was going on, Pottinger made a trip back to Hong Kong, which he found much changed. Here was now a town of thousands of people, a hive of activity, including a number of brothels. Many people lived on boats moored by the shore. Pottinger clearly wanted to keep the island. Though Aberdeen may have been dubious, Ellenborough was, like Elliot and now Pottinger himself, firmly of the view that Britain should keep it, if only for security reasons. The trouble just now was that while Hong Kong could give security to merchants, the tea business was at Canton and would stay there. The Americans and French were returning to the factories and even English ships were venturing as far upstream as Whampoa again. On the other hand, the opium business settled itself at Hong Kong contentedly enough. As did the opium/silver exchange business, since it was clear to everyone that silver earned by selling opium was the only way to buy tea. It was equally clear that the opium merchants were also able to function as highly respectable bankers. In fact, Gough himself banked with Jardine's, and by March 1842 was actually overdrawn to the tune of $1000 or so.[20] The prices for building or buying additional opium ships, from India or the United States, were actually going up.

At the end of February 1842 Pottinger decided to transfer the seat of the British Superintendency from Macao to Hong Kong. He must have been encouraged by some riots in Canton the previous December. Before leaving to return to Ningbo and the Yangzi, he also regulated the currency and organized a postal service. Some merchants followed Pottinger at once to the more secure island base. So did a few missionaries, some of whom were quite schizophrenic about the war and the opium trade. Protestant evangelicals were bound to believe that the state of the individual souls would determine the shape of society and its institutions, rather as Marxists would later attach much the same seminal significance to economic and class structures. Therefore spiritual reform in China was the condition precedent for abolishing the opium trade. Which meant that breaking down China's isolation – by war in this case – was also a blessing and the English forces were in effect doing God's work.[21] In the meantime, in that spring, the United States frigate *Constellation*, under Commodore Kearney, paid a peaceful visit to Whampoa for nine weeks, managed to get the Canton authorities to pay some hundreds of thousands of dollars in compensation to Americans who had endured illegal arrests or violence at the hand of Chinese mobs, and carefully did nothing to interfere in the Anglo-Chinese dispute.

The British 1842 campaign proper started at the beginning of May, even before Gough and Parker received their promised reinforcements. The main strategic issue had effectively been settled. It was understood that a move straight north to Bei Hei would be unwise. The fleet would be in broad shoal waters and among mud-flats, where major men-of-war would have to anchor out of sight of land, while the Bei He itself was only navigable by smaller boats and the weather was treacherous. So Ellenborough, like Gough and Pottinger, concluded that the expeditionary force should do what had always seemed the best tactic. It should move up the Yangzi to Nanjing (Nanking), block the Grand Canal and so, by threatening Beijing's food supplies, and especially its rice, compel the Chinese to come to terms. Neither Ellenborough nor Pottinger seem to have known that the general population of Beijing did not live on rice but on other foods. But the higher ranks of society and officialdom did need the rice, and the Chinese authorities, as a matter of policy, always kept a substantial supply of it stored in the city. In the event it did not matter.

Accordingly, troops were collected from Xiamen, Zoushan and Ningbo and the force moved across the estuary from Ningbo, to the north shore of Hangzhou Bay, to land and attack the fort of Chapu. It held some 8000 Chinese troops, including 1700 Tartars who were living, as usual, together with their families in a separate cantonment in the town. Two Royal Navy ships steamed into the bay for a preliminary probe. Next day, 18 May, the main attack went in. The immediate shore was marshy, but next to this were a few hills on which Chinese forces were strongly posted. The Tartars, many of them wielding a sword in each hand, formed up here, overlooking likely landing places. But Gough used his usual tactics by landing his infantry so as to attack the Chinese positions from flank and rear, and forcing many Chinese troops into the plain. The fighting was severe, but once again superior British fire-power meant heavy Chinese casualties compared with British losses of a mere nine killed and 55 wounded.[22] Only at one point were the British briefly checked. It was around a walled joss-house, manned by some 300 Tartars who threatened the flank of the British advance. Here the British suffered casualties. One of the dead was an especially popular officer, Lt-Colonel Robert Tomlinson of the 18th Royal Irish, a man for whom Rudyard Kipling's lines might have been written: 'And the Irish move to the sound of the guns / Like salmon to the sea…'.[23] When the British finally burned the joss-house and stormed the ruined walls, they found that all but 50 of the Tartars were dead. In the middle of the smoke and devastation sat an old Tartar colonel who, as soon as the redcoats loomed through the smoke, put down his pipe, took up his sword and cut his throat. But he failed to kill himself, was tended by British doctors and, to his own vast surprise, released in recognition of his bravery. In the meantime, the main assault entered the city, which was barely defended, and marched around its walls with bands playing and flags flying. There was much local looting while Yilibu (Ilipu) thanked Parker and Gough for the way their doctors had looked after Chinese wounded.

The battle also taught the British at least two grim lessons. One was discovering the mutilated body of a private in the Royal Irish. Some Chinese soldiers, even when themselves about to die, had taken the time to use the soldier's own razor to cut off his ears and nose and gouge out his eyes. The other was that the Tartars, preferring death to the dishonour of defeat, almost invariably committed mass suicide once defeat became inevitable. Most killed their wives and children before cutting their own throats. The entire captured Chapu was filled with corpses not just from death in battle but as a result of murder or suicide, including dead mandarins. It was an unforgettably disgusting spectacle. Even the British veterans, for all their unstinting admiration for the Tartars, were appalled and moved on quickly after destroying the batteries, magazines and other military facilities. But the bitter resistance had given Gough much to think about. In particular, he realized that the quicker the campaign could be ended, the easier it would be. The bitterness of the Chapu defence had reinforced the notion that the Chinese, if they were given time to learn and reorganize, would become altogether more formidable opponents. Others thought so too. As one American merchant had put it in a private letter a fortnight earlier, the Chinese 'have learned a great deal since the war began, and every six months shows they are harder to beat than they were before. If they had a few Russian or French officers, or West Point cadets, they would soon show a different face.'[24]

Then it was back to the main strategy of cutting the Grand Canal. In early June the fleet moved on to the mouth of the Yangzi. A path was found through the shoals there, and *Nemesis* captured some fishing smacks and, more to the point, fresh fish. On 13 June Parker began to work his way into the river mouth and on the 16th the force attacked some large-scale defensive works at Woosung, guarding Shanghai. The steamers towed warships into position and sailors and marines cleared the batteries, with slight loss even though the Chinese artillery was now much improved. They occupied Shanghai, without a fight since the defenders had left and many of the townspeople fled. Once again the English came in with bands playing. Shopkeepers brought poultry and vegetables to sell to the troops, and Gough made arrangements with leading merchants to try to stop widespread looting by Chinese mobs, as well as by some of the soldiers.

Then, towards the end of June, the expedition's promised reinforcements finally arrived. Ships came, carrying Major-General Lord Saltoun[25] (and, of course, the cello-playing Captain Hope Grant) and the other reinforcements for the Yangzi campaign, including the British 98th Regiment. Gough's rosters were now up to 9000 men. Most of the arrivals, moreover, were armed with the latest percussion musket, less prone to misfire than its predecessor (though the new and shorter bayonet issued with it was liable to bend). In addition, Gough had some 3000 sailors and ancillary personnel. By now, too, Yilibu was sending a junior official to sound the British out about negotiations. If the British would stop ravaging the river, the Chinese side would be willing to start talks. That came to nothing.

Before leaving Shanghai, Pottinger tried to set the tone for the rest of the campaign. On the one hand, he issued a proclamation declaring that the British were not fighting the Chinese people, but the imperial government. The war must go on until the Emperor sent an emissary to negotiate peace terms. Once again there was that insistence on cultural equivalence, political equality and what the English evangelicals would think of as the Brotherhood of Man: '...different countries... being...of one family, very plain is it that they should hold friendly and brotherly intercourse together, and not boast themselves one above the other.'[26] On the other, he wrote to Gough on 1 July pointing out that the period of operations was limited and the force could not resort to half-measures. It must be made clear to the Emperor's court that 'we have the means, and are prepared to exert them, of increasing pressure on the country to an unbearable degree.'[27] Indeed, the fleet was already intercepting all ships trying to get into or out of Shanghai.

By the time it left Shanghai on 23 June, reorganized and refreshed, it was also clear that there would be a strong search-and-destroy element in the Yangzi operation. That river, the English understood, was of more than regional importance, it was a central artery for the entire empire. Therefore they would stop the entire goods traffic, burn or sink or commandeer ships of all sizes or shapes. Even though, by the time the English got to the Grand Canal, the main Chinese rice fleet had passed by on its way north, there was a lot of other shipping to deal with. Throughout, many of the boats were promptly requisitioned to serve as storage ships, or to carry coal, or simply as houseboats for British officers, each with an English captain and a Chinese crew. In fact, throughout the Yangzi campaign numbers of Chinese worked for the fleet, as sailors, watchmen, lookouts or cooks. There were also the towns and villages along the bank. There, too, the British operated at will. Villages were plundered. Some Navy captains made a sport of seizing village elders and threatening that if cattle and other supplies were not delivered at once, the man's pigtail would be cut off. Nor, in view of Pottinger's views about 'unbearable pressure', was that sort of thing merely frivolous. Yangzhou (Yangchow), for instance, paid $500,000 in silver to be left alone and other places also ransomed themselves. On the other hand, with the diappearance of so much civil authority along the river, and a wave of Chinese theft and robbery, the overall damage done by Chinese to Chinese may well have been more than the damage done by the British.

After Shanghai, the next major objective was, of course, Nanjing itself, the ancient capital of the Ming dynasty and its Chinese – as distinct from Manchu – empire. Admiral Parker now had a fleet of 11 men-of-war, including the *Cornwallis* herself, 10 steamers, some troopships and 48 transports of all sizes, piled high with troops, weapons, coal, stores of all kinds. In a remarkable feat of seamanship he brought that fleet safely along almost 300 miles of the uncharted Yangzi with its heavy currents, rapids and sharp bends. Nothing like it had ever been seen along that great river or, for that matter, anywhere in Chinese waters. It had to be a highly disciplined operation. No night sailing. Almost everyone ran aground at some point, on a sandbank or in mud; and each time the entire fleet train was held up, in the lower and tidal reaches perhaps waiting for the tide to turn. Sometimes it was delayed for days. The whole fleet train could stretch for ten, even twenty miles.

For the most part, there was little resistance: only the odd fire-raft or pop-gun. But then the fleet arrived at the walled city of Zhenjiang (Chinkiang), at the confluence of the Yangzi and the Grand Canal. It managed to take the town on 21 July, in a major engagement, with much heavier fighting than the British force had so far experienced. Gough put two brigades ashore to attack Zhenjiang itself, with one more sent to take some nearby hills. Once again, the English came up against a Tartar garrison which conducted a fierce and skilful defence, even after the English had crossed the city wall. Once again, after a desperate and heroic resistance, many Tartar soldiers killed their wives and children before taking their own lives. Some of this was extraordinarily dramatic and painful. As the British entered the town, one Tartar general retired to his house, sat himself in a chair amid his papers, and ordered his servants to set fire to the building, burning himself to death. After seeing the carnage, Gough wrote home – not for the first time – 'I am sick at heart of war and its fearful consequences.'[28] The Chinese, for their part, quite failed to understand the British dismay at a spectacle of mass suicide, and their refusal to be held responsible for behaviour so different from European codes of war-fighting. Once again, too, widespread Chinese looting ravaged a conquered town. The British commanders tried to restrain their troops. In fact, the diary of the poet Chu Shih-yun noted that the British executed two of their own sepoys and put up a placard warning against rape and looting.[29] What could not, of course, be restrained were the private opium ships which followed the Royal Navy up the great river.

After Zhenjiang the British were obviously in a position to stop all Chinese traffic on the Grand Canal as well as the Yangzi itself. They wanted to avoid delays, to get on. By now, their British ships, which also served as floating hospitals, were filling up with soldiers down with dysentery or malaria. But Nanjing was plainly threatened. For the Chinese, its possible fall brought a number of issues to a head. During the whole British move up the Yangzi, Beijing had been seriously worried on several grounds. Even Nanjing itself was less important than stopping the barbarians before they got to the gates of Beijing. If the British advance continued – and China's forces seemed quite unable to stop them – and actually occupied the capital, it would inevitably be the end of the dynasty. More troops were accordingly rushed to Tianjin (Tientsin) and the northern coast to protect the capital against new and possibly direct attack. Furthermore, it seemed obvious that the British could not possibly mount such a campaign without wanting to acquire Chinese land. Their seizure of Hong Kong had demonstrated as much. So, when news of Chingkiang's fall reached Beijing on 26 July by special courier, the court told Qiying and Yilibu to start serious negotiations. But Palmerston had already made it clear to Pottinger that any agreement must be with the Emperor himself, not some provincial official. 'Her Majesty's Government' Palmerston wrote, 'cannot allow that, in a transaction between Great Britain and China, the unreasonable practice of the Chinese should supersede the reasonable practice of all the rest of mankind'.[30] So Pottinger was firm. He would not, like previous negotiators, tolerate endless Chinese prevarication. He had therefore already made it clear that he would only talk with plenipotentiaries carrying full powers. That created difficulties, since Qiying had no such powers in a Western legal sense. He had general instructions and would be judged, as senior Chinese officials always were, by the results he managed to obtain. Qiying and Yilibu rather helplessly followed the fleet as it sailed on to Nanjing.

On 5 August Pottinger joined the *Cornwallis* before the walls of the city. Three days later Yilibu consulted with the Nanjing governor, Niu Chien, who made it clear that the city could not be defended. Now the negotiators' reports to Beijing sketched the stark realities. 'Should we fail to ... ease the situation by soothing the barbarians, they will run over our country like beasts, doing anything they like.' All too clearly, China was in no position to haggle. Furthermore, Qiying, after tactful exploration, reported to the court that some of the acute earlier fears were unjustified. He had become convinced that the foreigners really only sought trade, not conquest. He would therefore accept personal responsibility for the conclusion of a peace treaty based on the assumption that British demands were merely commercial. Only then, and after some further difficulties about the precise powers given to the Chinese plenipotentiaries, and with British ships moving closer to the city walls and troops going ashore, did matters move towards closure.

On 12 August, Major Malcolm, Pottinger's secretary, produced a draft treaty which the Chinese agreed to consider. The British thought they saw more signs of Chinese 'humbug' and prepared to move against the city, perhaps because the Emperor was sending orders saying his negotiators must not meet Pottinger until after a settlement had been reached, and the barbarians had actually left the Yangzi. Still, by Sunday 14 August the Chinese, now bearing full commissions, agreed to negotiate on the basis of Pottinger's terms. All they wanted was for the British to go away. On 17 August the two Manchu notables arrived, together with Niu Chien, carrying the necessary mandates. The impending attack on the city was called off and hostilities suspended. Within two days a draft document had been agreed that could be sent to Beijing for approval. The following day Yilibu, Qiying and Niu Chien paid a visit to *Cornwallis*, were offered refreshments and bowed before a portrait of Queen Victoria. All that was left for the British was that there should now be an agreed and unambiguous treaty text. It was just a year since the expeditionary force had left Hong Kong.

Pending Beijing's reply, the two sides exchanged courtesy visits. In one of them, Pottinger again raised the issue of opium, which the proposed treaty text did not mention. Barely three weeks earlier, on 27 July 1842, the Chinese negotiators had written plaintively to Pottinger:

We have been united, by a friendly commercial intercourse, for two hundred years. How, then, at this time, are our old relations so suddenly changed as to be the cause of a national quarrel? It arose, most assuredly, from the spreading opium poison. Opium is neither pulse nor grain, and yet multitudes of our Chinese subjects consume it, wasting their property and destroying their lives; and the calamities arising therefrom are unutterable. How is it possible for us to refrain from forbidding our people to use it?[31]

Also at some point during the summer, it seems, the Chinese had already mentioned the possibility of legalizing the trade, provided that Britain would guarantee the payment of a fixed tax. Not surprisingly, the British had no intention of becoming tax collectors for the imperial treasury, still less to be formally associated with the opium trade. So Pottinger now raised the subject merely as a matter of private conversation. The Chinese cautiously asked why the British did not stop Indian production. Pottinger did not bother to explain that any attempt to do that would involve a slow and lengthy change in agricultural practices and even land tenure over large parts of India, with unpredictable social and political consequences. He simply pointed out the obvious: if supplies from India stopped, Chinese dealers would import opium from somewhere else. It was for the Chinese to stop the 'evil practice' and if China's officers and officials did their job, opium imports would stop. If that was not possible, why not legalize the trade and tax and control it?[32]

By 27 August the British learned that Beijing had agreed to the proposed treaty text and two days later, on 29 August, the three Chinese principals came aboard HMS *Cornwallis*, again bowed before a picture of Queen Victoria as a sign that they accepted state equality, and signed four copies of the Treaty of Nanjing. After the ceremony the British and Chinese delegations mingled amiably on the quarter-deck of the great British ship. Colonel Mountain noted that the occasion promised '... future visions of God's purposes, and ... the hope that this day has begun an era of blessing to China.'[33] The Emperor's formal approval came back in the first week of September, while Major Malcolm hurried to London by steam-frigate, and then overland, to arrive in record time on 10 December. Queen Victoria ratified the treaty at the end of December and the documents of ratification were exchanged at Hong Kong on 26 June 1843.

Of the two senior Chinese negotiators, Yilibu was appointed High Commissioner at Canton. He had been quite unwell during the final treaty negotiations, and at Canton lived towards death, a destination he reached in March 1843. His successor was Qiying who had, in the meantime, been titular governor of Nanjing. For political London, there were once again much more important issues to deal with, not least some good news from Afghanistan. Still, people were pleased by a decisive and victorious outcome and the fact that the Chinese had very properly been taken down a peg. The Queen, the government and Palmerston, by then temporarily out of office, were all delighted with the Nanjing settlement. Queen Victoria noted of Pottinger that 'very great confidence may be placed in him'.[34] Pottinger himself was told that 'Her Majesty highly appreciates the ability and zeal which you have displayed'.[35] Palmerston noted that 'There is no doubt that this event, which will form an epoch in the progress of the civilization of the human races, must be attended with the most important advantages to the commercial interests of England.'

Meanwhile Pottinger and the expedition slowly withdrew from China, Gough was promoted to Commander-in-Chief in India, and everyone's opinions about China's fundamental barbarism were reconfirmed by late news of their dealings with British captives. There was, for instance, the way the Chinese dealt with the survivors from two ships, the troop-ship *Nerbudda* and the *Ann*, which had been shipwrecked on the coasts of Formosa during the campaign. The people who reached the shore, mostly Indian sepoys, were taken prisoner. Eventually, the Taiwan gaols seem to have held 149 sepoys and 19 white folk. The local governor, Yao Ying, lied to Beijing, claiming the *Nerbudda* had been sunk by shore batteries under his command, and requested permission to execute the captives. It was given and most of the prisoners were killed on 12 and 13 August 1842, just before the Treaty of Nanjing was signed. Only nine prisoners survived. When the story reached London, it was not calculated to make anyone regret any part of the campaign.

8
Almost a Settlement

Nanjing was the first treaty China had concluded with any foreign state for over one hundred and fifty years: since the 1689 Treaty of Nerchinsk with the Russians. But it was quickly followed by a series of other agreements over the next two years. It has been fairly argued that until 1839 it was the Chinese who set the tone and terms for their dealings with other countries. From 1842 that framework began, slowly, to change.

The most remarkable aspect of that 1842 treaty, though, is what it did not do. Given that China had suffered a complete and unmitigated defeat – indeed, the most decisive defeat the Manchu empire had ever suffered – the terms imposed were remarkably moderate and limited; a point largely obscured in the decades of condemnation of Britain and British attitudes which were to follow very much later. After a war which the Chinese claimed, and went on claiming, had been caused by Britain's opium trade, the treaty did not mention it. Though the British wanted freer trade, no merchants or traders were involved in the preparation or conduct of the negotiations. There was not even any pressure to open up China to Western missionaries.

Palmerston's demand to have a British ambassador installed at Beijing was tacitly dropped. Four trading ports, Xiamen (Amoy), Ningbo, Fouzhou and Shanghai were opened, in addition to Canton. China also agreed to accept foreign 'superintendents or consular officers' at each of them. Moreover, British and Chinese officials of corresponding rank would in future be treated as equals. Foreign consuls would be 'the medium of communication between the Chinese authorities and the said merchants.'[1] As for the old style of communication, those foreign 'petitions', which had caused such difficulty and resentment, would be replaced by using words like 'communication' or 'statement.' On the other hand, the consuls themselves would see to it that

British subjects would pay the proper duties and other dues owed to the Chinese government. And '... the consul will be security for all British merchant ships entering any of the five ports.'

It was further agreed that in all of these ports foreign merchants 'with their families and establishments, shall be allowed to reside, for the purpose of carrying on their mercantile pursuits, without molestation or restraint'. Furthermore, 'in future at all ports where British merchants may reside [they would be permitted] to carry on their mercantile transactions with whatever persons they please.' That tied in naturally with the abolition of the old Canton Cohong monopoly, and meant freeing foreigners to trade with anyone, to bargain about price, or to rent accommodation or servants, as they might please. However, it was accepted that if a ship was caught smuggling, it and its contraband could be confiscated or the ship banned from further trading.

Palmerston's original treaty draft had wanted Britain to acquire one or more islands next to the coast, able to serve as a commercial and military base. The idea had been to have some piece of territory on which a British magistrate could properly operate to control British subjects; also a place of refuge. Territorial cession only came up once it was seen to be impracticable to have Chinese residents on any such British-controlled territory remain under Chinese jurisdiction. And once cession became the object, it was Zoushan that Palmerston had especially in mind. It had been recommended by the East India Company's people, as well as by others who understood the China trade. It was ideally placed for the hugely rich and important trade of the whole Yangzi river basin and, beyond that, to serve as a base for trade all along China's northern coasts. For all its hostile population and difficult wind conditions, it was sizeable and an important strategic asset. In the event, however, Pottinger, like Elliot before him, preferred the little rocky island of Hong Kong, with its deep, sheltered harbour and easy approaches. In spite of the fact that both Lord Stanley, now at the Colonial Office, and Lord Aberdeen, the new Foreign Secretary, remained unconvinced about it, foreign trade was centred at Canton and seemed likely to remain so. But circumstances at Hong Kong itself forced British hands. As Chinese merchants poured onto the island under British control, the British found themselves with a *de facto* Sino-British settlement on their hands. London finally accepted the Hong Kong acquisition by letter from Aberdeen on 4 January 1843, and Pottinger became the island's first governor.

As for the indemnities payable by China, London demanded $21 million: $6 million for British property destroyed by the Chinese,

$3 million to discharge the outstanding debts of the Hong merchants, and $12 million for the costs of the war. The money was to be paid in instalments over three and a half years. The Chinese did not argue about the figures. In fact, their negotiators told the Emperor that the relief from blockade and other pressures on China was cheap at the price.[2] The debt, as well as the May 1841 'ransom' of Canton, was paid in silver shipped to London or Calcutta – which may say a good deal about the 'drain' of silver from which China was alleged to suffer.

Trading taxes and duties were now set at around 5 per cent on both exports and imports, except for a 10 per cent duty on exports of tea, a commodity on which China still had a monopoly until the British got round to planting tea in Ceylon and Assam. In fact, Pottinger saw clearly enough that though the traders had complained long and bitterly about severe and eccentric Chinese tax demands, they did not actually know how much they were paying. They only knew about the overall prices-plus-charges which they had to pay to – and through – the Chinese merchants. Consequently the Chinese had no difficulty in accepting a British proposal for duty at 5 per cent. It was actually higher than the average of existing official rates, though less than the previous combination of formal duties and illegal exactions. Anyway, while the British insisted on reasonable trading conditions, they relied on a natural evolution of trade and other contacts to produce happier long-term political relations.

For the Chinese, the essence of the Treaty of Nanjing was that it merely made fresh but not very novel frontier arrangements. In fact, it was an echo of an 1835 treaty with Kokand, in the far north-west. That had allowed Kokand to station political residents at Kashgar as well as commercial officers in other places, who had extra-territorial jurisdiction over foreigners. Nor did the new treaty at Nanjing accept parity of esteem by letting foreign ambassadors come to Beijing. There would be more treaty ports, but the arrangements at five of them merely reproduced what was already happening at Canton. The foreigners continued to be constrained in ways which the treaty did not dispute and which were much more important than the constraints the treaty now removed. The opening of more ports to trade did not mean foreign access to any part of China beyond those port cities, or a right to acquire property or land anywhere else. Nor could foreigners engage in manufacturing or mining. Only the old embargo on the entry of Western women into Chinese territory was abandoned after Qiying delicately explained to the Emperor that the barbarians were influenced by natural affection for their women. 'The presence of females at the ports would therefore soften their natures and give us less anxiety as to outbreaks.' That may have been a significant concession, for the Chinese continued to be shocked by the clothes, and the free-and-easy behaviour, of Western women, as even Pottinger understood.

As for the admission of consuls at these ports, and their duties *vis à vis* their own citizens, that also chimed well enough with the traditional Chinese view that foreign headmen should supervise their own people. The heated condemnation of the extra-territoriality provisions by Chinese nationalists and Western sympathizers many decades later differs sharply from the views and tempers of the 1830s and 1840s. Neither the Chinese negotiators at the time, nor the imperial government, were greatly worried about extra-territoriality. Indeed, the provisions were to be more fully defined in the 1876 Convention of Chefoo (Yentai). To be sure, Hong Kong was a worry – not so much because of the territory involved as because ceding the island meant that Chinese people would come under foreign rule, the very issue that had made the Emperor so angry about Qishan's agreement with Elliot 18 months earlier. In fact, the Chinese text of the Treaty of Nanjing left the status of Hong Kong ambiguous. It was the English text, agreed to be authoritative, which provided for cession. Still, there had been no formal transfer of sovereignty, so Hong Kong looked like becoming, if anything, another Macao.

Of course the new system had its problems. Once the treaty was concluded, the Foreign Office had to find suitable consular officials in a hurry. So, in 1843 the China Consular Service was set up.[3] Since it would obviously be useful for consuls to speak Chinese, several were recruited from among missionaries or the Hong Kong merchants. And although the Hong Kong governor, as the senior British official in China, was soon put in charge of all consulates, the consuls themselves had tiny staffs, small and rickety prisons and could impose no punishments beyond 12-months' imprisonment or deportation. Anyway, offenders tended to be treated leniently, especially if the offences were against Chinese – much to the disgust of Palmerston in London.

The treaty also left a number of loose ends, as treaty documents in such complicated circumstances often do. And one major difficulty remained, and was still out of anyone's control. That was opium, with which the treaty had conspicuously not dealt. In time, these strands became interlaced with each other.

So far as opium was concerned, the Chinese of course assumed that the treaty's silence on the subject, which effectively left control of the opium traffic to the ineffective Chinese authorities, was merely another way of encouraging the trade. That idea was needlessly devious. Pottinger may have been instructed not to press the legalization solution formally, and been rebuffed about it in private conversation. Nevertheless, he continued to take an interest in the possibilities of legalization, probably feeling, like many others before him, that here was the best way to avoid friction between the two governments. At the end of December 1842 he told the British merchants that he still hoped to get the Emperor to go the legalization route. Yet the Acting British Consul at Canton wrote to him, tartly pointing out that the Emperor had opposed the introduction of opium, and cut off the heads of people selling or even just smoking it. If, having done all that, he were now to turn around and make himself the chief salesman of the drug, 'he would not last one month on the throne.'[4]

The opium situation therefore remained thoroughly confused. In April 1843 Pottinger wrote to the Chinese, offering to co-operate in suppressing the traffic, with the obvious proviso that '... the suppression of smuggling must depend on the activity and integrity of the Chinese customs-house officers; that neither British officers, nor people, nor vessels can be employed in it; and that, however deeply I may deplore such disreputable and disgraceful conduct, the remedy does not lie in my hands.'[5] By mid-1843 he had to explain firmly to his own people that the opium trade was still illegal and British officials would not protect anyone engaged in it.[6] But he also explained to the Chinese at Canton that, while there was no objection to China taking action against smuggling ships or their cargoes, British subjects must not be molested and the Chinese could not expect British officials to enforce Chinese laws against British people or ships. And while the British consuls at the newly opened trading ports were now duty-bound to help suppress smuggling – as no British official in China had previously been – Chinese officials in mainland ports would, he said, no doubt make similar efforts to stop smuggling in general and opium trading in particular. He himself would not allow opium into Hong Kong or its waters.

That could not last, though, once the Chinese themselves said they could do nothing about smuggling. Which made attempts to keep opium out of Hong Kong quite pointless. There was similar confusion among the Americans. Their own treaty with China, concluded soon after the British one, flatly forbade the traffic. But that did not stop their merchants from happily continuing with it. The French treaty, too, declared opium to be contraband, though that did not actually stop all trade. After the signing at Nanjing, therefore, smuggling went on more or less as before.

As for the many loose ends, Qiying and Pottinger began work on those as soon as treaty ratification had been completed. Tariff rates were fixed and other important regulations issued on 22 July 1843. Three months later the Treaty of the Bogue dealt, among other things, with co-operative discouragement of smuggling, the limitation of China's inland transport duties and the establishment of British courts in China to try offences committed by British nationals. That last point had already been conceded by the Chinese commissioners, but was now formalized. Parliament in London had, of course, passed its own Act a decade earlier claiming the right to set up such courts, and this was now confirmed in the Act for the Better Government of her Majesty's Subjects Resorting to China, which became law on 22 August 1843. It provided for courts to be set up, and authorized the Superintendent of Trade to make and enforce laws to control British subjects. Other matters to be clarified included the limits of Chinese jurisdiction. The treaty had not dealt with the details. True, the British had for long refused to have their people surrendered to Chinese criminal justice. But it was the American Ttreaty of Wangxia in 1844 which dealt with the issue in greater detail, and in consequence set matters for the British as well. The Chinese again accepted what British legislation had already provided for British subjects: that accused people could only be tried under the laws, and by the officials, of their own country. As to civil matters, the foreign powers claimed exclusive jurisdiction in cases involving foreign nationals only. Where Chinese were also involved, there would be a kind of arbitral procedure between the local consul and the Chinese authorities.

There was also the notion of freedom of trade for everyone, which had been part of Britain's aims, and of Palmerston's thinking in particular, from the beginning. Conversely, both he and Elliot had also wanted to include a Most Favoured Nation clause that would allow Britain to claim all the privileges that might in future be granted to any other country trading with China. In the event, the Nanjing Treaty did not deal with this, but the Treaty of the Bogue did,[7] as did the Sino-American and Sino-French treaties that followed in 1844. The Chinese might have raised eyebrows about whether such a provision was really necessary, since the Son of Heaven would surely refuse to differentiate between various kinds of barbarian, but to the Westerners a written agreement seemed more reassuring than a promise of imperial benevolence.

Other matters concerned the commercial relations between foreign and Chinese merchants. Although the Cohong monopoly at Canton had been ended, Nanjing did not change the way in which British merchants had to deal with the Hong merchants. These later agreements added that all duties and dues were to be paid to specially licensed bankers before trading vessels could be cleared. Other constraints were removed. Under the old system, the Cohong merchant had been responsible for each and every act of the foreign trader, or of his ships. Not only could that merchant alone sell to the foreigner or buy from him, but it was he who provided the foreigner with accommodation and servants. Now, foreigners would have to make their own arrangements with Chinese citizens. That was accompanied by details on the treatment of foreign traders and limitations on the transit of goods from Hong Kong to China's interior.

Then there was the question of what to do about foreign warships in Chinese waters and, more importantly, ports. It was agreed that the British would station a naval ship at each of the five trading ports, to provide '... the means of restraining sailors and preventing disturbance', and the Chinese would be informed whenever one ship was due to arrive to replace another. Soon afterwards, the Americans and French extended this to say that any ship of war cruising for commerce protection should be well received at any Chinese port.[8]

So once Britain had opened China's doors, other trading nations followed and a host of fresh political and strategic interests began to press on the celestial empire.

The first foreigners to follow the British arrangements were the Americans. They had for some years kept a close eye on developments. A US Navy squadron under Commodore Kearney had been in Chinese waters virtually throughout the war. Not only did Kearney, as we have seen, manage to get some compensation payments from Canton for US citizens, but both during and after the war a good deal of British opium traffic got help and protection from the United States Navy.[9] Even before the Treaty of Nanjing was signed, Kearney succeeded in urging on the Chinese that the Americans should participate equally in any new trade or tariff arrangements that might emerge from talks with the British. Now they clearly saw in the opening of China's ports great new opportunities for trade. At the end of December 1842, just as Queen Victoria was ratifying the Treaty of Nanjing, President Tyler asked Congress for money to send a mission to China to negotiate a commercial treaty. The first American appointed as Envoy Extraordinary and Minister Plenipotentiary – but to Beijing, not Canton or Shanghai – was a Massachusetts lawyer, Caleb Cushing. President John Tyler wrote to the Chinese on 12 July 1843, 'Our minister is authorized to make a treaty to regulate trade. Let it be just. Let there be no unfair advantage on either side.' But the Secretary of State, Daniel Webster, was more specific and instructed Cushing in terms that might have been drafted by Palmerston himself. 'You will,' Webster wrote,

> assert and maintain, on all occasions, the equality and independence of your own country. The Chinese are apt to speak of persons coming into their empire … as tribute bearers to the emperor … All ideas of this kind … must, should they arise, be immediately met by a declaration … that you are no tribute bearer; that your government pays tribute to none, and expects tribute from none …[10]

He added that Chinese regulations should be obeyed by all persons and ships visiting China and that if US citizens broke those laws, the United States would not protect them.

The Court understood that the barbarians needed to be 'soothed'. In November the Emperor issued an edict saying that 'Now that the English barbarians have been allowed to trade, whatever other countries there are, the United States and others, should naturally be allowed to trade without discrimination, in order to show Our tranquilising purpose.'[11]

Cushing arrived at Macao on the last day of February 1844, escorted by two ships of the United States Navy and accompanied by Dr Peter Parker and the son of the Secretary of State, young Fletcher Webster. Cushing's nomination and commission had been communicated to the Chinese through the United States consul at Canton, for he had no intention of imitating Napier's arrival a decade earlier. But he quickly discovered that the Chinese had made no arrangements to receive him. Three days after arriving, Cushing told the acting governor that he had come to negotiate a treaty and been instructed to travel to Beijing to deliver a letter from the President to the Emperor. The Chinese prevaricated and Cushing failed to get permission to travel beyond Canton. Indeed, he found himself obstructed in ways all too reminiscent of the Chinese treatment of Napier a decade earlier. So much so that on 24 April 1844 he wrote to the governor with a stark reminder of the results of China's continuing frustration of the British. If they were going to do the same thing now '… it can be regarded in no other light than as evidence that (China) invites and desires war with the other great Western powers. The United States would sincerely regret such a result. We have no desire whatever to dismember the territory of the empire. 'Our citizens' he went on, evidently quite willing to engage in a spot of diplomatic mendacity, 'have at all times deported themselves here in a just and respectful manner.' He hoped that the Chinese government would respond cordially 'to the amicable assurances' of the United States government.[12]

The Chinese were not moved, being coldly determined that the Americans, who had never paid tribute, should not be able to send an emissary to Beijing. Cushing was simply informed that Qiying, newly promoted to Governor-General of Guangxi and Guangdong, would negotiate with him and arrive in Canton, probably within a month. In the meantime other officials were not authorized to negotiate. This Cushing had to accept. Not only that, but Qiying explained that he was not empowered either to facilitate or to resist any move by Cushing to travel to Beijing. But if Cushing did go, Qiying would at once cease to negotiate.[13] On the last day of May 1844, Qiying finally arrived at Canton, and negotiations began at the end of June. By then, issues of protocol had once again reared their heads. Qiying sent a message on 3 June in which the American name had, respectfully, been raised one space above the line of text. But the names of China and the Emperor had been raised two spaces, so Cushing returned the document remarking '...that your Excellency will see the evident propriety of adhering to the forms of national equality, the observance of which is indispensable to the maintenance of peace and harmony between the two governments....'[14]

The Americans found there were other close parallels between their problems and Charles Elliot's difficulties before the war. For instance, Cushing, like the Englishman, found himself compelled to exercise a jurisdiction over US nationals in China which his own government had not actually given him. For at Canton the Americans, like the British, found themselves occasionally attacked by groups of Chinese, and in one struggle a Chinese man was killed. Cushing appealed to Qiying, asking that the foreigners be given protection.[15] Qiying replied that the Cantonese were a violent and overbearing lot and would probably demand a life in return for the Chinese who had died.[16] But Cushing refused, like the British before him, to accept Chinese jurisdiction. He set out the principles involved in a letter of 22 June 1844 to the United States Consul at Canton. It is a document which might make a politically correct American or British eye uneasy a hundred and fifty years later, but was eminently sensible at the time. Cushing pointed out that since the nations of Europe and America were a family associated by civilization, religion, treaties and the law of nations, foreigners residing in one of those countries were clearly subject to its municipal law. In relations between Christian and Moslem states, on the other hand, Christians were not subject to the local jurisdiction but to the authorities of their own country. That principle should also apply in China. 'Accordingly,' Cushing wrote, 'I shall refuse at once all applications for the surrender of the party (who had killed the Chinese at Canton)' but he would, instead, have the matter examined by US officers. Accordingly, he summoned a jury of Americans from Canton on 11 July. It decided unanimously that the Chinese death had been the result of legitimate American self-defence.[17]

In the substantive treaty negotiations Cushing, at Qiying's request, produced a draft treaty, accompanied by a statement of its general principles. This emphasized that the United States did not seek Chinese territory, but wanted reciprocity in Sino-US commercial relations, along the same lines as those now applying to China's relations with the British. On that basis the Treaty of Wangxia – a suburb of Macao – was signed on 3 July 1844, covering, in a rather more elaborate way, much the same points as the Treaty of Nanjing. It also allowed the Americans to acquire sites to build Protestant mission churches, hospitals and cemeteries, and to employ Chinese. It was further agreed[18] that any American accused of crimes should be tried by the consul 'according to the laws of the United States', although opium traders could be dealt with by the Chinese authorities. Cushing also introduced a clause providing for the revision of the Treaty in 12 years' time.[19] Under the Most Favoured Nation principle this, of course, became applicable to the British also. Later on, in the 1850s, China's rejection of British claims for such treaty revisions would lead to further serious friction between the two countries.

When the Chinese negotiators reported back to the Emperor, they were thoroughly dismissive of the Americans but thought the agreement might help to have one lot of barbarians contain another. Cushing, of course, was aware that his treaty offered some hope of future benefits rather than any immediate profit. On the other hand, the British having done the fighting, the treaty would cost the Americans nothing. In transmitting his treaty text to Washington, he noted that:

> I ascribe all possible honor to the ability displayed by Sir Henry Pottinger in China, and to the success which attended his negotiations; and I recognize the debt of gratitude which the United States and all other nations owe to England for what she has accomplished in China. From all this much benefit has accrued to the United States. But, in return, the treaty of Wang Hiya [sic] in the new provisions it makes, confers a great benefit on the commerce of the British empire. … and thus whatever progress either government makes in opening up this vast empire to the influence of foreign commerce is for the common good of each other and of all Christendom.[20]

He also pointed out that the treaty did not imitate Nanjing in that it did not compel consuls to stand surety for the payment of duties, nor did it charge them with prosecuting any of their own citizens who broke Chinese laws. On the contrary, US citizens were placed under Chinese protection. Also, while the British treaty had not mentioned opium, the treaty which he, Cushing, had negotiated stated clearly that the United States would not intervene on behalf of any of its citizens involved in opium or other contraband trade.

The Americans were followed, a few months later, by the French, as M. de Lagrené concluded the Treaty of Whampoa with China on 24 October 1844. It closely followed the United States model. Here, too, it was made quite explicit that in the case of any crimes committed by a Frenchman, he would be subject only to French laws. Only in three significant respects did the French treaty differ from the American precedent. First, it emphasized the commonality of Western nations by providing that in places where there was no French consul, French ships and people could seek the help of the consul of a friendly power. Second, it spelled out more fully the principle of extra-territoriality in criminal cases, so that French citizens would be judged by French law.[21] Third, and perhaps most important for the French government, was the matter of religious toleration. Roman Catholic missions had been tolerated in China for over a century before 1724, when all priests of alien religions were expelled. So now, at Lagrené's request, the Chinese duly issued an edict granting toleration, followed at the start of 1846 by the restoration of church property which had been seized long before. Toleration was extended from the Catholics to other Christian denominations once Qiying discovered that there were differences in the religions of the Western nations.

What these treaties, and most particularly the Treaty of Nanjing, make abundantly clear, is that the war had not been about opium. Although the Chinese elite remained unconvinced that there had ever been any other kind of dispute worth mentioning, let alone fighting about, for London opium was not the issue. In British eyes, the conflict had been about how relations between China and the West should be shaped as they moved from the merely commercial sphere into state-to-state diplomacy, politics and strategy. In that sense, English aims were deeply conservative, as indeed was England itself. Not only did opium play no part in the Treaty of Nanjing but it had no impact on the diplomacy of any of the major Western governments concerned with China before 1858–60, except in so far as they disavowed any interest in that trade.

In fact, these basic points were made, long before the war ended, by a distinguished American. It was John Quincy Adams, currently Chairman of the House of Representatives Committee on Foreign Affairs, and a former Secretary of State and 6th President of the United States. He told the Massachusetts Historical Society in 1841 that he could see nothing wrong in British attempts to secure equal rights for independent nations as against China's insolent assumption of supremacy. 'Opium,' he said

> is a mere incident to the dispute, but no more the cause of the war than the throwing overboard of tea in Boston harbor was the cause of the North American revolution ... the cause of the war is the kowtow – the arrogant and insupportable pretensions of China that she will hold commercial intercourse with the rest of mankind not upon terms of equal reciprocity, but upon the insulting and degrading forms of the relation between lord and vassal.[22]

His lecture was greeted with howls of outrage and one prominent journal refused to publish it.

In London, too, when *The Times* looked back on the war 15 years after Nanjing, its view was equally calm and unexcited. What, it asked, remained of the furious debates of 1840? Only

> the great historical fact ... that in the year 1840 the advancing enterprise of England came in contact with the isolated fabric of Chinese society. The paltry details whether this act was legal or the other act judicious have passed into oblivion. In the regular and inevitable development of the world it was necessary that at some period an adventurous maritime people like the English should force themselves into connexion with (the) feeble ... Chinese, inhabiting a rich country open to our trade. That period came in 1840 and certain disputes, ending in the success of (the English) nation, and the settlement of an English colony, were the natural result. The change of Ministry (in London) produced no change of policy. The Conservatives under Sir Robert Peel soon succeeded in upsetting the Whig Government, which had begun the war, but they did not hesitate to carry out all that the Whigs had begun.[23]

How, then, did the view take hold, not only among Chinese but in the United States and among the British themselves, that the 1840–42 conflict had been an 'Opium War' and that, more generally, the British had behaved wickedly and disgracefully in China? The answer has to do with complex and widely divergent domestic developments in Britain and China. But these only emerged long after the war, and their impact was distorted by the fact that the issues that had led to conflict remained unresolved – treaty or no treaty – for a further two decades.

But Nanjing had very different effects within China, depending on whether one considers the short or the long term. In the short term, so far as the Chinese Court and governing classes were concerned, and apart from the injuries done to the empire's pride and self-perception by repeated defeats, neither the war nor the Nanjing Treaty changed anything very much. The Middle Kingdom was still self-evidently the Middle Kingdom. The barbarians were still barbarians, to be ignored where possible. The power of the English force might have proved irresistible for the time being, but nothing had happened to cause any major change in China's view of itself and the world. Most of China had anyway been unaffected by the small war in the South. Even during the negotiations Beijing had been getting messages from various parts of the empire pleading for 'no concessions' and the treaty, in fact, made no concessions of great substance. That view prevailed until 1860, the more so since domestic troubles and rebellion not only overshadowed foreign issues but eroded the empire's capacity to deal with them.

In the longer perspective, however, Nanjing began a fundamental alteration in the structure of China's relations with foreign powers and even with foreigners living in China. It inaugurated a treaty port system that was to have very large consequences for China over the following century, until it was swept away by Japan in 1941. And it therefore triggered an attitude to foreigners that, over time, helped both to promote a resentful nationalism and to fuel the drive for modernization.

The treaty created channels for formal communication between the Chinese and British authorities. In the treaty ports, merchants could bring their families and stay the whole year rather than move with the seasons. They had a consul to look after their interests and were subject to laws against evading duties. To be sure, the trade concessions to the British would benefit other foreign traders, too. Long before the war the British government had claimed not to be seeking special trading advantages. The treaty confirmed it. But that was a matter for the foreigners, not for China herself.

9
Clashes Continue: Britain and China after the War

The British took some time to understand all that, for once the Treaty of Nanjing was signed, China again fell below London's political horizon. For the rest of the decade, British politics focused on domestic issues of the first importance, like church affairs or social problems. Probably the most urgent of all was the question of food supplies and agricultural protection, highlighted by potato and corn blights which led, among other things, to large-scale starvation in Ireland. Then Peel's government managed to repeal the Corn Laws, and so dismantle a critical barrier to food imports. That achievement broke his Tory party for a generation. But by 1851 one-quarter of Britain's bread was made with foreign grain and flour. The country was transformed into the world's leading free market economy, with the gospel of work one of the main principles of public affairs. As Samuel Smiles said 'An endless significance lies in Work: properly speaking all true work is Religion.'[1] Methods of public finance changed, too. Income tax, for example, first adopted as a war tax in 1799, allowed Britain to underpin its naval and military power with commercial muscle. But, as usually happens with convenient taxes, it stayed. And once Peel became Prime Minister, he used it to reduce indirect taxes and, by means of freer trade, stimulate consumption and growth. But beyond all that, more trade continued to mean peace, prosperity and the spread of civilization itself. It was not mere cynicism when, in 1858, the foreign merchants of Tianjin proposed a mission to 'develop the vast resources of China, and to expand among her people the elevating influence of a higher civilization.'[2]

Abroad, London continued to want stability and the status quo, as dominant powers usually do. That still meant preserving the European balance, containing French ambitions, Russian expansion, and propping up the Ottoman Empire. There was also the Europe-wide revolutionary upsurge of 1848, the problem of Poland and of governments in Spain and Portugal. In the 1850s there were several wars in quick succession. The most important was the Crimean War of 1854/56, so hopelessly mismanaged by Prime Minister Aberdeen that Palmerston was the obvious man to succeed him, and the Queen had, with considerable reluctance, to send for him. There was also the horrific Indian Mutiny of 1857, with its butchery of English women and children, or the spectacle of Indian mutineers blown from the mouths of cannon by the vengeful British. It was thought an honourable military punishment, in the tradition of the old Mogul empire, and a more soldierly death than mere hanging. Anyway, the British never again totally trusted Indian troops. For a long time the Indian Army was allowed no artillery and every Indian brigade had one British battalion to keep an eye on things. And British units in India carried their rifles and ammunition on church parade, just in case someone tried to use the Lord's Day to start another mutiny.

At the same time, there were powerful and growing religious and humanitarian elements in policy debates in England. Many people continued to see Britain as the representative of Western Christian civilization, in East Asia as elsewhere, whose honourable conduct would resonate around the world. Palmerston himself still wanted to establish and maintain Britain as the exemplar of constitutionalism, promoting freedom and free enterprise, with other constitutional states as 'the natural Allies of this country', rather as the United States and Britain in the early twenty-first century see every 'democracy' as an ally.

So that in the two decades after Nanjing, Britain's China policies remained much the same: equality, diplomacy, security and trade, in a general context of morality and justice. That also came to mean trying to maintain the unity and integrity of the Chinese empire. Which was not an easy matter when its borders were, at best, vague and uncertain and when France and Russia were advancing in those border regions. In 1849, for instance, the Russian Governor of Siberia, N.N. Muraviev, raised the flag at the mouth of the Amur river, and ten years later the French began to make serious inroads into Indo-China. But right, justice and morality also meant Britain's own treaty rights, including China's duty to protect British people on her soil. With monotonous regularity London went on demanding diplomatic equality and resisting China's claims to superiority in language or behaviour. Beyond that, however, the British remained interested in commerce, not territory or governance. Palmerston particularly welcomed the new openings for more trade: 'a greater benefit to British manufactures could hardly be conceived'.[3] Moreover, London continued to maintain, open and non-discriminatory trade was as much in China's interests as England's, not least because it meant so much more than profits.

Reactions in China were very different. Chinese pride and assertiveness were outraged at the ease with which the empire had been defeated, and by the tiny forces of a vastly inferior civilization at that. To be sure, much of the senior Manchu administrative class understood that China's defeat had been real and that the British must be given no excuse to start fighting again. For half a dozen years, policy was set by a small group around the Emperor, dedicated to that principle. It was followed, more or less, through the various Sino-Western agreements of 1842–44, into an 1848 Chinese agreement to compensate three British missionaries injured during an unauthorized incursion into Shanghai's hinterland. And many senior Chinese officials were persons of utmost probity. As a governor of Hong Kong remarked of Qiying, he was '... by far the most elevated in rank, as well as the most estimable in character, of any persons with whom the representatives of European states in China had ever come in contact.'

But official courtesy did not mask local resentment; and the growing Western presence, in treaty ports and soon elsewhere, made things worse. In November 1843, for instance, an English settlement was opened at Shanghai and, being open to all, quickly became an international settlement. The Americans and French created settlements, too. And as more and more people, including Chinese, came to these concessions to take advantage of their security, order and prosperity, they evolved into self-contained Western enclosures with their own manners and habits. These things made Western assertions of equality doubly objectionable.

So, as long as the British were given no excuses for war, imperial officials, almost as a matter of course, tried to ignore or circumvent the treaty provisions. That had to do with more than generalized resentment. It also rested on some traditional Chinese views about agreements and contracts which were – and remain to this day – very different from legalized British and Western attitudes. For the West, in the immortal words of Shakespeare's Shylock, it is a case of 'give me the bond.' Not that, in dealings between states, that principle is always observed. As the late President de Gaulle of France once explained, treaties are like young girls and roses: they last as long as they last. But in China, for an old-fashioned mandarin or merchant, a written contract could legitimately be a sometime thing. As and when conditions change, the partner in an arrangement based on mutual trust is expected to agree to a renegotiation or change. No less a man than John Stuart Mill glimpsed some of that when he commented, almost twenty years later and after a number of other painful Western contacts with China: 'Probably a Chinese statesman thinks that when concessions galling to national pride, or adverse to national policy, have been extorted by force of arms, and as it were under duress, he is doing no more than his duty in regarding the treaty as a nullity.'[4] Here was an attitude that would re-surface many times, not least in the period after 1949 when Communist China made claims against, variously, the Russians, the British and the Japanese, for the return of territories originally yielded up under what were now condemned as 'unequal treaties'. From the start, it deepened resentment at the treaties with the Westerners, in spite of the official commitment to upholding them. At the same time, here were attitudes sure to lead to disputes and clashes. On the one hand, they made it more difficult for China to adapt to Western norms of international practice. On the other, they not only violated Western notions about the binding nature of contract, but carried the highly unsettling implication that any treaty could at any time be challenged as having been, in some way, 'unequal'.

Even more important, Chinese officialdom was quite unable to take in the idea that the outcome of the war had demonstrated fatal shortcomings in China's military and political systems. By the end of the war China had begun to copy British 18-pounder guns and had built a two-decker man-of-war and even some new paddle-wheel boats. But there were no larger military changes. Major reforms of Chinese governmental affairs seemed entirely unnecessary, and especially undesirable in a period of growing domestic stresses and difficulties. The idea that foreign governments might be in any serious sense equals also remained wholly unacceptable; and the mandarinate could not even see that foreign chiefs actually represented governments. Foreign policy therefore remained very much a public-order issue, a matter of dealing with borders or pirates, as well as a tool for handling domestic issues. Western talk of a family of nations conjured up visions of the head of a (Confucian) family surrounded by devoted children. Many officials therefore continued to try simply ignoring the foreigners and Chinese treaty obligations. When that did not work, they tried extreme rudeness, with American officials as much as with the British. The result was continuing delay and obstruction in dealing with treaty provisions.

It also quickly became clear that Chinese opposition to the treaty was growing at all levels of society, especially in popular resentment in some regions. Hostility to Europeans and Americans continued throughout the 1840s, at times violently. At a time of generally weakening social discipline, losing the war made it more difficult still for Beijing to contain popular opposition, or even to rely on local officials. It was true that in many places the old, easy assumption continued that foreigners would, as they always had, end up adopting Chinese civilization and Chinese ways. So resentment centred on those places where the foreigners were not behaving like that, but visibly exacting privileges.

In the Canton region, anti-foreigner feeling and local militancy were particularly strong, fuelled by those hundred flowery legends about the people's heroically successful defeat of the British. There was a growing conviction that irregular war-fighting ('People's War') and defensive tactics had actually been victorious. By the later 1840s, fantastic and imaginary accounts of Chinese victories on land and sea inflamed the popular imagination. The belief also gained ground everywhere that the British had no military staying power: they could only meet the costs of a campaign from local commerce in China or by plain looting. There were even theories that China might be able to exploit British vulnerability in South Asia by stimulating local rebellions. Commissioner Lin had been right all along: military resistance to the West was entirely feasible. China's defeat had stemmed not from British action but from within, from domestic sabotage and bureaucratic betrayal. So there were not only anti-foreigner riots but muggings, robbery and once or twice even murder. Though access to other treaty ports was easy, at Canton the British failed to gain entry at all.

Central government control along the southern coasts, which had rarely been strong, became erratic and fitful. The war, and post-war unrest, also accentuated the conflict between the Manchu political world and the Han Chinese elite, with its disdain for legalistic uniformity and desire for local autonomy, and made it hard to pursue any kind of coherent policy. In Guangdong, the war particularly weakened local officialdom, while the commercial classes acutely resented Beijing's agreement to open more ports to foreigners, a move bound to undercut Canton. In these areas, in practice, the conduct of Chinese diplomacy devolved on the tough-minded and fairly xenophobic local gentry.

Qiying, as Governor-General of Guangdong and Guangxi, tried to make himself agreeable and became a great tamer of barbarians. But even he could not tame the Cantonese. Trouble once again came to a head in early 1846. Popular feeling forced him to make difficulties about the British right of access to the city. The British, with good sense, postponed entry indefinitely. But Lord Palmerston was less patient. When, in mid-1846, there were riots and local British officials temporized, Palmerston immediately insisted that: '... whenever British subjects are placed in danger, in a situation which is accessible to a British ship of war, thither a British ship of war ought to be and will be ordered...'.[5] By the start of 1847 he went on:

> We shall lose all the vantage ground which we have gained by our victories in China, if we take the low tone which seems to have been adopted of late by us at Canton... if we permit the Chinese, either at Canton or elsewhere, to resume, as they will no doubt always be endeavouring to do, their former tone of affected superiority, we shall very soon be compelled to come to blows with them again... we must stop... any attempt on their part to treat us otherwise than as their equals, and we must make them all clearly understand, though in the civilest terms, that our treaty rights must be respected. The Chinese must learn and be convinced, that if they attack our people and our factories, they will be shot... Depend upon it that the best way of keeping any men quiet, is to let them see that you are able and determined to repel force by force....[6]

So the governor of Hong Kong, Sir John Davis, finally tried to use force to get entry to Canton. British troops reduced some of the Chinese forts, leaving the city vulnerable. Qiying now agreed that he would let the British into the city two years hence, in 1849, once local people had been allowed a cooling-off period. But trouble continued throughout 1847 and 1848. And for the Chinese administration trouble not only included the murder of some Englishmen – which Qiying promptly punished with executions – but went well beyond the sphere of Sino-British relations. Qiying found himself trying to deal with growing piracy on the coast, as well as with civil disturbances in several parts of the provinces under his jurisdiction. In early 1848 the official Chinese position hardened. By 1849 the Emperor issued a rescript declaring that he could not oppose the unanimous opinion of the people of Canton and could not force a right of entry into the city.

By that time, much else had also changed. The Chinese war indemnity had been paid off and the British had finally evacuated Zoushan island, removing any threat to the Yangzi. In 1848 Qiying, who had made himself suspect as being too friendly to the foreigners, was recalled and replaced, in July, by Xu Guangqin as governor-general of Guangxi and Guangdong, with Ye Mingshen as governor of Guangdong. They now flatly refused to carry out the agreement on entry. British protests were treated with disdain, as the Chinese could see that the British were not really willing to use force again. They also had reports of a business depression in Britain and an increase of Anglo-French tensions. In addition to which, there was some idea that the Americans, as Britain's commercial rivals, might come to China's support. So Canton's merchants were encouraged to organize a full trade boycott, and there was talk of mobilizing the local irregular forces again.

The British, for their part, could see well enough that peaceful commerce would be impossible if they simply forced their way in. So they stepped back. The Chinese were delighted, and produced yet another tale of triumphant popular resistance. Clearly, it was now said, the British feared the people more than they did the imperial armies. The Emperor sent congratulations to the senior officials at Canton and a victory tablet was put up by local scholars and gentry. When Palmerston, by then back in office, heard about it, he remarked tartly that if this represented the view of the Chinese government, the British government 'would despair of being able to continue to maintain relations of peace between Great Britain and China'.[7] He also sent a protest to Beijing. It reminded the court plainly of the 'mistake which was committed by their predecessors in 1839', and of the war that had followed. His government would not tolerate what seemed to be official encouragement to the people of Canton to behave in hostile fashion to the British. By September 1850, after various other difficulties, he was even more impatient, foreseeing that if the Chinese were really trying to unravel the results of the war, there might have to be another fight: 'The Time is fast coming when we shall be obliged to strike another Blow in China... These half-civilized governments... require a Dressing every eight or ten years to keep them in order. Their minds are too shallow to receive an Impression that will last longer... and warning is of little use...'.[8]

By this time the 19-year-old Xianfeng had ascended the imperial throne, becoming the seventh emperor of the Qing dynasty. A year later he took as concubine and consort the 16-year-old Cixi, of whom much more would be heard. But the social, economic and agricultural disintegration of China – once again especially in the South – was growing worse. The underlying causes were largely structural. Population growth had outstripped the capacity of the traditional rural economy to absorb more people, increased poverty and encouraged ecological decline. At the same time, the mandarinate increasingly focused on its own bureaucracy rather than larger problems.[9] There was a government finance crisis, enhanced by British indemnity demands. There were crop failures in 1847 and again in 1848/49. Rebellions flared, many of them peasant-based, in ways that, tradition suggested, foreshadowed dynastic decline. By this time, too, the Chinese had begun to learn something of the West, its countries and histories. A trickle of young Chinese began to go abroad to study. At Beijing, where the new young emperor was determined to resist the foreigners, some court factions now concluded that British power was already overextended in places like Nepal and India. But in the paradoxical fashion that seemed to characterize events in China in this period, a foreign-staffed and managed Chinese Maritime Customs Service was created.[10] Fortunately for China it became an honest and reliable provider of increasing revenues to Beijing. The Chinese also felt free to continue to ask for British help in dealing with piracy on the coast. The Royal Navy duly obliged – and profited handsomely. It was offered £20 (tv: £1030) for every pirate, dead or captured, and even £5 (tv: £257) for each one that escaped. In 1848/49 one squadron earned £42,000 (tv: over £2 million) in that kind of head-money. The business grew even bigger after 1854, with the suppression of risings in Guangdong, when many ex-rebels became pirates.

The British also became aware, slowly and reluctantly, that their whole stress on trade in dealing with China had been rather pointless. Though they had won the war, after 1843 or so the China trade actually contracted. The 1847 House of Commons Select Committee on Commercial Relations with China had to accept that, in this business, traders' losses of 30–40 per cent were normal. In 1852 the Shanghai consul, Rutherford Alcock, pointed out that it was simply unprofitable to try to sell British manufactures in China. That being so, and since £23 million (tv: £1.2 billion) worth of British Eastern commerce depended entirely on the opium trade for the money to buy Chinese goods, that trade should be legalized. An obscure assistant magistrate at Hong Kong was even blunter two years later. His name was Mitchell and he wrote a report for the Governor of Hong Kong on the potential of trading with China. He pointed out 'that the export of manufacturing stuffs to China was less by nearly three quarters of a million sterling at the close of 1850 than at the close of 1844.' The fact that foreign trade was confined to treaty ports was irrelevant. The limitations were due to the self-sufficiency of the Chinese economy. 'When we opened the seaboard provinces of this country to British trade ten years ago,' Mitchell wrote,

the most preposterous notions were formed as to the demand that was to spring up for our manufactures. Our friends in Manchester and even their counterparts on the spot here … seem to have all gone mad together upon the idea of an open trade with 'three or four hundred millions of human beings.' They straightaway began to bargain and barter, in imagination, with 'a third of the human race', and would not be convinced that it was not possible to throw more into the newly opened markets. Sir Henry Pottinger told them that he had opened up a whole new world to their trade, so vast 'that all the mills in Lancashire could not make stocking-stuff sufficient for one of its provinces', and they pinned implicit faith in a statement to which their own fondness stood sponsor. Now as we could not possibly find a better one, I take Sir Henry Pottinger's hyperbole and try to exhibit how utterly unfounded from first to last was this splendid fabric of His Excellency's imagination.

The fact was that China would not abandon its own markets, methods and products.[11] And indeed, it turned out that while global trade volumes grew, the China trade remained a small percentage of the Chinese economy as well as of Britain's global trading.

However, what matters most with intelligence information and analysis is the way it is used. In this case, it was simply ignored. The merchants refused to believe Mitchell's assessment. The report was pigeon-holed and not even rediscovered and sent on to the Foreign Office until six years later. Still, it is a report that, in 2003/4, London and New York corporations might still find instructive.

There remained, too, the matter of opium. After the war its consumption increased, and it may well be – direct evidence, either way, would be hard to find – that demand was bolstered by the effects of general social turmoil, as well as by personal and public distress at China's humiliations. In any case, Commissioner Lin's 1839 ban on the Canton trade had made every large and small harbour along the coast into a potential smugglers' haven; and more and more fast and handy opium clippers were built throughout the 1840s and 1850s, not least in American shipyards like Baltimore, New York and Boston,[12] and operated under a variety of flags. As early as April 1843 Sir Henry Pottinger wrote:

> it is a matter of public notoriety that the chief mercantile houses engaged in the opium trade in China have already provided themselves with vessels built in America and sailing under American colours with American masters and crews, and it is also well known that any vessel may obtain a Portuguese register and the right to carry the Portuguese flag.[13]

So far as foreigners were concerned, Beijing's moral and political position had been thoroughly undermined by the offer, in the run-up to the 1842–44 treaties, to legalize the drug. Indeed, Beijing seemed flabbergasted that the British did not use their victory to enforce legalization. Some local authorities seemed no less surprised and even confused by the role of the new Western consuls. In 1845 the customs people at Ningbo were delighted and surprised in roughly equal proportions when, having reported to the consul the seizure of a small quantity of opium from a British vessel, the consul actually punished the ship by withdrawing its sailing-permit. On the other hand, the authorities at Shanghai simply did not want to know when the consul there denounced opium ships to them. The earlier British efforts to prevent Hong Kong from being an opium trading centre quickly lapsed, once ships from any quarter could carry opium to any coastal inlet. As early as 1845 Hong Kong, as one young English midshipman commented disgustedly, was 'a dreadful place for all kinds of roguery, being a complete second Sydney'.[14]

So when, in August 1850, the new young emperor issued fresh draconian decrees banning the use of opium, not a lot happened. The new penalties, which said offenders would lose their heads, with their families being sold into slavery, merely meant that foreign opium traders tried even harder to avoid the treaty ports and their own consuls. As the trade spread around the coast, a host of local officials still vied with one another to attract it and openly expected payment to allow the drug to land. Not only did that bolster their incomes, it often had to replace their official pay in a period when rebel activities could make regular salary payments impossible. In most places, even Shanghai, opium was traded openly and in daylight. Indeed, by the mid-1850s official directories listed the names of the opium-receiving ships beyond the ports, of their captains and the names of the firms controlling them. There were even formal negotiations between the traders and the Shanghai authorities about the level of duty on the opium. These duties became very useful for Beijing itself, as rebellion increased its expenses and reduced revenues. Not surprisingly, in February 1854 the Foreign Secretary, Lord Clarendon, urged the Governor of Hong Kong to try once more to get the trade legalized.[15] He said the same thing three years later to Lord Elgin, by then the British negotiator. He was urged

> to ascertain whether the government of China would revoke its prohibition of the opium trade, which the high officers of the Chinese government never practically enforce. Whether the legalisation of the trade would tend to augment that trade may be doubtful, as it seems now to be carried on to the full extent of the demand in China, with the sanction and connivance of the local authorities. But there would be obvious advantages in placing the trade upon a legal

footing by the imposition of a duty, instead of its being carried on in the present irregular manner.[16]

Even the American Minister now decided to support legalization. He concluded that the existing situation was 'insufferable' and an 'inconvenient masquarade', and it was necessary to act in flat contradiction of his express anti-opium instructions from Washington.

In these circumstances, it is hardly surprising that Chinese opium imports continued to increase. In Shanghai alone, for example, demand doubled in the decade from 1847 to 1857 to some 32,000 chests, or more than China's total opium imports had been in the later 1830s. By 1855 the total consumption along the coast from Canton to Shanghai seems to have risen to some 65,350 chests.[17]

Yet the empire was so far in crisis that even the foreign or opium problems were secondary. Amid simmering discontent a number of rebel movements had flared up from time to time ever since the White Lotus rebellion had ended around 1806. Most were anti-Manchu, some were Moslem, others mere bandits. But now one of the most dangerous and long-lasting rebellions in China's history, the Taiping movement, was gaining ground. Much of the evidence we have about them is from their enemies or from foreigners, because the empire later destroyed all of the Taiping documents it could find. But they were founded and led by Hong Xiuqan, a Hakka from the Canton region. He was deeply impressed by a Christian pamphlet, had a mental breakdown, saw visions, and later spent a month with an American Baptist missionary, Issachar Roberts, from whom he learned some of the practices of fundamentalist Protestantism. His movement began by basing itself in the distant southern province of Guangxi and by late 1850 numbered 20,000 believers, largely fellow-Hakka. It was an attempt to create a new Christian community, puritan, egalitarian, offering support to the lower classes and to social rejects, but also committed to the destruction of the Manchus. For the Manchus were demons, fighting against the true God. Support came from the poor, the uneducated, from gangs of river pirates, Qing deserters, clerks and even women bandits. On Hong's 38th birthday, in January 1851, he proclaimed his new Heavenly Kingdom of Great Peace, with himself as the Heavenly King. Some have interpreted this as a sinified version of the Christian Kingdom of God upon Earth.

The Taiping armies moved on their feet and lived off the land. They were fiercely disciplined, immensely brave and ruthless. Though at first armed only with swords, knives and a few muskets for hand-to-hand fighting, from the start they won important battles against imperial troops. As they moved to strike north, capturing several cities, thousands more rallied to the movement, bringing not only people but resources and treasure, especially once they moved into the rich Yangzi provinces where grievances against taxes and landlords were strong. In March 1853 they bloodily stormed Nanjing itself. The Manchu population and garrison, including women and children, amounted to some 40,000. The Taipings massacred them. Possibly 100 may have survived.[18] The city became the Taipings' Heavenly capital.

Yet in time the Taiping leaders fell to quarrelling among themselves, often murderously. No less important, with all their utopianism they were never a constructive force. What they set up was a theocracy, with some elements organized in ways oddly similar to the Maoist communes of the 1950s and 1960s. The basic unit was 25 families living, farming and fighting together, with a head who was leader and administrator as well as preacher, not entirely unlike a local Maoist Party Secretary. On the other hand, they formed no comprehensive or regular civil administration, not even of the countryside as their base. Moreover, their religiosity continued to offend scholars and gentry everywhere, for their beliefs represented a fundamental challenge to the Confucian state and its values. At the same time, their lower-class leadership was offensive to the local and provincial gentry.

The movement attracted a good deal of foreign attention. The British and Americans, especially, were at first attracted by the notion of millions of Chinese converting to something like Protestant Christianity and, in the process, subverting the corrupt and arrogant Manchu administration. But three weeks after the Taipings took Nanjing Sir George Bonham, the Governor of Hong Kong, visited them. He was not impressed. He did not think they would be able to form an effective administration and there was little sign of a willingness to trade. On the other hand, by that time the Taipings controlled so much territory that Washington authorized the American Minister, Robert M. McLane, to recognize them as the *de facto* government of the empire if he thought that justified. Even the French were at first sympathetic. But on closer inspection all three powers decided to remain strictly neutral in this Chinese civil war. Yet neutrality turned out to be impossible. For one thing, the Yangzi river region, which became the seat of Taiping power, was a major silk- and tea-producing region and therefore of direct economic importance to the West.

Moreover, the various regional disturbances affected Shanghai, which had one of the fastest expanding foreign settlements. For instance, in

September 1853 the 'Small Sword' Society took the Chinese part of the city, while leaving the foreign settlements alone. The Small Swords sought, like the Taipings with whom they claimed some alliance, to remove the foreign Manchu dynasty and restore proper Chinese rule. But they found themselves denounced once the Taipings looked at them more closely. Even though the foreign settlements were not molested, the city and its inhabitants were closely beleaguered, not only at first by the Small Swords, but by the imperial army which besieged the Small Swords in turn. In the meantime, the Shanghai merchants, both foreign and Chinese, cheerfully sold weapons and supplies to all sides, imperial, Small Swords and Taiping. But with the whole region in turmoil, large numbers of people from the countryside took refuge in Shanghai and thousands crowded for safety into those foreign settlements. Indeed, for the next century, whether in times of rebellion or, much later on, of Japanese invasion, thousands of refugees would seek safety there.[19] Protection became a very live issue.

Given their continuing big and small difficulties with local turmoil and Chinese officialdom, by the early 1850s the British decided to press for a revision of the whole body of Sino-Western agreements. It was very clear that this was no selfish British effort. The Foreign Office sent instructions that the negotiators were to work with the French and Americans for the general Western interest. That was not always easy. In late 1852 Humphrey Marshall of Kentucky became the American Minister. Educated at West Point, he had got his colonelcy during the Mexican war and later gone into the House of Representatives. He was deeply suspicious of the British and all their works, and thought they harboured convoluted and devious plans about forming a special relationship with the Taipings and dominating the Yangzi basin and Western China. In fact, the British continued to be deeply afraid of any such development. In 1854 a new Governor of Hong Kong and Plenipotentiary was appointed: Sir John Bowring, a 62-year-old, much-travelled Westcountryman with a face, as someone said, remarkably ugly and shining with intelligence. He was an exuberantly Christian fellow and had much experience in commerce. He once remarked that 'Jesus Christ is free trade and free trade is Jesus Christ.' He was a considerable linguist, a founder of the Peace Society and a close friend of London radicals like Bentham and Cobden. He feared, like Lenin, J.A. Hobson and other anti-imperialists half a century later, that expanding trade would lead to governance, as British efforts had done in India. His view of Marshall was not kind. The man was not only suspicious but 'is a very coarse, headstrong man – has never been out of Kentucky before he came here...'.[20] Palmerston now told Bowring to try to secure British access to the entire China coast and to the cities, people and products of the Yangzi region. He should also revive, yet again, ideas about legalizing the opium trade. Most essential of all, a British Ambassador should at last be sent to Beijing. Only then would the Chinese, and their Emperor, recognize the state equality Palmerston had been pressing for since the 1830s.

But the Governor-General of Guangxi and Guangdong, and imperial commissioner for relations with foreign powers, was now the very Ye Mingchen who had been largely instrumental in refusing British entry to Canton back in 1849. A fat, intelligent, sourpuss of a man with a taste for astrology and a reputation for cruelty, he was especially hard on rebels and their families, whom he seems to have executed as soon as he could lay hands on them. At times he probably had up to 200 heads a day lopped off. Commissioner Ye now flatly refused to see the Western officials, let alone to consider treaty revision. He treated Bowring and Marshall's successor, Robert M. McLane, with studied contempt. He of course knew that the British had, for a decade or more, not thought their treaty rights, or treaty revision, worth a war. But he did not understand the hardening of English views, and especially those of John Bowring. Now, in the critical period of the mid-1850s, 'The pivotal consideration in London, made obvious by Palmerston and Clarendon, was Yeh's final rejection of the British demand for treaty revision...'.[21]

However, even now there was no crisis. The British sought to avoid using force, in manoeuvres reminiscent of the futilities of 1838–40. Bowring, accompanied by American and French envoys, travelled north to Tianjin, on the approaches to Beijing, to try and by-pass Ye. They all had to retreat empty-handed and 1855 was spent in more fruitless efforts to get Beijing to renegotiate. By this time the British and French, and even some of the Americans on the spot, began to accept that there might have to be another fight. It was impossible to deal with the Chinese and nothing since Nanjing had persuaded the Chinese to accept the Western powers as equals. As long as foreign relations were handled by a Canton commissioner, instead of centrally, the imperial court would remain at arm's length from the foreigners and keep up the traditional pretence of foreign inferiority – on which, to be sure, domestic order as well as universal standing might depend.

By 1856, with the Americans, French and Russians all wanting greater access to the Chinese market, new difficulties arose and mutual irritation increased. At the end of February a French missionary, Auguste Chapdelaine, was arrested, tried for preaching the Christian gospel, caged, beheaded and his head thrown to the dogs. In early October, a member of the local gentry at Canton reported to officials that at Whampoa, among the crew of a lorcha[22] named the *Arrow*, he had recognized a pirate or the father of a pirate. Four mandarins and 60 soldiers boarded the ship, which was Chinese-owned but registered under British papers, arrested 12 sailors and hauled down the flag. There has been endless dispute about details. The ship was captained by Tom Kennedy, a 21-year old Irishman from Belfast. But he, and many like him, were captains of convenience, used like foreign flags merely to divert the attentions of the Chinese maritime police from a Chinese-built, Chinese-owned, Chinese-crewed ship. However, the tough, impetuous and pushy local consul, Harry Parkes, complained that the ship's British registration (which had, technically, just expired) was still valid, and the Chinese had no right to board a British vessel without going through him, still less a right to haul down the flag. He demanded an apology, and Ye's assurance that nothing of the kind would happen again. Of course Ye refused, and would have been bound to refuse even if he had not been, as the American medical missionary Dr Peter Parker noted, 'alone and pre-eminent in his insane and insufferable conduct towards foreigners...'.

The incident may have been fairly trivial, but it was the straw that broke the camel's back. Bowring decided to back Harry Parkes and called in the Royal Navy. Its local commander was Rear-Admiral Sir Michael Seymour. He was 54 years old, slow, pompous and one-eyed, having lost the other eye when a Russian mine picked up in the Baltic blew up on him. Now, on 23 October 1856, he captured and dismantled four barrier forts a few miles down-river from Canton and bombarded the walls and parts of the town, destroying perhaps 1000 houses and killing civilians. On the 31st Ye issued a proclamation offering $30 (tv: roughly £260) for every English head. In mid-December the British factories were burned down. On 29 December there was a mutiny on the small steamer *Thistle*, and the 11 Europeans on board were beheaded by men apparently wearing uniforms. War junks attacked civilian ships. In mid-January 1857 arsenic was found in bread supplied to Westerners at Hong Kong, now also inhabited by up to 80,000 merchants, smugglers, fishermen, shopkeepers, coolies and ruffians of every kind. Some British people were assaulted. By then, too, British troops had burned some hundreds of houses in Canton.

The Americans became involved as well. Most of their officials on the spot had long ago concluded that the only way to make China meet Western demands would be by using force. McLane, who was willing to ignore the distant instructions of his Secretary of State, had already said plainly that 'diplomatic intercourse can only be had with this government at the cannon's mouth'. He was not alone in concluding that America ought to co-operate with Britain.[23] Dr Parker, who succeeded him, also wrote home to recommend that the United States should take action together with the British. Washington refused, but the US Navy became involved anyway. In mid-November 1856 Chinese forts fired on a US corvette, conspicuously flying the Stars and Stripes, while she was on her way to Canton. Commodore Armstrong demanded an explanation and apology from Ye. None came. As the Chinese prepared for further action, Armstrong used his three ships to capture and dismantle the barrier forts which had done the shooting. Seven Americans were killed and 22 wounded, but Chinese casualties were around 300. Washington, however, refused a general use of force, and the French similarly ruled themselves out from active measures.

To the Chinese, it seemed entirely absurd that the *Arrow* affair, a small infringement in the process of arresting suspected pirates – something on which the Chinese and British were actually co-operating – should bring on conflict. To the British, it was equally absurd that the Chinese should flatly refuse satisfaction for yet another insult to their flag, and military operations seemed to be the only way to get somewhere with the Chinese. When news of the business reached London in January 1857, discussion immediately focused on the broader issues of the observance of treaty arrangements and securing proper diplomatic links and easier trade arrangements. *The Times* published extended accounts of both British and Chinese versions of events.[24] But it thought the affair at Canton was only the latest instance of a much more general Chinese ill will: '... the affair of the Arrow was but the expression ... of an animosity long entertained, and sure to explode, sooner or later, into active hostility.'[25] The paper accused the Chinese of 'arrogant and insulting' behaviour and added 'We have no interest in ruining the (Chinese) government or disorganizing the society of that vast country ... All we want is liberty and security for our commerce and a prompt and efficient redress of grievances as they arise.' It added '... we must teach (the Chinese) to treat us in every matter of social consideration as at least their equals.' Britain was entitled to claim the right of peaceful civilian residence at Canton which had been granted not just in 1842 at Nanjing but in supplementary agreements in 1843 and 1846.[26] Since the Nanjing agreements had not prevented new clashes, there ought to be a fresh treaty, and this time peace should not be concluded 'till we have eliminated from it the conditions of a future war.' And since matters could not be left at the mercy of provincial authorities, there simply must be a resident Ambassador at Beijing with access to the Emperor.

Altogether, *The Times* thought, it was time to place relations on a new footing.[27] 'China must be brought into full communication with the civilized world, and the task of dragging her from seclusion can be best performed by Englishmen ... we do not want to conquer China (but) we should, then, prepare ... to assert our position and to enforce the right of civilized nations to free commerce and communication ...'. The British authorities should demand 'free entrance for men of all nations into the country ...'.

The Times was not alone. *The Globe*, which normally took very different political positions, thought the British had given a number of openings for a Chinese apology over the *Arrow* business, but they had been refused. So 'now ... will be a favourable opportunity for forcing on the attention of the Chinese Government those concessions [i.e. foreign access to Canton] that are required in the interest, not only of the larger commerce of England, but of the other European nations and of the United States' since '[n]either the true welfare of the Chinese nor of ourselves is promoted by a policy of exclusion'.[28]

The paper returned to the point. 'Our aim,' it wrote 'has not been to obtain any exclusive privileges, but simply to procure access to a country ...'. On that, the Americans, Australians and New Zealanders were co-operating with Britain.[29] A couple of weeks later it went on, 'The fact is, that the Chinese authorities have presumed on our moderation and forbearance. We did not enforce the treaty at Canton as we did at Shanghai and elsewhere ... Neither France nor America is in a better position, nor better satisfied with the state of their relations with the Chinese.'[30] Nor were official relations everything. *The Globe* worried about the general impression of disorder at Canton, the way in which individuals could find themselves carried off by soldiers or bandits, or merchant ships be simply shot at.

The matter reached the floor of Parliament towards the end of February, by which time the government had produced a 'blue book' of British and Chinese documents. A motion was tabled in the House of Lords complaining that no military activities should have been started at Canton without express authorization from London. The Chinese actions over the *Arrow* did not justify military operations.[31] The Tory leader, Lord Derby, for instance, argued that there had been no need to use force and it was far from clear that forcing entry to Canton would promote trade, let alone benefit the general British position in South China. Still, on 27 February, the Lords approved the actions at Canton by 146 votes to 110.

In the Commons, matters were different. There, the renowned Liberal MP, Richard Cobden, took a lead. His attack was fundamental: 'No foreign politics.' The whole business of a balance of power, he said nine years later, was a 'foul idol', bound to condemn Britain to ineffective but costly interventions. Years earlier, in 1846, he had declared that 'the free trade principle (was) that which shall act on the moral world as the principle of gravitation in the universe – drawing together, thrusting aside the antagonism of race, and creed, and language, and uniting us in the bonds of eternal peace.'[32] And he never wavered from his passionate advocacy of free trade as 'God's diplomacy' which would, if implemented, make international conflict and war, let alone colonies, redundant.[33] So he now put down a motion criticizing not just Bowring but the government that had appointed him. All sides agreed that this was now a Motion of Confidence; and the government found itself confronted by some of the most formidable members of the House. They included not only Cobden but Sir James Graham and two men who would be among the century's greatest prime ministers, Benjamin Disraeli and William Gladstone who had, together with Graham, been so prominent in the China debate 15 years earlier. A few instances will give the flavour of the exchanges. They include assertions about Chinese behaviour which, at times exaggerated or even untrue, were firmly believed in London and so broadly influenced British opinion.

Cobden himself put pragmatic arguments. Whatever else the British bombardment at Canton might or might not achieve, it would not remove the obstacles to trade. In fact, the hostilities had no clear aim and no good could possibly come from them. He was supported by the forceful radical populist, John Arthur Roebuck QC, member for Sheffield, who took a more elevated view. Britain, he said, was the only great power with a constitutional government. Every act condemned by world opinion would therefore be taken as evidence against liberal institutions. In the East, Britain was the only Western power with a large dominion, so her acts would reflect on the whole of Christianity and Western civilization. As for the actions of the Canton police in boarding the *Arrow*, distinguished people in England thought them entirely legal. So 'will you punish the unfortunate people of Canton for an action which has been considered right by some of the greatest lawyers in England?' There was more. Parliament should look at the blue book and 'Compare the truculent manner in which the English papers are written...mark the courtesy and intelligence that distinguish (the Chinese)...(so) which is the civilized man and which the barbarian?' Moreover, '[t]he Chinese looking on our progress in India, say we are an aggressive people – that where we plant our foot we extend our administration, and therefore they will not let us enter their cities ... (that fact) ought to be viewed by us with tenderness and respect.'

Perhaps the weightiest critique came from Gladstone. He quoted that tough old Canton merchant, William Jardine, as saying that, in general, China's 'treatment of the English community was one of kindness and justice.' The government had never told Parliament that access to Canton was an adequate cause for war. Commissioner Ye was probably right to say that British entry to the city 'would be more mischievous than beneficial.' It was quite wrong for Britain to use force to try to increase trade, or spread her influence. If there had to be British reprisals at Canton at all, they should have been proportionate and not have included bombarding civilians. The British had compelled the Chinese to divert to Canton troops needed to fight domestic rebellion elsewhere, with devastating consequences in places. There were also the larger repercussions for the international balance. 'Great powers have been brought into contact with us in the East. We have the Russian Empire and the American Republic there, and a political compromise developing itself like the balance of power in Europe.' The violence of British conduct might therefore end up giving the leading influence in China to the United States. All this, and especially the emphasis on public morality, was well calculated to appeal to current British opinion. Yet Gladstone was surely wrong in his underlying assumption: that one could treat the Chinese as just another state within the accepted international system. It was a fundamental misunderstanding of Chinese self-perceptions and views of world order.

Palmerston may by now have been something over 70 years old, short-sighted, slightly deaf and with dyed hair, but he responded with his customary vigour. So far as the Opposition was concerned '...everything that was English was wrong, and everything that was hostile to England was right.' Of course '...if we had a Minister at Pekin who could have addressed himself to the servants of the Emperor...this and other local difficulties would have been surmounted and accommodated without difficulty...'. Admiral Seymour had been quite right to seek direct communication with the local Chinese authorities. But the *Arrow* business was only '...one of many acts of deliberate violation of our treaty rights.' In fact,

> there was a systematic determination on the part of the Canton authorities to refuse to us all our treaty rights as far as it was possible

to deny them ... I say that the violation of our treaty rights ... was part of a deliberate system to strip us step by step of our treaty rights, to set the population of the city against us ... and to give undue advantage to others against British subjects .... .

It was significant, too, that the trouble was confined to Canton. There were no difficulties elsewhere: in Shanghai everything was 'good humoured and humane.' In any case, Commissioner Ye '... is one of the most savage barbarians that ever disgraced a nation.' He was guilty of wholesale executions of Chinese. And 'the first act of Yeh upon the breaking out of the dispute was to issue a reward for the heads of Englishmen, and he next put out a proclamation declaring that he had taken secret means of extirpating that hated race.' He had murdered Europeans and poisoned food meant for them. In this matter the Chinese had combined cruelty and treachery. Should Parliament now tell Ye that he had been right after all? What would be the consequences of such a vote for the entire British position in the East?

The government certainly had an '... ardent wish that these disputes should speedily and satisfactorily terminate.' It would be

... to the great and manifest advantage of the people of China if a larger commercial intercourse were established with them. And if these unfortunate events had not happened we should have been in communication with the Government of France – and I think the United States would join us – with the view of sending a friendly diplomatic mission to Pekin for the purpose of making fresh arrangements with the Chinese for securing more extended commercial relations with them .... .

In the end, though, Palmerston's own Cabinet colleague, Sir George Cornwall Lewis, noted in his diary that the weight of argument favoured the Opposition.[34] It was perhaps also a sign of wider and growing doubts about the morality of Britain's position that the government lost the vote of confidence by 263 to 247. Queen Victoria was seriously annoyed and deplored the House's lack of patrotism.[35] In her journal she noted 'the wretched cant and humbug displayed in the debates.' But it was even more a sign of popular opinion that Palmerston promptly called a general election and could fight his campaign largely on the grounds of patriotism and the honour of the flag. As *Punch* wickedly recorded the Commons vote:

For hauling down the British flag, apologizing to the Chinese and putting Derby, Dizzy and Gladstone in office	263
For maintaining the honour of England and keeping Pam in place	247
Chinese majority:	16

Or, as Palmerston himself told his voters at Tiverton, in Devon '… an insolent barbarian … had violated the British flag, broken the engagement of treaties, offered reward for the heads of British subjects … and planned their destruction by murder, assassination and poisons.'[36] As far as the public was concerned, here was the man who stood up to foreigners and for England. He was returned to power with a comfortable majority.

So the China issue would be pursued and Beijing compelled to come to terms. The French decided to join in. There were, of course, difficulties. There was a shortage of money after the Crimean War, people were busy with trouble – yet again – in Afghanistan[37] and there was the major disaster of the 1857 Indian Mutiny. The government also had to find a new man to take charge at Hong Kong. London and the Foreign Office understood that Canton was now beside the point. Only once a British Ambassador was by right at Beijing would Britain be recognized as an equal. On 9 February 1857 the Foreign Secretary, Lord Clarendon, explained that to Bowring. 'Without such a guarantee for ready access to the Supreme Government, all other concessions will be more or less precarious.' So Palmerston appointed James Bruce, 8th Earl of Elgin, as 'Special Plenipotentiary' for China. Elgin was 45, stout, white-haired and looked, as someone said, like a 'bewhiskered cherub'. Rather like Napier before him, he was a Scottish nobleman of ancient lineage. Also like Napier, he needed money to support his family and his estate, because his father had spent so much on acquiring the famous 'Elgin Marbles' from Greece. He was not enthusiastic about fighting the Chinese, and privately described the *Arrow* affair as 'a scandal to us, and so considered … by all except the few who are personally compromised.' And: '… nothing could be more contemptible than the origin of our existing quarrel … That wretched question of the 'Arrow' (was) a scandal to us.'[38] Still, he had a distinguished colonial career behind him, including a successful Governor-Generalship of Canada, and however pleasant and humane he might be personally, was going to do his duty.

He was appointed in April 1857 and given his marching orders. He should not occupy Canton unless that became absolutely necessary and there should be no unnecessary destruction of Chinese life or property. He should rather sail north to Bei He so as to deal with the central government. He should request complete observance of the existing treaties. He should also ask Beijing for access for an accredited British representative, and the opening of more ports to commerce. He was also told that the British government had 'no desire to obtain any exclusive advantage for British trade in China but are only desirous to share with all other nations any benefits which they may acquire in the first instance, specifically for British commerce.'[39]

By mid-1857 enough of a force had been collected to deal with the Chinese. It included a number of officers who had served in the earlier China war. The French having decided to co-operate, their High Commissioner, Baron Gros, joined Elgin in October. Two other governments sent missions: Count Poutiatine from Russia and William B. Reed, Parker's successor as American Minister. The Canton river was blockaded while British and French forces took the city in December 1857. Ye was discovered, taken prisoner, sent to Calcutta, and died soon afterwards, possibly by starving himself to death. By the end of March 1858, Elgin was in Shanghai where he was severe with the merchants and those missionaries who travelled without permission into the Chinese interior. In fact, the more he saw of the British in the East, the more disillusioned he became. 'I have seen more to disgust me with my fellow-countrymen than I saw during the whole course of my previous life', he remarked.[40] Before sailing north to the Bei He river mouth he told them plainly that 'Neither our own consciences nor the judgement of mankind will acquit us if, when we are asked to what use we have turned our opportunities, we can only say that we have filled our pockets from among the ruins we have found or made.'[41]

On arriving at Bei He the four powers demanded once more that the Chinese should do what they had long promised. At minimum, that should include direct foreign representation in Bejing. In addition, Christianity should be tolerated. Though the Chinese were willing to compromise on some matters, the Emperor had fundamental objections to accepting state equality or admitting ambassadors to Beijing – thereby denying his own universal sovereignty – or even the idea that he should give the Chinese negotiators full powers to make agreements.[42] By then Reed, who had begun by deploring the war, was shown documents from Ye's office proving that Beijing had entirely approved of what he had done, and decided that the British and French were justified after all.

In fact, he came round to the view of his predecessors. 'Steadfast neutrality and consistent friendship,' he wrote to Washington 'make no impression on the isolated obduracy of this empire.'[43]

On 20 May 1858 the British and French took the Dagu forts at the mouth of the Bei He.[44] The Chinese now faced twofold dangers, for a few weeks later they were compelled to cede the entire north bank of the Amur river to Russia. Two high-ranking Manchus were therefore sent to negotiate with the British. Qiying also came to try to cajole them. The British ruthlessly produced his own earlier confidential memorials, taken from the Canton archives, proving his deviousness and pretence. The old man left, disgraced and in tears, and the Emperor ordered him to commit suicide. In June the Chinese agreed the Treaties of Tientsin (Tianjin) with the four powers. In these documents, which explicitly forbade the use of the term 'barbarians' to describe Europeans in future, it was agreed that foreign ambassadors would reside in Beijing. Christianity could be openly preached. Persons with valid passports, including missionaries, could travel freely throughout the empire. Ten new ports would be opened to foreign trade and foreigners could do business along the Yangzi for 1000 miles or more, up as far as Hankou. China would pay war indemnities to the French and British. Extraterritorial privileges were confirmed and new rules for trade and tariff levels were drawn up.

Furthermore, it was finally and formally agreed that the restrictions on opium trading would be relaxed and a set import duty demanded. But importers could only bring it ashore. Within China, it would be handled solely by Chinese and constitute Chinese property. The Chinese finally accepted all this without argument. In fact, they were already admitting opium freely, including through Russia, and imposing taxes on it. By mid-1858 the Emperor noted with satisfaction that there was now peace in the South between the barbarian forces and Chinese officials. 'The fact that the barbarians are opposed to each other and kill each other [presumably in places like the Crimea] has nothing to do with the larger matter.'[45]

Not that this was the end of it, since making agreements with China was, as usual, one thing, having them carried out quite another. The Chinese did not really accept this agreement either and ratification kept being postponed. On the British side, Lord Elgin's brother, Frederick Bruce, was appointed as first Minister to China. A year after the treaties, in June 1859, Bruce arrived at the Bei He, escorted by a Royal Navy flotilla, and accompanied by the Frenchman de Bourboulon and a new American Minister, John E. Ward. The Chinese refused to let him land at the river mouth and proceed to Beijing. A few days later the British and French tried to force the passage. But the Chinese had a new commander, the Mongol Senggelinqin,[46] who had strengthened the river defences and the Dagu forts. The British, to their huge surprise, were severely rebuffed and suffered considerable losses: four gunboats and well over 400 men. During the fight the American naval commander, Commodore Josiah Tatnall, paid a friendly visit to the wounded British Admiral, Hope. While he was at it, his boat's crew helped to work the British guns; and Tatnall used his steamer to tow into action several barges of British marines, which could make no headway against the tide. He explained that kinsmen had been in distress and 'blood is thicker than water.' In the meantime, John Ward landed peacefully on the coast beyond the river, was received and escorted to Beijing. He was treated civilly but without honour, and refused an audience with the Emperor when he would not kneel, let alone kowtow. Ward was a Southerner from Georgia, and coolly explained 'I kneel only to God and woman.'

In London, Prime Minister Palmerston was confirmed in his strong views about China. In March 1860 Lord Elgin, who had earlier come home, was sent back to China. He should now get an apology from the Chinese for the firing on British ships, a ratification, at last, of the Treaty of Tientsin (Tianjin), and an indemnity to the allies for their military expenses. In an aside he was also informed that it would be nice if he could acquire the Kowloon peninsula, opposite Hong Kong. By June 1860 the British and French notified the other Western powers that they were at war with China. But the war was to be limited. Lord John Russell, the Foreign Secretary, sent instructions that 'there are no reasons for interrupting friendly relations with the Chinese at Shanghai, Canton, or elsewhere.'[47] Elgin was told not to press the imperial authorities to the point where they lost control of a China where authority and grip were already threatened by the Taiping rebellion.

As for forces, Britain sent out 10,000 British and Indian troops. Their commander was Hope Grant – presumably still accompanied by his cello – but by now a Lieutenant General, a knight and a veteran of the Sikh wars and the Indian Mutiny. The French envoy, Baron Gros, also returned, together with 5800 men under General de Montauban. This time, too, everyone had learned lessons from the Crimea and medical and supply arrangements were excellent. Wounded soldiers were tended on board the ships and ample food supplies were available for purchase from the rich farmlands and villages along the Bei He. The force even had some Chinese support, in the shape of the Canton Coolie Corps which carried supplies and served faithfully and bravely, even in battle. The French even calculated that they and the British, between them, had some 5000 servants and coolies – almost as many as the entire French contingent.[48] It was said that these southern Chinese were quite happy to see their northern cousins defeated.

On his appointment, Elgin sent an ultimatum to Beijing, demanding the admission of a British envoy. It was rejected. In another of the confusions and paradoxes of Chinese affairs, in the meantime Beijing's fight against the Taipings in central China relied on foreign help. The allies landed, without resistance, and at the end of August, Anglo-French forces entered Tianjin. Beyond the city, on the approaches to Beijing itself, they found an army waiting for them, paused, and sought to negotiate. But the Chinese seized a party of British and French officials and soldiers operating under a flag of truce. Some were beheaded. Others died agonizingly in prison: their hands were so tightly bound that circulation was cut off, the hands and wrists rotted, and infection and maggots spread to their arms and bodies. When Elgin heard the news, he was deeply shocked and fiercely determined to exact revenge.

In the meantime the French and British, marching separately, agreed to meet at the Imperial Summer Palace outside Beijing (the Yuan Ming Yuan). The French got there first, on 6 October, to stare in wonder at the 80 square miles of park into which generations of Chinese emperors had poured love, artistry, wealth and imagination. Here were ingenious pavilions, 200 main buildings, lakes, chambers filled with silks, gold jewellery and ornaments of marvellous, delicate and often subtle beauty. There followed one of the century's most startling pieces of vandalism. First, the French went a little mad. One young officer wrote home that there were such treasures that nothing like it had been seen since the sack of Rome by the barbarians.[49] One of Britain's rising military stars was amazed. Lieutenant Colonel Garnet Wolseley was another of those fervent Anglo-Irish Protestants, pious, socially ambitious and – a rarity in the mid-nineteenth-century British officer corps – an intellectual. He campaigned with the Bible, the Book of Common Prayer and the *Meditations of Marcus Aurelius* in his knapsack. He remembered later that French 'officers and men seemed to have been seized with a temporary insanity; in body and soul they were absorbed in one pursuit, which was plunder, plunder.'[50] The French had arrived virtually without transport; when they left they moved with 300 heaped wagons. Once the British arrived on the scene, they were only slightly more organized and some troops also went out of control. But order was restored and the three British commanders renounced plunder and loot for themselves.

The rest of the bullion and the objects were auctioned within the British force, with one-third of the proceeds going to the officers and two thirds to the other ranks.

That was not the end. Elgin still had to exact revenge for the killings of the British and French prisoners, and wanted to do it by finding a way to strike at the prestige of the Emperor himself, not at the Chinese populace. As he explained 'It was necessary ... to discover some act of retribution and punishment, without attacking Peking ... to make the blow fall on the Emperor, who was clearly responsible for the crime committed ...'. The French wanted to burn down the imperial palace, but Elgin thought that might just drive the Chinese from Beijing altogether, and away from negotiations. Instead, on 18 and 19 October, he had British troops set fire to the already plundered and badly damaged Summer Palace buildings. Mostly made of wood, they went up at once, leaving a desolation. (For some years Chinese and a few Europeans went on pillaging the remnants.) In London, almost everyone approved. Sidney Herbert wrote to Hope Grant 'The public here are ... very pleased with the way everything has been done in China – firmness, temper, skill, success ... .' But in Paris, Victor Hugo wrote 'We Europeans are civilized, and to us the Chinese are barbarians. Here is what civilization has done to barbarism! History shall call one of these bandits France, the other England ...'.[51]

It was, at any rate, the end of the war. On 24 October Elgin was carried ceremoniously in a red sedan chair through Beijing's central artery, carefully preserved from the time when Kublai Khan had founded the city almost exactly 600 years earlier, to be received by the Emperor's brother, Prince Gong, in the Hall of Audience. A new Convention of Beijing was signed – providing for payments of eight million *taels* of silver each to the British and French – the Sino-British Treaty of Tientsin (Tianjin) was finally ratified and the next day Baron Gros had the same ceremony for the French. Elgin left Beijing on 10 November, and on 21 January, two days after formally annexing the Kowloon peninsula to Hong Kong, finally left China. In London, he was received in triumph and quickly sent on to serve as Viceroy of India.

There is not the slightest doubt that Elgin saw himself, throughout, as an honourable man, seaching for justice in Sino-British dealings and determined to limit the sufferings of the Chinese people. All his life he believed that he had acted 'as China's friend in all this.' At the same time he continued, privately, to condemn both sides in the war. The Chinese, he wrote, were fools to bring such calamities on themselves by their pride and treachery, while British policy consisted merely of 'resorting

to the most violent measures of coercion and repression on the slender-
est provocation.'[52]

Others, too, recorded their respect and even sometimes affection for
China and its people. Garnet Wolseley for one. He spent some 45 years
fighting in one or another of Britain's small wars. He served in the Burma
War of 1852, in the Crimea, in the Indian Mutiny, in Elgin's march to
Beijing, in the American Civil War, the Canadian Rebellion of 1869, the
Ashanti war in Africa in 1873, in the Zulu War of 1879, and achieved
fame in 1882 when he defeated the Arabi Pasha rebellion against the government of Egypt and established the British presence there. At the start
of the twentieth century, in the heyday of Britain's imperial glory, he was
a Field Marshal, a Viscount, and Commander-in-Chief of the British
army. But he looked back with admiration at the China where he had
served forty years earlier. The Chinese, he wrote in 1903,

> are the most remarkable race on earth, and I have always thought and
> still believe them to be the great coming rulers of the world. They
> only want a Chinese Peter the Great or Napoleon to make them so.
> They have every quality required for the good soldier and the good
> sailor, and ... I have long selected them as the combatants on one side
> of the great battle of Armageddon, the people of the United States of
> America being their opponents.[53]

Such men were not alone in their respect or good will for the Chinese.
In 1857 and again in 1860, Queen Victoria herself sent handwritten letters of friendship to the Chinese emperor. Neither could be delivered
and a century later, in the 1960s, a young man destined to become
another British Foreign Secretary, Douglas Hurd, found them again. He
was writing about the 'Arrow War' and discovered the letters, still stored
in Elgin's old home, still unopened.[54]

10
China: Resentment Congeals into Nationalism

As late as 1860, therefore, the notion of British wickedness in China and, more particularly, of guilt for an 'Opium War', was very much a fringe opinion, certainly in England. To understand the later and retrospective condemnation, we must look at the growth of a resentful anti-foreign nationalism in China and the transformation of some influential British views of empire.

The Chinese empire had been gravely weakened, by 1860, through twenty years of wars and rebellions. The population was declining from – estimates vary – some 410 million in 1850 to perhaps 350 million a quarter of a century later. And in 1861 the Xianfeng emperor died. His successor being a five-year old child, who became the Emperor Tongzhi, there was a power struggle in which three princes were killed or forced to commit suicide. The key ruler became the infant emperor's mother, the Dowager Empress Cixi, once his father's concubine. After she bore her son in 1856 the Emperor allowed her to read state papers and discuss policy with him. Cixi was a tiny woman, tough, highly intelligent, ruthless and almost certainly murderous, albeit charming when she wanted to be. Corrupt and absurdly extravagant, in so far as she had a policy it was to restore and maintain the power and standing of the Manchu dynasty and to maintain Confucian verities. Although she was deeply ignorant of the world beyond court politics and intrigue, she came to wield all the executive, legislative and judicial powers of the Chinese state and therefore to be the indispensable arbiter among others' views and policies. When Tongzhi died in 1875 she chose her four-year-old nephew Guangxu to succeed him, effectively confirming her own power.

Her drive to shore up and maintain familiar structures and habits was in constant conflict with the evident need for modernization and reform.[1] Repeated defeats at the hands of the West had eroded Manchu prestige and the Manchu grip on the empire. That meant a shift of power to the provinces, the local gentry and from the Manchus to the properly Chinese Han. Weakness was accentuated by many factors, including the limitations of the central civil service. As late as 1900 there were only 40,000 of them for the entire empire, each one responsible for financial, public and legal affairs in his region. That alone meant mandarin reliance on the local gentry. The system of mandarin rotation made things worse by giving a good deal of effective power to the permanent clerks, familiar with the details of local affairs, who outnumbered the mandarins by almost 20:1 – and diverted much revenue into their own pockets.

There was also the deadly threat of the Taiping rebellion. Here were much the most important of the empire's foes. Some time before, the 28-year-old Prince Gong – the very man who had signed the Beijing Convention with Elgin and who now became Cixi's chief minister, or Royal Councillor – had written to his elder brother, the Xianfeng emperor, that 'The British are merely a threat to our limbs. First of all we must extirpate the rebels.' Indeed, in a series of victorious campaigns in the 1850s the Taipings achieved command of much of central China, even though the empire kept a network of local magistrates, who sometimes even collected taxes. Nevertheless, there were moments when the imperial government seemed reduced to some local regimes holding scattered bits of territory against the rebels. By 1860 the Taipings had spent seven years dominating and ravaging the countryside on both sides of the Yangzi down as far as Chinjiang.

However, their northern campaign was destroyed, its leaders being given the death of a thousand cuts. The main force then broke out from their capital, Nanjing, and advanced towards Shanghai. By August 1860 the Chinese authorities asked the British and French to protect the city. Once again, irony coloured Sino-Western relations: while imperial forces were trying to deal with Elgin's troops outside Beijing, other Anglo-French forces – mainly Madras and Sikh soldiers and British marines – were fighting off determined Taiping attacks at Shanghai and defending the Yangzi delta. Even as the rebels withdrew, they left Hangzhou after holding it for six days, with 70,000 corpses of Manchu troops and civilians.

But in time, Taiping strategies led nowhere, their collective leadership fell murderously apart, and their region of control narrowed as it was besieged by imperial forces. The empire had started to fight them with – frequently ineffective – local forces. But after 1860 Beijing started to put in new commanders and the imperial troops, newly reorganized on

Confucian disciplines, started to win. Some years later, yet more Western help played an important part in finally crushing the Taiping rebellion. It came most effectively with foreign merchants selling howitzers and Remington rifles to the imperial armies, and most colourfully in the person of a British artillery officer, Charles Gordon. Another passionate Christian fundamentalist, he had piercing blue eyes, total self-reliance and became, to many, a legend of perfection. He now took command of a mercenary army fighting alongside the Qing, acquired the nickname of 'Chinese' Gordon and, years later, went on to suffer a legendary martyr's death at Khartoum in the Sudan. In 1864 Nanjing finally fell to imperial forces. No quarter was asked or given, and 100,000 Taipings chose death rather than surrender. But if the Taipings disappeared, they left behind heroic legends about a movement inspired by egalitarian dreams, legends that had an important influence on China's twentieth-century socialists.

War, revolution and the self-evident weaknesses of the empire brought several kinds of dilemma. Weakness produced a popular hunger for strong leadership and a stronger China. Not that temporary weakness could mean changes in governing principles and policies. In 1861 the throne was once again urged to 'resort to peace and friendship when temporarily obliged to do so; use war and defence as your actual policy.'[2] But there were difficulties. A powerful 'self-strengthening' could not be satisfied merely by political theatre. Yet in so far as self-strengthening meant administrative and educational reforms, industrialism and modern weapons, its principles and impulses were often diametrically opposed to Confucian principles and values. Moreover, since weakness at Beijing produced several centres, each with at best regional authority, efforts at domestic reform were also in constant conflict not only with efforts to shore up and maintain familiar Manchu structures and habits, but also with local assertiveness. Reform also depended, at least temporarily, on foreign technologies, industry, trade and people, but that was bound to be unpopular at home. Cixi herself, like so many others before and since, detested 'truckling to foreigners'. Moreover, the government, being weak at home, and with unrest simmering around the empire, had to cater to the patriotic feelings, not only of the general populace but of the gentry who were the key to local order. So, while weakness compelled a catering to foreign demands, popular support at home depended on a defiance of foreigners and their treaties. These two pressures were irreconcilable. Amid such tensions a reformist like Prince Gong stood little chance.

Disruption extended from politics and administration into every sector of the economy. The sectors that relied on commerce were especially affected. Demand for imported manufactures fell, opium imports grew and exports of both tea and silks soared. Since exports now far exceeded imports, foreign payments to China had once more to be made largely in silver. And since there was only one kind of coin the Chinese still had confidence in, the Spanish dollar, outside sources of it soon dried up. Worse still, the Chinese hoarded their silver, as people usually hoard precious metals in times of trouble. The result was an acute shortage of money and the growth of barter trade. Furthermore, the value of money became quite erratic, and few things cause greater social unrest than unreliable money.

Yet a number of brilliant and loyal officials in the provinces did manage to promote reform and industry. And Chinese development and modernization did rely on foreign help. Possibly the most useful foreign contribution came in the field of ideas. From the 1860s onwards came translations of Western works on history, science and law, so that by the 1890s most major Western ideas were known in China, even discussed in newspapers. The Imperial Customs Service, under the sensitive and cultured Irishman Robert Hart, began to provide a large and steady government revenue, its foreign supervisors faithful to their Chinese masters.[3] Other British, American and other foreign advisers helped with administration, or took a hand in running newspapers, building ships, arsenals, modern medical services, and, of course, building railways soon after the great railway booms in England in the 1840s and America around the time of the Civil War. China's obvious need for modern weapons helped to promote modern industry. So did the example of the 1868 Meiji Restoration across the water in Japan. Not that foreign comment or advice was always helpful. At the end of the 1870s, with Russian pressures on northern and western China, Hart invited Charles Gordon to advise on China's defence. Gordon, who was by now in India, came, saw and was appalled. 'If you will make war,' he said, 'burn the suburbs of Peking, remove the archives and the emperor from Peking, put them in the centre of the country and fight (a guerrilla war) for five years; Russia will not be able to hurt you.'[4]

But in general the Western powers, for all their faith in freer trade, derived little benefit. There were tight Chinese rules on foreign activities. Foreign investment was rejected, labour saving resisted, students were only reluctantly sent abroad and, when they returned, apt to be treated with disdain. There was no general industrial development, no export effort, no encouragement to private enterprise. Just as Mitchell had foretold years earlier, there was much Chinese market resistance to Western goods and much 'buy Chinese' sentiment. Anyway, locals were apt to know more about local conditions and tastes and to be better at labour relations. And beyond the treaty ports the population, which had little 'disposable income' anyway, relied mainly on local handicrafts, as it always had, rather than on foreign goods. Even the expansion of treaty port trade towards the end of the century turned out to be quite largely a revival of pre-rebellion Chinese domestic commerce.

Still, once the foreigners were established in the treaty ports, and their settlements allowed special extra-territorial status, they expanded, economically and territorially. The foreigners wanted, whether for reasons of comfort, or hygiene, or simple peace and quiet, to have special resident areas in the suburbs of these cities. Such 'concessions' were leased from the Chinese government by the foreign power concerned, which then sublet plots to its own citizens, with the Chinese accepting foreign self-determination on things like rates, roads and property leases.[5] The local consul was at first the highest judicial and executive authority, though the treaty ports gradually established their own municipal councils. Some people also came to own land privately, outside the concessions.

The concessions expanded in both number and significance. By 1878 Britain had six of them, the smallest of some 25 acres at Kiukiang on the Yangzi.[6] But the largest, and much the most important of the international settlements, was at Shanghai. Not that life in them was always blissful. The consuls kept running into difficulties. As stout Christians they had to try, though without much success, to condemn the brokers who procured indentured Chinese labourers for Cuba, Chile, Australia, California or Peru. They also had to cope with missionaries and others making unauthorized forays into the Chinese interior; or with customs issues; or with quarrels between Protestants and Catholics. Or there could be quite serious health and sanitation problems. For instance, residents had to rely on local facilities and local water. But at Shanghai the river water was so filthy that before 1880 it became very difficult to keep persons or clothes clean. Only in that year did Shanghai start to get proper mains and water pipes. Before that, many Westerners preferred to get their clothes laundered in a two-week round trip to Japan.

But from the start there was no doubting that the new treaty ports played a vital role. Their mere presence gave China access to modern ships, the telegraph, technology and to foreign customs. Even in the midst of financial confusion, modern Western banking houses began to appear in Shanghai as early as the mid-1850s. Western merchants could issue payment orders, known as 'chits', to *compradors*. These chits, in effect cheques, became widely accepted by the locals, even the peasants. Indeed, Shanghai quickly became the great Far Eastern metropolis and a major centre not just for trade but, later, investment for the entire Yangzi region and beyond. Once the 1895 Sino-Japanese Treaty of Shimonoseki opened the gates of the treaty ports to manufacturing, Shanghai's industrialization took off as well.

Given all this, the increasing number of foreigners and the way in which Chinese tried to live or work in these international settlements, it is not surprising that by 1899 the settlement at Shanghai covered over 8½ square miles or that by the end of the 1920s something like four-fifths of Britain's direct foreign investment in China was directed there. None of this was covered by formal treaties and China's sovereign rights remained, formally, fully in place.

It even took a long time for the Chinese government to make a coherent effort to manage formal foreign relations. At first, Prince Gong, who understood China's weakness, and learned to trust the British and French, established the Zongli Yamen in 1861. It was a kind of Foreign Office, able finally to start dealing with other countries as equal sovereign states. Yet the greater his success in creating amiable relations with foreigners, the more his power eroded within a Beijing system whose *literati* and officials steadily refused to conceive of such things as equality of states, or any other derogation from the unique status of the Chinese empire. So the Zongli Yamen remained marginal to Beijing's centres of real power. The result was, that as late as the 1870s, foreign affairs were still treated as frontier politics, not as a serious preoccupation of the central government. Chinese envoys might be received with helpful courtesy in London and Washington, but there was no serious follow-up on the Chinese side and no machinery to develop one. Even at the end of the century foreigners were largely seen as exotic and dangerous, and Chinese diplomats who returned from overseas postings were often forced into early retirement. Even China's first major modern war, in 1894/95 against the newly modernized Japan, was largely conducted by provincial governors as if it were a matter of frontier defence. Only after China had been routed – and by a small and often despised fellow-Asian country at that[7] – did the dam against Western ideas and standards of international relations begin seriously to break.

And yet, for all its weaknesses, China possessed some priceless assets. One was that the empire was simply too big and populous for any other country to try to govern it. Realistically, therefore, outside powers had no alternative to supporting imperial governance unless they were prepared to court the huge risks of trying to partition the empire. Another was the mutual jealousy of these powers: none would allow another to acquire special advantages. Finally, China's problems could not be seen in isolation. They had large implications for the entire Asian, Pacific and therefore also the European balance of power.

As far as the British were concerned, from 1860 onwards and with the establishment of a regular mission at Beijing, they found themselves, for the next three or four decades, the most important foreign influence in China. And for all its primary focus on British self-interest, the interpretation of that influence was often enlightened, even with an occasional dash of benevolence. It included hopes for domestic reform and modernization in the empire; consolidation of the regime against domestic rebellion; greatly expanded trade and investment; and Chinese recognition of Britain as the empire's best foreign friend. It remained determined to avoid responsibilities smacking of governance. Nevertheless, British gunboats, keeping order on the southern coasts in the interests of trade, made Britain something like an active prop of the imperial order in that whole region. British governments tried to promote their interests with some care for imperial cohesion and therefore keeping any pressures on China well short of demands that might destabilize the government. So when, in the late 1860s, they sought a revision of the Tianjin treaty, the British Ambassador, Sir Rutherford Alcock, was told to accept any arrangement that would satisfy the Chinese, even though British mercantile resistance ultimately prevented any agreement being finalized. Yet by 1914 the British empire remained China's principal trading partner and most important foreign investor. Only at the very end of the nineteenth century did the British, too, take part in the scramble for concessions and spheres of influence by various foreign powers.

Moreover, such British strategies meant favouring multilateral approaches and co-operation, especially, with the French and Americans. Not that foreign nibbling at China could be stopped – especially after the explosive modernization programme of Japan that began with the 'Meiji Restoration' of 1868. In the mid-1870s, under British pressure, China opened more ports to trade. In 1878 China had to surrender the Ryukyu islands to Japanese power. Although Russia kept pressing on China's west and north – no wonder Hart wanted Charles Gordon to help in China's defence planning – in 1881 the empire paid an indemnity to Russia for the recovery of some bits of Inner Asia. In 1884 Sino-French discussions over Vietnam and the French occupation of Hanoi and its harbour, Haiphong, broke down. The French confirmed their control of China's tributary Vietnam, which they had gradually strengthened since 1870, by defeating the Chinese, in the process taking just one hour to sink the 11 ships of the new Chinese 'self-strengthened' southern fleet.

Prince Gong was finally dismissed. And in 1894–95 came the disastrous war with Japan that cost China an indemnity of 200 million silver *taels*, the cession of Formosa to Japan and Korean independence, and deep hurt to China's national pride.

After that the pace of change quickened. Most of the encroachments on the empire, especially those in the south and the west, had not touched China proper, merely periphery and borderlands that were anyway not strongly under Beijing's control. And the powers had tacitly agreed to preserve the unity and integrity of that core China, since it could not be allowed to become the satellite of any one of them and was too large and important to be partitioned. But defeat by Japan made it even more painfully clear that the modalities of the Far Eastern and Pacific balance had changed. As industries, technologies and communications developed, especially in Japan, Russia and America, they brought with them much greater power, including more advanced naval and military capabilities. As the balance altered, so did the competition for commercial and strategic access to China. That produced, in the later 1890s, a competition for special 'spheres of influence' and, after 1898, substantial 'concessions'. The most important of these became the dominant Russian position in Manchuria. Foreigners also financed, and often controlled, many of the new strategic railways.

Still, British interests remained centred on international equilibrium on the one hand and British prestige, the security of British subjects, and commerce on the other, not on territory or governance. In the words of London's 1858 instructions to Lord Elgin, the British 'have no desire to obtain any exclusive advantages for British trade in China but are only desirous to share with all other nations any benefits which they acquire in the first instance, specifically for British commerce.' In 1911 the Foreign Secretary, Sir Edward Grey, said much the same. China should suppress rebellion and resist demands from other powers. What Britain wanted was 'a strong and stable government which would ensure conditions favourable to trade.'[8] Even the 'Open Door' idea, that China's territorial and political integrity should be respected, while everyone was allowed to trade there, began life as an idea around London. It was a British customs official, a Mr Hippisley, who happened to pass through Baltimore in 1899, called on his friend, Assistant Secretary of State William Rockhill, and mentioned the idea. Why should not the United States circulate an 'Open Door' appeal to the powers? The new Secretary of State, John Hay, turned out to love the notion and his first Open Door note was cabled to all the great powers on 6 September that year.

In the meantime, for China the defeat by Japan had changed every-thing. Although Russia, France and Germany had intervened to limit Japanese gains, now, finally, imperial officials reacted with brutal politi-cal realism. It had, of course, long been clear that the central political problems stemmed from the structures and habits of the highest levels of government and had much less to do with any civil service, or man-darin, incompetence. The administrative classes, while not free from corruption, remained a remarkably tough, intelligent, and wholly unsentimental bunch of men. Western eighteenth-century negotiators had sensed as much. In 1860 Garnet Wolseley made the same discovery. He and his colleagues examined captured Chinese documents. 'Some of [these] papers were very clever,' he recalled

> and showed an extraordinary amount of diplomatic ability. Having no regard whatever for truth, bound by no fine feelings of humanity, but ready at any moment to sacrifice their innocent agents to the expediency of the moment, their political system is eminently calcu-lated for all the complex situations of diplomacy. The cold-blooded rules for government enunciated in 'The Prince'[9] appear to be well understood in China.[10]

So now, facing serious threats from both Japan and an expansionist Russia, the Chinese tried to get Western help and American mediation on the peace terms Japan wanted to impose. They even cold-bloodedly made a pact with their most dangerous enemy and neighbour, Russia, while continuing a long-term process to fend off Russian power by Han migration into the borderlands, especially Mongolia. Not long after the Sino-Japanese war, Britain formed an alliance with Japan to look after Pacific security and contain Russian power but also maintain the Chinese empire. It was patterns like these which dominated the 1898 for-eign scramble for Chinese concessions or even the politics of the eight-nation occupation of Beijing as part of the anti-Boxer campaign of 1900.

But the most important changes were domestic, and grew partly from self-examination and attempts to discover what had gone wrong. From that sprang the rehabilitation programme of 1861.[11] By 1890, and even more decisively after the 1895 defeat by Japan, out of that grew the pri-mary and overriding aim of politically conscious Chinese to create new state institutions and political forms, a strong state and a strong central government to safeguard China's sovereignty. On 30 June 1895 Kang Youwei, a leading Confucian reformer, who believed that political and economic modernization were feasible within a Confucian framework, wrote to the emperor.

> The pressure upon us from the nations of the Great West represents a changed situation that China has not known in thousands of years. Previously, barbarian invasions from all directions meant no more than the menace of a strongly armed force; state craft and literature did not come into play. Now the nations of the Great West vie with us in the art of government and surpass us in knowledge.

At the same time, the group of senior examination candidates assembled in Beijing submitted a reform memorial stressing China's need for a modern army, the development of an industrial base, increased taxation, the development of a state banking system and the need to bring China's railways into state ownership.

Even allowing for the traumas of war and defeat, no such nationalist drive could have come out of the blue. And in fact, assertiveness, and resentment of foreigners and foreign ways, had built up for many years, not just in line with foreign encroachments but in tandem with China's need for foreign ideas, technologies and people. Even deeper roots in issues of ethnicity, culture and values fed into the dark and sullen resentments of the Chinese. Within the imperial context, the Chinese were already resentful of the Manchus, and anti-foreigner resentments contributed strongly to the mix that congealed into a generalized and eventually coherent nationalism. In any case, the more China was dragged into the modern international and inter-state world, the more would her governing classes be compelled to adopt modern nation-state principles and a modern nation-state outlook. A concept of nationhood had to be forged, a concept of citizenship and of national unity, with all its possibilities for national and citizen mobilization. It would all be a world away from the 1860 experience of having Canton coolies supporting foreigners fighting against the government and northern Chinese troops.

National and nationalist principles are usually defined, and always strengthened, by what the nation is not, quite as much as by what it is; and in defining them a great energizing principle is often a sense of injury. So it was in the case of China which, for over a century after 1850, cultivated a sense that China and Chinese culture had been unfairly and unjustly deprived of their proper pride of place among men. Over time, the portmanteau of resentments began to bulge. The 'unequal treaties' had been resented and rejected from the beginning.

But in time the Chinese began to list even private agreements by foreign companies as 'unequal treaties'. The foreign concessions, and unofficial local agreements on their regulation, aroused special anger as a derogation from Chinese sovereign rights. The foreigners' extra-territorial arrangements, once simply practical agreements to cater for foreign trade or residence and an administrative convenience for all concerned, came to look, through the new nationalist spectacles, deeply offensive. It might once have been a Chinese custom to allow foreigners to control foreigners, but these treaties and concession arrangements gave foreigners privileges over locals and protection against the legitimate authority of the Chinese state and its officials. So the treaties became a convenient focus for a whole range of anti-imperialist criticisms. The cause of treaty revision or abolition came, in time, to unite what were otherwise widely divergent schools of Chinese political opinion. It also resonated strongly with Western liberals and anti-imperialists.

Other old arrangements were also now reinterpreted as deliberately and inherently malign. The British might try to say that Hong Kong had only been acquired as a tiny, secure base for ships and merchants, but that was a lie. The spheres of influence and concession arrangements of the 1890s demonstrated that Hong Kong had always been intended as only first of a series of territorial claims. The Imperial Maritime Customs Service, controlled by foreigners, was just another example of Western imperialism using China for its own ends. Then there was the presence of Western gunboats in China's waters and rivers. That might originally have been merely to protect foreign residents amid Chinese turbulence, or – often at the request of Chinese officials themselves – to help suppress piracy. In reality, it was only another example of imperialist arrogance and aggression. Treaty tariffs, invented merely to regularize erratic, ad hoc and corrupt local exactions, were now seen as hurdles, deliberately erected to prevent protection of China's infant industries. Even clearer demonstrations of Western greed and ruthlessness had come in the foreign ownership and control of stategic railways or the simply outrageous occupation of Beijing in 1900, by troops of eight nations marching against the Boxers.

Perhaps the deepest offence was caused, not by Western political or economic power, which might pragmatically have been put up with, but by the intrusion of foreign values and cultures. Modernization, industry, technology – all the things that China needed to reassert her place among the nations – meant deep changes in social habits, philosophies and values. That made the foreign pressure for modernization, deliberate or otherwise, doubly offensive. Western economic and industrial ethics of individualism and competition simply contradicted the Confucian principles of hierarchy and ordered rule, which continued to be a badge of identity of a proper Han. They were part of nothing less than an attack on the Confucian state. It was a matter of deep shame that, given the inherent superiority of Chinese culture and society, of her place at the core of civilization, China should be suffering such a drastic fall from grace. Foreigners, who should be approaching China with reverence, acknowledging her cultural superiority, had humiliated and victimized the Celestial Empire. China was still the 'Middle Kingdom'. That had once meant she was the centre of human civiliza- tion, but now it meant an ancient, civilized but weak China, surrounded on almost all sides by actual or potential enemies like a pack of hungry dogs. So that the greater the foreign impact became, the more it created resentment, except perhaps among some small, urbanized, educated elites, administrators and intellectuals. In any case, and too often, Western people behaved in arrogantly superior fashion and even seemed contemptuous of Chinese ways. For instance, the free-and-easy manners of Western women remained offensive to Chinese notions of decorum.

In some ways the deepest offence of all came from Christianity with its socially disturbing heterodoxies and seditious teachings. The Christian missionaries were particularly to blame. Their enthusiasm stemmed quite largely from Wilberforce's old insistence that the intro- duction of England's religion, and therefore of English morals, was the only source of all other social and political improvement. The results were sadly ironic. Young men and women, mostly British and American, went to China full of idealism, with a passion to uplift the poor and ignorant, to demonstrate in word and deed the superior qualities of Christianity, to improve education and health. Their num- bers rose fairly rapidly after 1860, from – the numbers are uncertain – around 400 to possibly some 4000 around 1900–5. And, to be sure, the clinics and schools were often welcome. Yet for the most part, these well-meant efforts ran into a brick wall of non-acceptance. There were few converts. As late as 1949, before the communist revolution, out of 450–500 million Chinese there may have been at most 800,000 Christians.[12]

In many cases the very vocabulary the missionaries used carried estab- lished Buddhist connotations, producing misunderstandings of just what the Christians were trying to say. Concepts like 'redemption' were incomprehensible. Calling people 'sheep' was insulting, and shepherds were at the very bottom of the Chinese social ladder. Missionary attacks on established ancestor worship and idolatries were deeply offensive and the condemnation of concubinage – and therefore the bearing of more sons – worse still. In any case, the Taiping version of Christianity had destroyed the image of Christianity proper, for all the missionaries' rejection of Hong's teachings. So the local Confucian gentry were the missionaries' natural enemies. Both were privileged groups. Each taught competing and, in principle, universalist ideologies. But the missionaries were agents of foreign powers, protected by foreign gunboats, directly threatening the Chinese ruling class. Christianity was clearly just part and parcel of Western imperialist industrial and military power – a link made clear every time there were foreign demands for indemnities following anti-Christian riots.

Resentment spread more widely after missionaries were admitted into China's interior. It is true that the often irritating self-righteousness of humanitarian and missionary evangelism had very little influence on tough imperial administrators who thought the Western social sentimentalities merely odd. But vicious and often obscene anti-missionary tracts started to circulate at popular levels, accusing them of everything from perverted sex to causing poverty. There were hundreds of incidents, with missionaries sometimes attacked, occasionally killed. The final anti-Christian paroxysm came in the Boxer rising of 1899–1900, that fearsome yet essentially pathetic movement which practised old-fashioned magic arts and preferred lances and swords to guns but, in addition, was anti-foreign and pro-dynastic and had the patronage of the old empress Cixi herself. Yet the more the Boxers became anti-foreign, the more the anti-foreign local gentry tolerated them.

The failure of the Boxer rebellion – which coincided with the first discussion of Karl Marx in Chinese publications – helped to compel the monarchy finally to yield ground to the reformers. There was talk of a constitutional monarchy and sweeping reforms of education and the civil service as the high road to strengthening 'the wealth and power of the nation.' Social Darwinism – the notion that 'survival of the fittest' applied to social and state affairs – gained ground. In fact, state reform became inevitable as nationalism allied itself with political liberals, just as it had done in Europe.

The Manchus could not, in the end, avoid the pressures for popular and parliamentary institutions, for the Mandate of Heaven had come to an end. From 1904 the Russians and Japanese were fighting each other on Chinese soil, with Beijing impotent to interfere or prevent. It was the year of Cixi's 70th birthday, which had already been celebrated with feasting and theatrical performances. But in 1907 she suffered a slight stroke and by the following year she realized that the end was coming.

On 15 November 1908, having presided over China's decline for half a century, she died at the Hour of the Goat (1–3 p.m.). Her funeral costs are said to have been some 1½ million *taels* of silver. It was a bare three years before the end of the dynasty and the empire.

The empire may have been collapsing for some time, but nationalism was slow to develop a coherent doctrine or to form an organized mass movement. And that in spite of the many examples of nationalist formation, not only in Japan but from the American and French revolutions and, more recently, the unification of Italy and Germany in the 1860s and 1870s. Objections to foreign power and arrogance, even events like the 1905 anti-American boycott, were not enough. Only by 1910 or so did political nationalism become programmatic and acquire an explicitly anti-foreign colouring. That came in a revolutionary movement first created by overseas Chinese and led by Sun Yatsen. He spread it to the junior officers and non-commissioned officers of the army and helped to promote the revolution of 1911 and the creation of the Republic the following year. Once a more violent anti-foreignism emerged in the mid-1920s, there were loud demands for the immediate abolition of the 'unequal treaties' and immediate restitution of foreign concessions. By then Sun Yat-sen's successor, Chiang Kai-shek (Jian Jieshi) and his people regarded Britain as their worst imperialist enemy, though after 1928 Japan was even more feared. The fact that in 1920 the infant Soviet Union abruptly abandoned Russia's 'unequal treaties' certainly helped it to win a much larger political battle. By the later 1920s and 1930s it was the Soviets who were the guiding spirit behind the more radical elements of Chinese nationalism, helped rather than hindered by China's general domestic turmoil of the 1930s.

In all these discussions and programmes, the Chinese politics of resentment echoed strongly. If China had been, and still was, lamentably weak, where should blame lie? Where could relief be found? The most obvious, congenial and programmatic explanations were two. Each resonated with traditional Chinese attitudes and each blamed barbarian wickedness. Both agreed on the corruption and inefficiency of the old regime. But beyond that, one following Karl Marx and Lenin focused by 1919 on anti-imperialism, the other on the political and strategic greed of particular Western powers. After all, Marx had ascribed the rise of the Taipings to the British opium trade as well as to British guns, all of which had corrupted the mandarins and wrecked Manchu authority. Mao Zedong encapsulated these various inchoate notions about domestic corruption, combined with Western wickedness, in a brilliant and evocative phrase. The notion of China 'standing up', implied at one and the same time deep resentment of the country's previous condition and an expectation of revival once the unconquerable 'people' put out their united strength. Not that he ignored other lessons of Chinese history. On the contrary: the pattern of his last campaigns strongly echoed the patterns of the original Manchu conquest.

Where did opium, and Western opium trading, fit into all this politics and diplomacy of resentment? Given the scope and scale of the resentments of patriotic Chinese, opium *per se* remained a fairly minor item in the list of indictments. The reasons are not far to seek. China's political and moral position on opium, so forcibly asserted by Commissioner Lin in 1839, was fatally undermined by the 1842 offer to legalize it. And once legalization actually came, in 1857/58, not only was opium sold quite legally at treaty ports but China's own production grew by leaps and bounds, with considerable benefits to government coffers. There was even some pro-opium agitation. Attempts to stem foreign imports naturally encouraged domestic production.[13] By 1879, with import substitution, domestic production may have been over three times as much as opium imports,[14] and by 1900 eight times as much.[15]

Some change came. In November 1906 there was a decree to suppress the entire trade. Four years later, in 1910, the first meeting of China's brand-new National Assembly tried to reinforce the anti-opium laws. With Sun Yatsen's revolution a year later, anti-opium activity was made a patriotic crusade. Yet opium remained important to Chinese warlords in the period after 1912 and, later, to Chiang's Guomindang party. Bejing kept being fed entirely bogus reports from the regions. In 1912, for instance, shortly after the province of Szechuan reported complete eradication of the opium poppy, it harvested a bumper crop. As the *North China Daily News* mournfully commented, Beijing did not control the provinces any more than provincial governors controlled the farmers.[16] A decade or two later, production and use were still plentiful. There were open opium monopolies in places like Canton and Xiamen (Amoy), with public regulations and officers appointed to run them. Indeed, so far as opium suppression was concerned, the growers 'are no more affected by the mandates of the Central Government than are the tribes of Central Africa. They simply disregard Peking...'.[17] Hong Kong was awash with Chinese opium. By 1937 it was estimated that, in a population of about one million, 40,000 were opium smokers and 24,000 used heroin. Western observers were sadly agreed that the net result of the official anti-opium campaign had been to increase poppy growing, and particularly the use of heroin, cocaine and morphine.[18] In the 1930s matters became much worse with the deliberate promotion of drugs by the invading Japanese army.

In the middle 1930s, the communist forces led by Mao Zedong staged their legendary 'Long March' through the peripheries of China to the fastnesses of Yanan. The soldiers found themselves marching through whole provinces, for instance Guizhou, Hunan and parts of Yunnan, where opium was the only currency. The warlord troops of dirt-poor Guizhou were known as 'two-gun men': one rifle and one opium pipe. And though the Red Army tried not to recruit opium addicts, it also had to use opium as currency to buy supplies as it marched through fields of poppies, at times 'as far as the eye could see.'[19] Even after the march, at their retreat in Yanan, the communists may have grown and sold opium to the local population to make money,[20] though they tried to ban it once they were in power. And at the end of the twentieth century China together with India were reckoned to be the fastest-growing large markets in the world for the opium derivative, heroin. World production of farmed drugs was by then concentrated just beyond China's borders, with two-thirds of heroin coming from Afghanistan and one-third from Myanmar (Burma). Quantities reached China's interior, once again by way of smuggling.[21]

But if opium played only a minor part in the whole litany of complaints, real or imaginary, about Western imperialist wickedness, the British part in opium trading was not forgotten. In part, no doubt, the very prominence of Britain's role in China in the second half of the nineteenth century ensured that her real or imagined sins would be heavily underlined. Certainly the Chinese education system, at least until the end of the twentieth century, was careful to keep that grievance alive. And perhaps, also in part, given the role of drugs in Britain's and America's domestic affairs as the twentieth century wore on, harping on opium created, from China's point of view, politically helpful possibilities of moral pressure.

11
Britain: Evangelicals, Humanitarians and Guilt

The tides of opinion in Britain and the United States were very different from those in China. Naturally, opinions were not uniform. Strong commercial or strategic interests were often highly influential. Nevertheless, so far as China and opium were concerned, in both countries the critique of Britain grew. So did a mood of self-criticism, even of guilt.

To begin with, in Britain during the middle decades of the nineteenth century, organized religion became a central social and intellectual force. The Victorians became more ideological, more radical and more evangelical, while the middle classes, with growing political and social clout in an industrializing and urbanizing country, were becoming more toffee-nosed and intolerant of deviant behaviour. That produced a frequently prissy humanitarian interventionism, with humanitarianism becoming an essential component of British national and imperial identity. It helped to produce a code of fair play, a sense of British brotherhood, a determination to keep upper lips stiff and avoid complaints; and a somewhat neurotic determination to keep up appearances. But it also produced social relief efforts, ranging from poor relief or child labour laws to prison reform, the Factory Acts or the fervent anti-slavery campaign. By the end of the century, that developed into a general social service ethos. Together with that, also late in the century, came concerns about public health and a growing influence for the medical profession, with its *penchant* for general rules – and equally important, its ability, at a time of the Darwinian revolution, to clothe moral or even class concerns in the garments of disinterested science.

In imperial affairs these attitudes dovetailed without difficulty with the conviction that the British were a special people, destined to command, naturally selected by birth and breeding to change the surroundings and habits in which they found themselves. The spread of

British power was, naturally, good in itself for both rulers and ruled, and could only be undermined by displays of uncertainty or weakness. In that context the sense of religious and social obligation brought a growing emphasis on trusteeship, doing good and the welfare of native peoples. For the evangelicals, in particular, it was Christianity that could bring order to the savage places of the earth and opportunity to the oppressed. Did it not follow that it was the empire's noble task to awaken men everywhere to the ideals and principles of the West? Moreover, since religion was basic, and Hindus, Buddhists and others were merely superstitious, was it not clear that bringing Christianity to them was the condition of all progress? As early as the 1830s Parliament was being told that the British empire was a structure 'on whose extension and improvement, as far as human judgement can predict, depends the happiness of the world.' Queen Victoria's own definition of the imperial mission was 'to protect the poor natives and advance civilisation.' The House of Commons heard repeated motions calling on colonial officers to spread civilization and Christianity among natives everywhere, perhaps an early version of the Anglo-American 'human rights' imperialism a century and a half later. Under James Stephen, who headed the Colonial Office from 1837–46, it became a stronghold of such ideas. Many officers sent to serve overseas, military as well as civilian, were deeply religious people, who carried bibles and talked in biblical terms. So were many of their wives, who brought very similarly Christian moral and social attitudes to bear not just on their own families but on the societies around them.

Altogether, by mid-century, there arrived in various parts of the empire a whole new generation of English women, much less tolerant and worldly than their predecessors, much more censorious, earnest and devout, insistent on respectability and social niceties. Many of them were full of practical energy and hugely influential in changing habits, mores and relations with locals throughout the empire.

By the same token, critiques of empire ranged widely and were always a counterpoint to imperial enthusiasms. They could feed on a variety of Christian and humanitarian views, including anti-slavery passions. Quite early on the Edmund Burke wing of the Conservatives worried that British power abroad must not be abused for private advantage and that traditional societies under British control should not be exploited. Mid-Victorian radicals, like Cobden and Henry Richard, not only saw free trade as a moral crusade, but consistently criticized what they regarded as abuses of British power.[1] So did John Bright, never lacking in self-confidence and self-regard. When someone pointed out that he was a self-made man, Disraeli remarked 'yes, and he adores his maker.' In time, the humanitarians' critiques of the shortcomings of imperial governments even helped to create a new scepticism about colonial rule as such.[2] Before the end of the century, liberal imperialists worried that existing empire practices were inadequately generous and familial; and some grew alarmed by the force of Chinese resentments. Even once notions of empire as 'family' had faded, there remained a generalized liberal guilt.[3] That could rest on Christian notions of the 'Brotherhood of Man', or the idea that one race has no business ruling over another. Others continued to urge powerfully that empire was quite simply a waste of time and money.

Altogether more powerful and influential was socialist anti-capitalism, ranging from milder social reformers to the principles of the 1848 'Communist Manifesto' and, later, to its altogether more vicious Leninist extensions. It was certainly Marxist thought which was to affect Western ideas most profoundly for the next century or more, even among schools of thought far from socialism proper. It spawned a number of immensely powerful political ideas, including the proposition that economic structures determine all social change and economics is not just a factor in, but the ruthless driving force behind, all government and business activity. Colonies, in this view, were simply mechanisms of piratical exploitation; and Christianity was merely one facet of imperialism. For such groups the most obvious and damning explanation for the British activities in India and China was, quite simply, the capitalist desire to make money irrespective of the cost in human suffering. Indeed, had not Marx himself directly ascribed the rise of the Taipings to the British opium trade and British armed power, both of which had ended China's isolation, corrupted the mandarinate and undermined Manchu authority?[4] Hobson, too, condemned: '... adventurous groups of profit-seekers ... driving their Government along the slippery path of commercial treaties, leases, railway and mining concessions, which must entail a growing process of political interference.'[5] And he noted, regretfully, that the Chinese suffered from the fact that the spirit of their nation was 'opposed to militant patriotism.'

Socialism had much less appeal in America, but religious and humanitarian ideas could often point in similar directions. Furthermore, in the 1840s and 1850s Americans had strong memories of their wars against the British, not just in 1776 but in 1812, and the burning of the White House and, indeed, all other public buildings in Washington, in 1814. It was on 24 August that year that Rear-Admiral Sir George Cockburn sat down in the White House, from which President and Mrs Madison had fled, ate their dinner, drank to the health of 'Jemmy' (the President), and burned the place down.[6] Suspicion of the British remained a major strand in American opinion for the entire nineteenth century and anti-imperialism an element in US policy until well after the Second World War.

In the middle decades of the century, so far as England's imperial mission was concerned, opium was simply not a major issue. It was a very minor element in an imperial task that had to do with strategic need, saving souls, spreading modernity and welfare, as well as with trade and commercial gain. True, opium was important for India's finances but neither the East India Company nor the Indian or British governments were engaged in anything remotely illegal or even, in the majority view, improper. For Britain itself, in the middle decades of the century, opium was simply not a major issue and almost everyone was relaxed about it. In fact, almost until 1900, in both Britain and America, most of the drugs that the late twentieth century declared illegal continued to be merely patent medicines. They remained on the free market, quite uncontrolled. In the industrializing world of nineteenth-century Britain, there might be some worries about working-class use of opium. But legislation on over-the-counter medicines only came when prescription-only methods were first introduced in the 1860s after general public-health worries produced an alliance between parts of the administration and reformist medical men. At the end of that decade Charles Dickens and some American friends still met an elderly pusher known as Opium Sal while touring the London underworld with a police escort, and visiting a Shadwell opium den.[7] The police even took the Prince of Wales round to have a look, and Scotland Yard escorted the French Prince Imperial and his tutor on a quite similar tour in the early 1870s.[8]

Opium was of course also used in Europe, as well as widely in the empire itself. The toughest Indian troops in British service regularly drank opium – widely thought equivalent to alcohol – without loss of efficiency. On the continent, too, the German Chancellor, Otto von Bismarck, and many others were open and regular morphine users. In Britain itself, in the last two or three decades before 1900 opium use soared because doctors used it in prescriptions.[9] It is true that by the late nineteenth century the Chinese in East London were thought by many to be a special and mysterious threat, and opium dangers featured in the pages of Conan Doyle and Oscar Wilde and, later, in Fu Manchu films. But before 1914, drugs were only vaguely regulated under the Pharmacy Acts. Heroin itself was widely regarded as 'a medicine without peer'. During the First World War department stores catalogues listed heroin and morphine pastilles and Harrods store offered morphine and cocaine gift baskets. As late as the 1950s people could buy, over the counter, cough medicines containing some opiate.

In America, as well, the use of opium as a painkiller became widespread after consumption soared during the Civil War. The first federal laws against opium smoking came only in 1887, but even then there were no proper drug laws in North America until the 1908 Opium Narcotic Act in Canada. In the United States, narcotics over-the-counter sales only ended with the 1906 Pure Food and Drugs Act. The effect of the 1909 Opium Exclusion Act seems to have been to switch users from the relatively harmless smoking of opium to using its derivative, heroin. The drug firm Bayer had introduced it in 1898, marketed as a cough-suppressant with the 'ability of morphine to relieve pain, yet is safer.'[10] Then, in 1914, came the Harrison Narcotics Act, though even that was commonly referred to as the drug medicalization act, since it provided for exemptions and doctors could prescribe drugs that were otherwise illegal.

Still, as time went by, the social climate changed. There was growing sympathy for China. It had to do with increasing knowledge, sympathy for China's general difficulties and old notions of 'justice' as between states and nations. As for the opium trade, it might be clear that control of China's imports was a matter for China alone, as was the business of dealing with Chinese officials who broke China's laws. But was there not something dubious about letting British subjects make large profits from a trade that seemed to cause much suffering there? Was it really acceptable for British governments to preach free trade but steer clear – as governments did for almost the entire century – from involvement with particular projects, firms or trades? There was, too, the sheer impetus that the success of Wilberforce's anti-slavery movement had given to the notion of empire as a Christian duty, with political structures in which the natives could be brought to Christ. The opium trade was clearly at odds with all of that.

Unease about the opium traffic surfaced quite early in Parliament and did not end with the strong references in the 1840 debate. At the beginning of April 1843 that well-known Anglican evangelical, Lord Ashley, later the Earl of Shaftesbury, put a motion in the House of Commons designed to suppress the trade. Though the motion was withdrawn – in order not to prejudice then ongoing talks with the Chinese – it combined moral with pragmatic arguments, put in a thoughtful way. The opium trade, Ashley said, endangered all other British political and commercial interests in China.[11] In the same month that shrewd Canton merchant, James Matheson, saw which way the wind was blowing. He told his opium ship captains to be cautious. The opium trade was now so unpopular in England that it should be kept as quiet and out of the public eye as possible.[12] Other memorials or parliamentary motions followed from time to time, including one in 1855 from Ashley again, by now Lord Shaftesbury. In the 1857 debate, Gladstone charged that Hong Kong, having been acquired for refitting British ships, had become a centre for promoting smuggling, especially of opium. Palmerston's answer was to point out that Britain's imports of tea had doubled since 1842 from 42 million lbs to over 80 million, with similar increases for silks. That had to be paid for, but it was China's own trade restrictions that prevented the outside world from selling there, and so earning the cash or bullion needed to pay for these things. China's own strict limits on other trade therefore increased everyone else's reliance on opium. 'The very limited extent of our dealings with the Chinese hitherto,' he told the Commons, 'has tended to stimulate the trade in opium.'[13] If China remained closed to proper trade, the problem would become even worse. It was precisely such an extension of normal trade with China that the government was pressing for. It would balance sales and purchases, secure Britain's imports, and greatly benefit Chinese consumers.

The balance of political opinion continued to concentrate on the impracticality of Britain trying to control Chinese imports, even illegal ones. So when, as late as 1870, Sir Wilfred Lawson put a motion in the Commons 'that this House condemns the system by which a large portion of the Indian revenue is raised by opium', he lost the vote by 150 to 46. It was a much wider margin than that by which Palmerston had trounced his opponents thirty years earlier.[14] Lawson's basic arguments were not novel. But he did point out that, since the East India Company's authority in India had ended in 1857/58, after the Indian Mutiny, Britain was now much more directly responsible for India, and therefore for Indian opium production. Ironically, it was Gladstone himself who now opposed him. The very man who had denounced the opium trade thirty years earlier was now Prime Minister and found that righteous indignation was not enough. Instead, he defended the opium trade and India's opium revenues. Back in 1840, he said, opium had been prohibited in China. Now, the Chinese government had, wisely in the Prime Minister's view, made opium into a dutiable commercial commodity. Moreover, he reiterated the argument, which had also been heard thirty year earlier and eerily foreshadowed the drug 'legalization' discussions some 130 years later: was it really true that using opium necessarily meant abuse? Was opium really damaging if taken in moderation, as so many people in China did? Was it so very different from alcohol and tobacco?

He also pointed out that if Parliament condemned the trade, it would have to deal with the financial consequences. Would it really be responsible for the Commons to condemn, at a moment's notice, some 15 per cent of India's existing revenue? And to do so without any notion of how it was to be done, or how the shortfall should be made good? As it was, some £6 million (tv: £270 million) were being paid, without complaints and as a contribution to India's welfare, by the inhabitants of another country. Would the British parliament be willing to replace this from new British taxes? In any case, what effect would a ban have on opium growers all over India and on transport systems? Indians were not British constituents. If India acted on a condemnation by the Commons, would that not throw Indian finances into confusion and prejudice India's welfare, even her peace? A mere dozen years after the Indian Mutiny crisis, such an argument was irresistible. (Five years later, a similar motion to Lawson's was equally lost.)

There were other, more subtle and far-reaching motives, not mentioned in the debate. They had to do with the dangers of over-extending Britain's strategic and other resources. Perhaps even, as John Seeley pointed out dramatically a few years later, with a sense of Britain's ultimate weakness in the face of rising industrial powers like the United States, Russia and Germany. In any event, Palmerston's old emphasis on what Britain could not do – like policing other peoples' frontiers – remained part of the empire's operational principles, even if no-one put it quite that way in public.

Nevertheless, by the time that Gladstone won that 1870 vote, the balance of public views was undergoing profound changes. Some of the reasons had to do with concerns about the physical effects of drink and drugs and produced, among other things, a powerful temperance movement later in the century. That tallied easily with objections to opium. It also went together with the growing role of evengelicalism in all facets of life. Churches and chapels became arenas for airing social unrest and demands for reform. As a group, they were by far the most important voluntary organizations in that period of growing emphasis on good works and social care. By the middle of the century clergy, and especially Anglicans, may well have been much the most numerous single profession, dwarfing the army, law or medicine. In the 1840s, it has been calculated, almost three-quarters of all Oxford and Cambridge graduates were ordained into the Church of England, and in the 1860s well over half of their graduates still went into the Church. These clergy were at the cutting edge of intellectual debates and had the means to spread their moral enthusiasms far beyond their parishioners. In the 1860s, for example, the Religious Tract Society printed some 33 million books and pamphlets each year. It is hardly surprising that this trend deeply affected attitudes throughout society. It certainly informed the general mood of social reform and amelioration in British politics and public opinion. Nor was fervour confined to Anglicans. Presbyterians – especially in Scotland – and other Nonconformist groups were equally energetic and dedicated.

On imperial issues, and on China, much the most important criticisms, producing rising waves of moral indignation, also came from the churches and the missionaries. It was mainly these religious and philanthropic groups who worried about native peoples and the spread of Christianity and civilization. It was they who gave to that English genius for interference all the passion of moral indignation. A number of missionary societies, in particular, had sprung up at the beginning of the nineteenth century: the Baptist Missionary Society in 1792, the London Missionary Society in 1795, the Church Missionary Society in 1799, the British and Foreign Bible Society in 1804 and the Methodist Missionary Society in 1813. Sometime later, in 1865, Dr J. Hudson Taylor founded the China Inland Mission which rejected elaborate funding and permanent missions. It attracted young middle-class volunteers, including many women; and by 1890 it was the largest of all British missions. In 1900, Britain may have had some 10,000 missionaries, of all denominations, serving abroad. The influence of these and other bodies on British society and politics was immense. Many denominations ran religious weeklies and many of them concentrated on the doings of foreign missions. Newspapers were interested, too.[15] As one scholar of the time has put it:

> the contribution of the religious laity, clerics and missionaries to Britain's knowledge and understanding of other peoples was immense ... [and] At the height of the so-called 'new imperialism' of the late nineteenth century, the influence of non-British strains of Protestantism ... scepticism about Western civilization, and greater attentiveness to the values of indigenous cultures combined to make British evangelicalism increasingly less nationalist and chauvinistic.[16]

So it was the Christian missionaries with their zeal and crusading spirit, especially after the 1857/58 treaties, who were most effective in agitating against the opium trade. The more they looked at local laws, habits, conditions, the more these looked barbarous and ripe for reform by enlightened Englishmen, Scots and Americans. They were appalled by the poverty and misery they found and deeply incensed by the damage opium was doing to the Chinese and by the difficulties that it, and other Western influences, put in the way of bringing the Chinese to Christianity. The Protestants were the most powerful and influential of these groups, more particularly the Nonconformists. In many cases they developed a deep respect and love for China and the Chinese people, together with deeply paternal attitudes. Indeed, they had strong views on the Christian duty of paternal guidance for natives in all regions subject to English or American influence. Race and class were largely irrelevant. Religion and civilization were what mattered. And among these folk, the substantial number of medical missionaries were motivated even further by contemporary advances, not only in medicine itself, but in the claims which medical men were making in broad areas of public health and social regulation. But many of them enthusiastically welcomed the outcome of the 1840–42 war – and, later, of the 1857–60 conflicts – since the opening of the treaty ports and, later, the interior, would allow missionaries to operate more widely within the Chinese empire. In the process they were sometimes a serious nuisance for the diplomats and soldiers who had to try to protect them.[17]

But the Protestant missionaries formed a strongly cohesive group with instruments ready at hand to co-ordinate their views and make their humanitarian opinions influential. There was that very large number of church publications in whose pages they could spread their message. There was also a constant flow of missionaries from the colonies visiting home. Given long travelling times, they often stayed for at least a year and could bring first-hand accounts of conditions in China. From the 1860s onwards they helped to organize a wave of meetings and pamphlets, condemning the whole business of opium out of hand. In that deeply religious age – religious at least for the Europeans and Americans – they had large and regular church attendances to impress with the moral implications of Chinese sufferings and Britain's role in the opium business. They tended to treat the opium trade, and its abolition, as a moral imperative in relation to which the practicalities and costs of policy were irrelevant. In fact, they strongly influenced Western interpretations of all Chinese affairs.

These missionary groups made themselves heard as early as the 1830s. The opium issue was raised in newspapers and journals like *The Times* and the *Gentleman's Magazine*, often quoting from Canton publications.[18] When Lord Ashley moved his motion in Parliament in 1843, he based it explicitly on three petitions sent to him: from the Committee of the Wesleyan Missionary Society, from the Baptist Missionary Society, and from the directors of the London Missionary Society. Then, in 1857/58 a philippic in the *Leeds Mercury* proclaimed that 'The opium trade is a national iniquity, an enormous injury deliberately inflicted by Great Britain upon China...'. Opium was the sole cause of Chinese hostility to the English and to Christianity.[19] A Committee for the Suppression of the Opium Trade was formed in Edinburgh in the following year. In the 1870s the campaign grew stronger. In 1874 The Anglo-Oriental Society for the Suppression of the Opium Trade was formed, largely by Quakers.[20] (By 1880 Lord Shaftesbury was its president.) A year later the Society held a major conference in London. In 1876, in the Commons, Mr Bourke lamented that 'Everything we have obtained by treaty from the Chinese we have obtained by force' and, as Sir Thomas Wade put it: 'extorted against the conscience of the nation.' By the 1880s it was widely accepted that Britain had been heartless and unscrupulous, had actually waged war in defence of the drug and had forced it on the Chinese. By the 1880s the argument was made even more forcibly that opium was actually strangling other forms of trade both because of the odium of the opium trade and because opium was making the Chinese too poor to buy British manufactures. In 1884 a Dr Fortescue Fox, reporting on a trip to the Far East, wrote that, in the eyes of the Chinese, the missionaries were 'representatives of a power which is their enemy both in peace and war, whose hostile armies are but succeeded by a hostile opium policy more ruinous than the sword.'[21] Though he also reported visiting 'brilliant emporiums', where opium was to be had in greatest comfort and where one could meet people who had smoked opium for 20–50 years, in moderation and without ill effects.[22]

There were a number of missionary conferences, for instance in London in 1888 and one of Methodists in Washington in 1891. In that same year, the Chairman of the Anti-Opium Society, Sir John Pease, finally won, by 160 votes to 130, a House of Commons motion, saying that Indian opium revenue was 'morally indefensible'. Two years later a Royal Commission on opium was appointed. Its Final Report – of 2500 pages, published in April 1895 – argued that Britain was guilty of immoral practices: 'The main purpose of the production and sale of opium in British India unquestionably is to supply the Chinese and other Eastern markets.'[23] In 1892 Henry H.T. Cleife wrote about 'England's Greatest National Sin',[24] while the Rev. Griffith John thought England needed 'to wash our hands clean of the iniquity... The trade is... a foul blot on England's escutcheon.' In 1896 missionaries in China proposed the formation of an anti-opium league. By the time of the 1906 parliamentary elections some 250 of the candidates were committed anti-opium folk and the new members of parliament were mostly middle class, with a good proportion of Nonconformists. (By then, opium had anyway declined to around 7 per cent of the revenue of British India. Even so, the Secretary of State for India, Lord Kimberley, opposed abolition.) In 1907 the Convocation of Canterbury agreed unanimously that Anglicans, and Britain, had an important moral and political obligation to help China eliminate the opium evil.[25] In 1909 there was a major international anti-opium conference and in 1913 it was the opium merchants themselves who asked that the trade from India be stopped, no doubt encouraged by the further decline of opium's importance in Indian revenue and commercial earnings. Yet even as late as the 1960s some British writers accepted, without question, that China was right to regard this episode in England's past as dishonourable.[26]

It is true that for much of this period the campaign, with its fierce debates about whether the British had forced opium on the Chinese, or whether the Chinese were really serious in wanting to suppress the traffic, created more noise than wide or deep popularity. Nevertheless, the moral bias in favour of prohibition gradually hardened and by the time of the 1912 Hague Convention on the subject it was agreed that only legitimate medical purposes could justify the use of opium.

Such opinions were even more important in the United States than in Britain itself. It is true that at the end of the nineteenth century Secretary of State John Hay had to fend off strong commerial and other pressures for active United States involvement in China. But it is also true that by then the Americans had for two or three decades had roughly twice as many Protestant missionaries in China as the British. Indeed, it has been suggested that the number of US missionaries in China doubled between 1890 and 1905, and doubled again by 1919 to some 3300. Prominent among them were leaders of the Student Volunteer Movement, like John R. Mott and A.T. Pierson, who entirely rejected any imperial outlook or even Western ways. Altogether, as early as the 1890s the Americans were much more visible than the British, especially in the major missionary universities like Shanghai and Beijing. Beneath the surface of US attitudes to politics and the world, there has always been a deep well of religious feeling. The same kind of universalist religiosity was one of the roots of the anti-slavery movement and hence of the US Civil War. It has been reflected in anti-drink campaigns and the twentieth-century effort at Prohibition. It has always done battle against drugs. In 1842 Catherine Beecher had written 'to American women, more than to any others on earth, is committed the exalted privilege of extending over the world those blessed influences, which are to renovate degraded man, and "to clothe all climes with beauty".'[27] Anti-opium trade views were reflected in the 1844 Sino-American treaty's support for China's opium prohibitions. Missionary reports, and their testimony during home visits, not only fuelled an anti-opium crusade but shaped opinion about China for at least the next century. It also fuelled some very odd American views about the British Empire and what made it work.[28]

Before 1890 missionaries were apt to occupy strategic positions not only in the general opinion-forming sphere, but even in forming American political positions on China. They even drafted some of the Sino-American agreements of the period. In fact, late in the century, the American missionary movement became a highly respected and respectable crusade under the leadership of charismatic persons such as Dwight L. Moody and Ira Sankey. After the Boxer rising, they tended to become defenders of China and sought – to be sure, not altogether successfully – to secure official American support in making China a strong state. More importantly, though, they made China into a moral problem rather than a matter of international relations. Around 1900 China still seemed, to Americans 'mired in the timeless dirt, death and degradation of the ages ... the respect paid to the dead, the public pathos of the dying – caused Americans deep distress'.[29] So one answer, from bodies like the American Bible Society, was to flood China with copies of the scriptures. Another was to encourage the adoption, not just of Christianity and the West's moral principles, but of its technologies, constitutionalism and democratic institutions.[30] That was part of the context in which, by 1900 or so, the American drive for general drug prohibitions gathered pace. In 1909, on the initiative of President Theodore Roosevelt, an International Opium Commission was convened at Shanghai to consider suppression measures. The successor conference, in 1911–12 at The Hague, produced the International Opium Convention of 1912. With increasing dogmatism it was asserted that drugs were an unmitigated evil. By the mid-1920s some missionaries had also discovered the sinfulness of the entire China treaty system – which earlier missionaries had actually helped to draft – and called for resolutions of repentance for creating such an unchristian structure.

Even then, nowhere in Europe or North America was there anything resembling the somewhat frantic, even hysterical, late-twentieth-century 'war on drugs'. It was not until the 1920s and 1930s that doctors, especially but not only in the USA, decided that drugs led to addiction and addiction to sociopathologies. It was only then that drug users began to be seen not as eccentrics but as criminal deviants, and that criminalization of drugs took root. It is hardly surprising that by the end of the twentieth century the 'war on drugs' produced an illegal drug business worth several hundred billion dollars and an estimated 8 per cent of world trade.

These waves of moral and religious fervour, of socialist condemnation of capitalism, even of simple disenchantment with empire, were bound to have large effects, especially in societies like Britain and the United States where popular opinion so often rules. So it is no surprise that general opinion in the West came to believe, long after the event, that Britain had behaved wickedly in China. It became conventional and not merely missionary wisdom to say she had made war on China just to force opium on the Chinese. Social chaos had been brought to that large empire for no better cause than selfish financial profit. The kind of pragmatic defence of British policy that Macaulay and Palmerston had given to Parliament in 1840, or even that of Gladstone in 1870, sounded increasingly implausible to late-Victorian and Edwardian ears. Such political or diplomatic considerations could not compete with the moral and religious passions that the opium issue aroused, or even with the general 'social conscience' considerations of twentieth-century England and America. Institutional changes indirectly strengthened condemnation. Few developments more clearly mark the late Victorian period at home than the growth of social relief efforts by regulation, a growth that for very different reasons dramatically increased during and after the First World War. To minds attuned to this, the Palmerstonian idea that it might be too costly, or politically harmful, or even legally dubious, for governments to regulate the details of imperial commercial activities, or patterns of Indian land use, let alone the use and distribution of drugs, seemed not just absurd but entirely reprehensible.

Yet the consequences of these Western religious and anti-opium passions were deeply ironic, in two divergent ways. The evangelical and humanitarian wish to do good, guilt feelings about the past, or government policies meant to protect China, produced a sense, in the United States even more than in Britain, of selfless Western benevolence, of China as the West's, and especially America's, protégé. That was reinforced during the 1930s and 1940s by American and British support for China against Japan, and the propping up of a weakened China's role as one of the 'Big Four' victors of the Second World War. It was reinforced further when American China policy in the 1940s and 1950s was critically influenced by groups of 'China experts' who were, in very many cases, the children of missionaries and had themselves spent some of their early years in China. All of which contributed to a deep sense of betrayal when the Communist Party took power in Beijing in 1949. Here were factors which coloured American and Western policies towards China into the 1970s.

In the meantime, neither missionary evangelism, nor Western humanitarians nor anti-drink campaigners had much influence on a Chinese political class deeply divided between the drive to reject foreign influences, and the wish to destroy the old order and imitate – and surpass? – foreign knowledge, technologies and institutions. These tensions led to some radical reversals of China's policies towards the West in the decades after 1900, including a clear-headed recognition that if China wanted to succeed in the modern diplomatic arena, it would have to adopt Western language and idioms. That helped to produce two competing versions of a burgeoning Chinese nationalism, personified in Chiang Kai-shek (Jiang Jiesgi) and Mao Zedong. Both versions were very willing to make political use of frequently naive Western religious or liberal enthusiasms. By the 1930s Chiang's version found itself being decisively weakened by the Japanese occupation of its main centres of strength, on the coast and in the great cities, as well as by its visible reliance on the West. It was a condition that Mao exploited with brilliance. Himself a lifelong student of ancient and modern Chinese history and strategy,[31] he found succinct phrases to dismiss all that had gone before as shameful and humiliating. 'The China of today,' he wrote in 1938, 'cannot be compared with the China of any other historical period. She is a semi-colony and a semi-feudal society. But at the same time, China is historically in an era of progress....'[32] Sympathetic foreigners harped on the theme that China was 'standing up'.[33] Mao may or may not have known the Latin tag *carpe diem* (seize the day) but he understood the principle very well. He could use the Japanese invasion as an intolerable assault on China's sovereignty, land, people and pride and as an effective rallying cry for all Chinese. Yet he also understood that he owed his own victory in 1949, not least, to those same Japanese. 'If Japan had not invaded China in the 1930s, the communists and the nationalists would never have cooperated,' he said '...and the Communist party would have remained too weak to seize power....'[34]

All in all, during the first half of the twentieth century China's leaders, with ruthless political *nous*, used the combination of her political, military and economic weakness, and views of China as innocent victim, to create one of the more brilliant strands of twentieth-century Chinese foreign policy. It was a diplomacy of resentment that successfully asserted China's status as victim, morally superior to her oppressors. Carefully keeping Chinese grievances alive in official propaganda and education was an important contribution to such a strategy *vis à vis* the outside world, as well as to the consolidation of national unity in an often fissiperous realm. It is not surprising that in such a process Commissioner Lin should have become an heroic figure. Or that the harping on real and imagined wrongs suffered before 'liberation' should have made the West into a useful scapegoat for all the very real miseries of translating a semi-feudal and agricultural society into a powerful modern state.

Notes

1 Mission to Canton

1. Quoted in Susanna Hoe and Derek Roebuck, *The Taking of Hong Kong; Charles and Clara Elliot in China Waters* (Richmond, Surrey: Curzon Press, 1999). This is a particularly careful and detailed study.
2. The equivalent figure in Aug. 2002 pounds sterling was over £291,000, according to comparative tables issued by the Bank of England. Throughout this book these comparisons are given in the following form: £6000 (tv: £291,000).
3. *London Gazette*, 12 Dec. 1833.
4. I have given contemporary nineteenth-century names/spellings, in brackets, where that seemed convenient.
5. *Quarterly Review*, Jan. 1834, quoted in the *Morning Post*, 3 Feb. 1835, p.3.
6. Quoted in the *Liverpool Dispatch* and cited in the *Morning Post*, 22 Jan. 1835, p.2.
7. In 1832 there were 26 British country traders at Canton. By 1837 there were 156.
8. Hosea Ballou Morse, *The International Relations of the Chinese Empire* (3 vols), vol.1, *The Period of Conflict 1834–1860* (London: Longmans, Green, and Co., 1910), p.120.
9. Correspondence relating to China (hereafter referred to as CRC), 1840, p.18; *Chinese Repository*, Aug. 1834.
10. CRC, 1840, p.18.
11. An English translation of the instructions, apparently in full, is printed in the *Morning Post*, 3 Feb. 1835, p.1.
12. *Chinese Repository*, Sept. 1834.
13. CRC, 1840, p.24; *Chinese Repository*, April 1839.
14. *North China Herald*, 15 March 1851, quoted in Morse, *The Period of Conflict*, p.132.
15. Jane Hunter, *The Gospel of Gentility* (New Haven, CT: Yale University Press, 1984).
16. Morse, *The Period of Conflict*, p.139–53.
17. Chang Hsin-Pao, *Commissioner Lin and the Opium War* (Cambridge, MA: Harvard University Press, 1964), p.57.
18. CRC, 1840, p.29.
19. *Gentleman's Magazine*, Jan. 1834, p.99.
20. Ibid. p.156.
21. Letter from Clara Elliot to her sister-in-law, dated 24 Aug. 1834, quoted in Hoe and Roebuck, *The Taking of Hong Kong*, p.27.
22. CRC, 1840, p.71.
23. Napier to Palmerston, CRC, 1840, p.15; also quoted in Morse, *The Period of Conflict*, p.142.

24. Napier to Lord Grey, CRC, 1840, p.28; also quoted in H.B. Morse and Harley F. McNair, *Far Eastern International Relations* (Boston: Houghton Mifflin, 1931), p.86.
25. His letter – the writer was not named – was dated 7 Sept. and summarized in the *Morning Post* in Feb. 1835.
26. Chang, *Commissioner Lin and the Opium War*, p.58.
27. *Quarterly Review*, see note 5 above.
28. *Morning Post,* 4 Feb. 1835, p.3. Similarly, a letter from Canton dated 19.8.34 and printed in the *Weekly Dispatch*, 1 Feb. 1835, p.1 said simply 'The British trade is at present stopped, as Lord Napier will not obey the order of the Viceroy to leave Canton.'
29. John W. Foster, *American Diplomacy in the Orient* (Boston: Houghton Mifflin, 1903, reprinted Da Capo Press, New York, 1970), p.63.
30. The Duke, by this time the Grand Old Man of British public affairs, was famously terse and to the point. Once, when asked by some clergyman what he would like the next sermon to be about, he replied 'about ten minutes.'
31. Chang, *Commissioner Lin and the Opium War*, p.61.
32. Quoted in Parliament by Sir James Graham, Hansard, House of Commons, 7 Apr. 1840, col.682.
33. Letter of 13 Sept. 1837 to the Secretary of the Admiralty, quoted in Hoe and Roebuck, *The Taking of Hong Kong*, p.65.
34. The *Gentleman's Magazine*, March 1835, pp.267–9.

2   Palmerston's England, the World and China

1. Lady Campbell to Emily Eden in 1822, Bourne Collection of Palmerston papers, London School of Economics Library (hereafter referred to as 'Bourne Papers').
2. Charles C.F. Greville, *Memoirs*, ed. Henry Reeve, 3 vols (London: Longmans Green, 1874).
3. See A. Aspinall, *Politics and the Press 1780–1850* (London: Home and Van Thal, 1949), pp.191, 238. More generally, Jeremy Black, *The English Press 1621–1861* (London: Sutton Publishing, 2001).
4. Donald Southgate aptly entitled his excellent work on Palmerston (using Lord Palmerston's obituary in the *Daily Telegraph*) *The Most English Minister* (London: Macmillan, 1966).
5. *West Somerset Free Press*, 7 Sept. 1861, quoted in a column by Paul Johnson, *Spectator*, 19 Aug. 2000, p.25.
6. *Leeds Mercury*, 24 June 1843.
7. Lord John Russell (later Earl Russell), *Early Correspondence*, ed. Rollo Russell, 2 vols (London: T. Fisher Unwin, 1913), vol.2, pp.238–9.
8. Kennan's famous 1946 'Long Telegram' from the Moscow Embassy to Washington was summarized as 'The Sources of Soviet Conduct' in the July 1947 issue of the journal *Foreign Affairs* under the pseudonym of 'Mr X'.
9. Hansard, House of Commons, 16 July 1844, col.931.
10. Hansard, House of Commons, 18 May 1841, cols 654–5.
11. Bentham, 'Emancipate your Colonies! addressed to the National Convention of France, Anno 1793. Showing the uselessness and mischievousness of

distant dependencies to an European State', *The Works of Jeremy Bentham*, ed. John Bowring, vol.IV (London: Simpkin Marshall, 1843), pp.407 et seq.

12. Thomas Babington Macaulay's review of Lord Mahon's *History of the War of Succession in Spain*, Edinburgh Review, vol.LVI, 1932, pp.499–541.

13. Sir William Molesworth, Hansard, House of Commons, 6 March 1838, cols 476 et seq.

14. Report from the Select Committee on Aborigines (British Settlements) *Parlimentary Papers* 1837 (425) VII, p.76.

15. To Bulwer 22 July 1840, in Henry Lytton Bulwer, *The Life of John Henry Temple, Viscount Palmerston: with Selections from his Diaries and Correspondence*, 2 vols (London, 1870), vol.2, pp.318–19.

16. Public Records Office (Gifts and Deposits) *The Russell Papers* 3. Lord John was the younger brother of the Duke of Bedford.

17. E. Baines, *History of the Cotton Manufacture in Great Britain* (London: H. Fisher, R. Fisher and P. Jackson, 1835), pp.360–1, 432.

18. Donald Read, *Cobden and Bright: A Victorian Political Partnership* (London: E. Arnold, 1967), p.110.

19. Cited in W. Baring Pemberton, *Lord Palmerston* (London: Batchworth Press, 1954), p.141.

20. Friedrich List, *The National System of Political Economy*, trans. Sampson S. Lloyd (London: Longmans Green, 1885), p.293. (This is a translation of List, *Das Nationale System der politischen Oekonomie*, Stuttgart, 1841.)

21. Even Sir Charles Webster's magisterial two-volume *The Foreign Policy of Palmerston* scarcely mentions the Celestial Empire. Wellington's biography by Elizabeth Longford has no mention of China either.

22. The underlying principles are hardly peculiar to China. As Gibbon reminds us in a comment on the Emperor Severus 'The true interest of an absolute monarch generally coincides with that of his people. Their numbers, their wealth, their order, and their security, are the best and only foundations of his real greatness; and were he totally devoid of virtue, prudence might supply its place, and would dictate the same rule of conduct.' *Decline and Fall of the Roman Empire* (London: Dent [Everyman's library], 1978), vol.I, Ch.V, p.118.

23. Joseph Fletcher, 'The Ch'ing in Inner Asia', in Denis Twitchett and John K. Fairbank (eds) *Cambridge History of China*, vol.10, The Late Ch'ing 1800–1911 Part I, ed. John K. Fairbank (Cambridge: Cambridge University Press, 1978), Ch.2, p.36.

24. 'In transliterating foreign names, the Chinese shrink from signifying them by using characters which should have a pleasing meaning or should simulate a Chinese, i.e. a truly civilized name ... This Chinese practice is not, perhaps, a direct insult, but it illustrates the national tendency to belittle the foreigner and to treat him as outside the pale of civilization.' Morse, *The Period of Conflict*, pp.126–7.

25. Michael Greenberg, *British Trade and the Opening of China 1800–1842* (New York: Monthly Review Press, 1979), p.42n5.

26. In Tsun's memorial of 1835 to the Emperor, quoted in Greenberg, *British Trade*, p.45.

27. J.L.Cranmer-Byng (ed.), *An Embassy to China: Lord Macartney's Journal 1793–94* (London: Routledge, 2000), p.340.

28. In addition, the port of Amoy (Xiamen), with its access to the tea production of Fukien (Fujian), was open to Spanish trade, but this was not of great significance, since Chinese ships could transport goods to and from the Philippines more cheaply than the Spaniards.
29. Greenberg, *British Trade* (quoting House of Lords Select Committee) p.3n3.
30. James B. Eames, *The English in China* (London: Pitman, 1909), p.448.
31. At first it was smoked like tobacco, giving the smoker around 0.2 per cent morphine. Then smokers began to put pills of pure opium into pipes over a flame, inhaling the combined water vapour and opium. That yielded 9–10 per cent morphine.
32. Greenberg, *British Trade*, pp.142–3; P.C. Kuo, *A Critical Study of the First Anglo-Chinese War, with Documents*, Shanghai, Commerical Press, 1935, Chs V&VI.
33. Jack Gray, *Rebellions and Revolutions: China from the 1800s to the 1980s* (Oxford: Oxford University Press), 1990.
34. Greenberg, *British Trade*, pp.14–15.
35. Quoted by Lord Ashley, Hansard, House of Commons 4 April 1843, cols 362 et seq.
36. One estimate suggests that the opium monopoly came to yield about one-seventh of the total revenue of British India. Cf. D.E. Owen, *British Opium Policy in China and India* (New Haven: Yale University Press, 1934).
37. Letter of 1 July 1835 from Sir George Robinson to Lord Palmerston, received in London 28 Jan. 1836 and quoted in Parliament by Sir W. Follett, Hansard, House of Commons, 7 April 1840, cols 721–2.
38. Quoted in Greenberg, *British Trade*, p.61. It seems that written contracts only became necessary once the Cohong was abolished following the 1842 Treaty of Nanking (Nanjing).
39. For the slow decline and surrender of the East India Company's China trade rights, in excruciating detail, see Patrick Tuck (ed.), *The East India Company: 1600–1858*, vol.VI, C.H. Phillips, *The East India Company 1784–1834* (Manchester: Manchester University Press, 1940).
40. Palmerston to Auckland 22 Jan. 1841, quoted in Martin Lynn, 'British Policy, Trade and Informal Empire in the Mid-Nineteenth Century', in Andrew Porter and Alaine Low (eds), *The Oxford History of the British Empire*, vol.III The Nineteenth Century (Oxford: Oxford University Press, 1999), p.105. Also D.C.M. Platt, *Finance, Trade and Politics in British Foreign Policy 1815–1914* (Oxford: Clarendon Press, 1968).

3 It's More Than Trade, Stupid! Canton 1835–38

1. CRC, 1840, pp.47, 55, 56, 89; also cited in Morse, *The Period of Conflict*, p.147.
2. Robinson, note of 29 Jan. 1836 to Palmerston, quoted in W.C. Costin, *Great Britain and China 1833–1860* (Oxford: Oxford University Press, 1937), p.31.
3. Morse, *The Period of Conflict*, p.169, citing CRC 1840, p.285.
4. Gerald S. Graham, *The China Station: War and Diplomacy 1830–1860* (Oxford: Oxford University Press, 1978), p.62.
5. See Palmerston's dispatch of 22 July 1836, CRC, 1840, p.121.

6. CRC, 1840, p.129.
7. Ibid., p.121.
8. For example, letter of 28 April 1835, quoted in Susanna Hoe and Derek Roebuck, *The Taking of Hong Kong; Charles and Clara Elliot in China Waters* (Richmond, Surrey: Curzon Press, 1999) p.44.
9. A summary of the views he put to Lennox Conyngham is in W.C. Costin, *Great Britain and China*, pp.31–4.
10. CRC, 1840, p.136.
11. Lord Palmerston to Captain Elliot, CRC, 1840, pp.123, 149, 192, 258, 319.
12. Collis suggests values, for 1831, of East India Company sales of $5 million, British firms under Company licence $0.5 million and the Americans $2 million.
13. Approximately £12,000 (tv: just over £500,000). One *tael* was around 1.2 ounces of pure silver.
14. Greenberg, *British Trade,* p.73.
15. James M. Polachek, *The Inner Opium War* (Cambridge, MA: Harvard University Press, for the Council on East Asian Studies, Harvard University, 1992), p.106.
16. Jonathan Spence, 'Opium Smoking in Ch'ing China', in Frederic Wakeman Jr and Carolyn Grant (eds) *Conflict and Control in Late Imperial China* (Berkeley: University of California Press, 1975), pp.150–1.
17. Polachek, *The Inner Opium War*, p.127.
18. Gideon Nye, *The Morning of my Life in China,* (Canton 1873), pp.51–2.
19. Wakeman, Frederick Jr, 'The Canton Trade and the Opium War' in Denis Twitchett and John K. Fairbank (eds), *The Cambridge History of China*, vol.10, *The Late Ch'ing 1800–1911 Pt I*, ed. John K. Fairbank (Cambridge: Cambridge University Press, 1978), Ch.4, pp.33–4.
20. Polachek, *The Inner Opium War*, p.123.
21. CRC, 1840, pp.173, 190/91.
22. Hoe and Roebuck, *The Taking of Hong Kong*, p.64.
23. H. Hamilton Lindsay, letter (of 1 March 1836) to the Rt. Hon. Viscount Palmerston on British Relations with China, published as a pamphlet by Saunders and Otley (London, 1836).
24. Ibid., pp.6–7.
25. Sir James Matheson, *The Present Position and Future Prospects of the British Trade with China* (London: Smith Elder and Co., 1836). Hoe and Roebuck suggest that it was ghost-written for him: see *The Taking of Hong Kong*, p.54.
26. Matheson, ibid., pp.15, 60.
27. Quoted in James Morris' delightful *Heaven's Command: An Imperial Progress* (New York/London: Harcourt, Brace, Jovanovich, 1973), p.31.
28. Justin McCarthy, *A History of Our Own Times*, vol.1 (London: Chatto and Windus, 1881), pp.175–6.
29. CRC, 1840, p.234.
30. Ibid.
31. J. Phipps, *A Practical Treatise on China and the Eastern Trade* (London: W.H. Allen, 1836), Introduction. A modern authority estimates that during the decade before 1842 opium made up about two-thirds of all British plus Indian imports into China. Greenberg, *British Trade…* p.50.
32. 'Chinese Affairs', *Quarterly Review*, March 1840, p.548.

33. This contempt for Chinese judicial methods persisted. Much later, in the 9th edition of the *Encyclopaedia Britannica*, the Professor of Chinese at King's College London, R.K. Douglas, remarked that 'the Chinese set little or no value upon truth … it is argued that where the value of an oath is not understood, some other means must be resorted to to exact evidence, and the readiest means to hand is doubtless torture … '.
34. Wellington memo of 24 March 1835, quoted in Costin, *Great Britain and China*, pp.40–1.
35. Quoted in Parliament by Sir James Graham, Hansard, House of Commons, 7 April 1840, col.682.
36. Note of 12 June 1837, quoted in Costin, *Great Britain and China*, p.41.
37. At the end of Dec. 1779 the accumulated debts of several such bankrupt firms were found to be some $4.3 million (or roughly £1 million (tv: £70 million)), since the Spanish dollar in this period varied between 4.44 and 4.18 to the pound (cf. Morse, *The Period of Conflict*, pp.16–67). In April 1837 the foreign merchants at Canton asked the Cohong to petition the Viceroy for an order that the debts of another bankrupt firm – a claim of some $2.7 million (£600,000; or tv: £25.6 million) – be paid. Other debts followed.
38. Greenberg, *British Trade*, p.204.
39. CRC, 1840, p.311.
40. Hansard, House of Commons, 28 July 1838.
41. Morse, *The Period of Conflict*, p.210 Table E.
42. Kuo Pin-chia, *A Critical Study of the First Anglo-Chinese War, with documents* (Shanghai: Commercial Press, 1935), p.213.
43. Quoted in Chang, *Commissioner Lin and the Opium War*, p.111.
44. Hansard, House of Commons, 4 April 1843 col.366.
45. Peter Ward Fay, *The Opium War 1840–1842* (Chapel Hill, NC: University of North Carolina Press, 1975), p.138.
46. Kuo, *A Critical Study of the First Anglo-Chinese War*, pp.250–1.
47. Polachek, *The Inner Opium War*, pp.133–5.

4 The British and Commissioner Lin 1839

1. *Quarterly Review*, March 1840, p.559.
2. Arthur Waley, *The Opium War Through Chinese Eyes* (London: Allen and Unwin, 1958), p.19.
3. His order of 18 March 1839 in CRC, 1840, p.350.
4. *Quarterly Review*, March 1840, p.541.
5. Quoted in Gray, *Rebellions and Revolutions*, p.41.
6. Hansard, House of Commons, 7 April 1840, cols 722–3.
7. CRC, 1840, p.352.
8. Ibid., p.350.
9. Maurice Collis, *Foreign Mud* (London: Faber and Faber, 1946), p.213.
10. It seems that Dent and Co. eventually surrendered 1700 chests of opium, second only to Jardine Matheson's 7000 chests. See Morse, *The Period of Conflict*, p.218n17.
11. CRC, 1840, p.363.

12. For the correspondence, see Hoe and Roebuck, *The Taking of Hong Kong*, pp.70–1.
13. Ibid., p.72.
14. Chang, *Commissioner Lin and the Opium War*, p.265n18.
15. John Slade, *Narrative of the Late Proceedings and Events in China* (Canton: Register Press, 1839; Wilmington, DE: Scholarly Resources, 1872), pp.53–4.
16. See, for instance, Morse, *The International Relations*, p.221n32.
17. Letter of 10 Aug. 1840, *The Times*, 19 Aug. 1840, p.3, reprinted in Chang, *Commissioner Lin and the Opium War*, Appendix D, pp.229–30.
18. CRC, 1840, pp.367–8.
19. CRC, 1840, p.370.
20. Hoe and Roebuck, *The Taking of Hong Kong*, pp.74–5.
21. Waley, *The Opium War Through Chinese Eyes*, p.39.
22. CRC, 1840, p.374.
23. Chang, *Commissioner Lin and the Opium War*, p.165.
24. H. Hamilton Lindsay, *Is the War with China a Just One?* (London: James Ridgway, 1840).
25. House of Commons Report of the Select Committee on Trade with China, 1840, pp.147, 359.
26. *Chinese Repository*, May 1839.
27. Chang, *Commissioner Lin and the Opium War*, p.195.
28. Waley, *The Opium War Through Chinese Eyes*, p.47.
29. Ibid., p.49.
30. *Chinese Repository*, June 1839.
31. Quoted in Collis, *Foreign Mud*, p.241.
32. *The Times*, 1 Nov. 1839; *Canton Press*, 20 July 1839, quoted in Waley, *The Opium War Through Chinese Eyes*, p.51n2.
33. Quoted in Wakeman, *The Canton Trade and the Opium War...* p.191.
34. CRC, 1840, p.451.
35. *Canton Register* and *Chinese Repository*, June 1839, quoted in Morse, *The International Relations*, p.232nn82–3.
36. *Chinese Repository*, Jan. and Oct. 1840.
37. CRC, 1840, p.431.
38. *Chinese Repository*, Jan. 1840.
39. Specifically, the Order in Council of 9 Dec. 1833.
40. Quoted in Collis, *Foreign Mud*, p.248.
41. CRC, 1840, p.448.
42. Collis, *Foreign Mud*, pp.254–5.
43. The letter is quoted in Chang, *Commissioner Lin and the Opium War*, p.207.
44. *Chinese Repository*, Oct. 1840. The death penalty was, of course, by no means unusual in China in this period.
45. *Friend of China*, issue of 14 July 1893, printing a 'Chinese statement on the Opium Traffic' and quoted in John K. Fairbank and Ssu-yu Teng, *China's Response to the West: A Documentary Survey 1839–1923* (Cambridge, MA: Harvard University Press, 1954), pp.24–7; see also *Chinese Repository*, vol.8, p.321.
46. For discussions, in June and Sept. 1839, between the Commissioner and the editor of the *Chinese Repository*, see *Chinese Repository*, Sept. 1839 and Jan. 1840.

47. Polachek, *The Inner Opium War*, p.153.
48. From documents captured during the war: John F. Davis, *China: During the War and Since the Peace*, 2 vols (London: Longmans, 1852), vol.1, pp.11–12.
49. Chang, *Commissioner Lin and the Opium War*, p.166.
50. Dispatch of 16 Nov. 1839, in Sir Henry Taylor, *Autobiography* (London: Harrison and Sons, 1874); also quoted in Hansard, House of Commons, 4 April 1843, col.368; and in Hoe and Roebuck, *The Taking of Hong Kong*, p.52.
51. John Ouchterlony, *The Chinese War* (London: Saunders and Otley, 1844), pp.34, 37.
52. Chang, *Commissioner Lin and the Opium War*, p.82.

5   London Debates 1839–40

1. Bourne Papers, box 1.
2. Still, a sense of uneasiness surrounded the march. At Jellalabad – to become notorious once more during the Anglo-American 'War on Terror' of 2002 – Colonel Dennie of the 13th Light Infantry remarked one day 'You will see, not a soul will reach here from Kabul except one man, who will come to tell us the rest are destroyed.' James Morris tells the story in his delightful *Heaven's Command; An Imperial Progress* , p.101.
3. One of them was Colonel Robert Warburton. The son of this marriage, Sir Robert Warburton, became one of the most famous frontier administrators of his day in British India.
4. Hansard, House of Commons, 18 May 1841, col.651.
5. Memorials presented to Parliament, Aug. 1840.
6. Palmerston's letter of 28 Nov. 1842 quoted in Collis, *Foreign Mud*, p.266, and Greenberg, *British Trade*, pp.214–15.
7. Hansard, House of Commons, 8 April 1840, col.751.
8. Quoted in Collis, *Foreign Mud*, pp.266–7.
9. *Chinese Repository*, 9, p.321.
10. Bourne Papers, box 9.
11. The text of the letters can be found in Morse, *The Period of Conflict*, Appendices A and B, pp.621–30.
12. Roy Porter, *The Greatest Benefit to Mankind: A Medical History of Humanity from Antiquity to the Present* (London: Fontana Press, 1999), p.194.
13. Morphia was isolated by Friedrich Wilhelm Stuermer in 1805 and the hypodermic needle invented by Dr Alexander Wood. See also Margaret Goldsmith, *The Trail of Opium: The Eleventh Plague* (London: Robert Hale, 1939), p.107.
14. For instance, *Quarterly Magazine*, March 1840, pp.568–9.
15. Lindsay, *Is the War With China a Just One?*
16. 'War With China and the Opium Question', *Blackwood's Magazine*, March 1840, pp.368–84.
17. *Quarterly Review*, June 1840, p.738.
18. The largest, by far, was *The Times,* with a circulation by the later 1840s of around 38,100. Its five chief rivals, combined, had only around 18,000. As for journals, the *Economist* had around 2000 and the *Spectator* only some 3500. See R.D. Edwards, *The Pursuit of Reason: The Economist 1843–1993*

(London: H. Hamilton, 1993), p.35; and T. Morley, 'The Arcana of that Great Machine: Politicians and The Times in the late 1840s', *History*, 73 (1988), pp.38–54.
19. Aspinall, *Politics and the Press*, pp.190–1, 238.
20. See a helpful but unexciting comment in David Brown, 'Compelling but not Controlling? Palmerston and the Press 1846–1855', *History*, vol.86, no.281, Jan. 2001, pp.41–61.
21. Palmerston's remarks in Hansard, House of Commons, 12 March 1840, cols 1155–6.
22. Hansard, House of Commons, 14 March 1840, col.1223.
23. See the comments of Sir G. Staunton in Hansard, House of Commons, 24 March 1840, cols 8–10; and a petition in the Lords, in similar terms, from Lord Stanhope, Hansard, House of Lords, 4 May 1840, col.1158.
24. For the debate see Hansard, House of Commons, 7, 8 and 9 April 1840, cols 669–951.
25. Hansard, House of Commons, 7 April 1840, cols 673–4.
26. An odd post, ranking well below the Secretary of State for War and the Colonies (Lord John Russell). Though carrying Cabinet rank, it was mainly concerned with piloting the army estimates through the House of Commons and had no concern with military policy, which was Russell's business, let alone with strategy.
27. Hansard, House of Commons, 7 April 1840, col.717.
28. Every member would instantly understand that he meant Oliver Cromwell, the victor of the civil war against King Charles I, and later 'Lord Protector' of England.
29. Hansard, House of Commons, 7 April 1840, col.719.
30. Ibid., col.728.
31. Ibid., col.731.
32. Ibid., col.742.
33. Ibid., col.808.
34. Hansard, House of Commons, 8 April 1840, cols 800–20.
35. As Lord John Russell wrote to the Queen, quoted in Edgar Holt, *The Opium Wars in China* (London: Putnam, 1964), p.103.
36. Roy Jenkins, *Gladstone* (New York: Random House, 1995), p.60.
37. Hansard, House of Commons, 9 April 1840, cols 898–925.
38. By Clause 6 of the China Trade Act of 1833.
39. Hansard, House of Commons, 9 April 1840, cols 925–48.
40. Cf. Bulwer, *The Life of John Henry Temple, Viscount Palmerston*, vol.III.
41. Baron Broughton (J.C. Hobhouse), *Recollections of a Long Life*, ed. Lady Dorchester, 6 vols (London: J. Murray, 1910), vol.V, p.257.

6 Fighting and Talking: Elliot 1840–41

1. *Chinese Repository*, June 1840.
2. Bridgman, who had served in China since 1830, was the founder and indefatigable publisher of the journal *Chinese Repository*, that recorded the events of this period with considerable accuracy. The quotation is from the *Repository*, 9, p.106.

3. For the letters to the Elliots, see Morse, *The Period of Conflict*, Appendix B, pp.626–30.
4. The text of the 4 March note can be found in ibid., Appendix D, pp.631–2.
5. The tale is once again told in Morris' *Heaven's Command*, p.201 and footnote 1.
6. Peter Ward Fay, *The Opium War 1840–1842* (Chapel Hill: University of North Carolina Press, 1975) p.239.
7. Ibid., p.238.
8. Morse, *The International Relations*, pp.263–4.
9. The remark was made to Morse personally, see *The Period of Conflict*, p.263n38.
10. Lord Jocelyn, *Six Months with the Chinese Expedition* (London: John Murray, 1841), pp.52–5.
11. Ibid., p.61n.
12. *Chinese Repository*, 9, p.251; also quoted in Fay, *The Opium War*, p.226.
13. The commanders had had warnings enough, but believed there was no alternative. A later Court of Inquiry found it had all just been an awful muddle. Cf. Surgeon McPherson, *Two Years in China, Narrative of the China Expedition 1840–1842* (London, 1842).
14. John Ouchterlony, *The Chinese War* (London, Saunders and Otley, 1844), p.85.
15. For Jardine's plan, see Fay, *The Opium War*, p.215; Polachek, *The Inner Opium War*, p.182.
16. Kuo, *A Critical Study of the First Anglo-Chinese War*, p.261, cited in Fay, *The Opium War*, p.230.
17. Elliot to Auckland 13 Dec. 1840, cited in Fay, *The Opium War*, p.270.
18. Morse, *The Period of Conflict*, Appendix E pp.632–36.
19. Ibid.
20. Hoe and Rebuck, *The Taking of Hong Kong*, pp.149–50.
21. Rait, Sir Robert S., *The Life and Campaigns of Hugh, First Viscount Gough, Field-Marshal*, 2 vols (London: A. Constable, 1903), vol.1, pp.230–1.
22. *Chinese Repository*, Jan. 1841; also cited in Edgar Holt, *The Opium Wars in China*, p.119.
23. Charles C.F. Greville, *The Greville Memoirs*, 8 vols (London: Longmans Green, 1875), vol.4, p.364 et seq.
24. Victoria, *Letters of Queen Victoria*, ed. Arthur C. Benson and Viscount Esher vol.I, 1837–43 (London: J. Murray, 1908), p.260.
25. Fay, *The Opium War*, p.276.
26. Morse, *The Period of Conflict*, Appendix G, pp.641–7.
27. *Chinese Repository*, Jan. 1841.
28. Later transferring to the Ross-shire Buffs, who were to become the Seaforth Highlanders, and from them, as a very proper Irishman, to the 18th Royal Irish.
29. *Chinese Repository*, March 1841.
30. *Chinese Repository*, 10, p.418.
31. Rait, *The Life and Campaigns of Hugh, First Viscount Gough*, pp.170–80.
32. Hoe and Roebuck, *The Taking of Hong Kong*, p.179.
33. Rait, *The Life and Campaigns of Hugh, First Viscount Gough*, p.168.
34. Ibid., pp.170, 179–80.
35. Gerald S. Graham, *The China Station: War and Diplomacy 1830–1860*, Ch.6.

36. See Morse, *The Period of Conflict*, p.286n140.
37. Hoe and Roebuck, *The Taking of Hong Kong*, p.193.
38. Morse, *The Period of Conflict*, p.275.
39. *The Times*, 22 Nov. 1842.
40. Hoe and Roebuck, *The Taking of Hong Kong*, pp.183, 202.

7   The Yangzi Campaign: Pottinger 1841–42

1. Bridgman correspondence, quoted in Fay, *The Opium War*, p.312.
2. Palmerston to Sir H. Pottinger 31 May 1841 printed in Morse, *The Period of Conflict*, Appendix K.
3. Auckland's letter to Pottinger, dated 24 June 1841, quoted in George Pottinger, *Sir Henry Pottinger, First Governor of Hong Kong* (Stroud, Glos: Sutton Publishing, 1997), p.72 and footnote.
4. *Chinese Repository*, July 1841, p.404.
5. He wrote as much to Auckland on 1 July. Rait, *The Life and Campaigns of Hugh, First Viscount Gough*, p.204.
6. The 55th had a chequered history. They did well enough in China and were reckoned to be one of the best-disciplined regiments of the army in the Crimea in the mid-1850s, though the regimental surgeon reported that venereal disease was a major problem. Yet by 1857 they were one of 64 Bengal regiments to join the Indian Mutiny. Their British colonel was so horrified that he shot himself.
7. *Chinese Repository*, Oct. 1841.
8. Armine S.H. Mountain, *Memoirs and Letters* (London, 1857), pp.199, 204.
9. Rait, *The Life and Campaigns of Hugh, First Viscount Gough*, pp.236–8.
10. Ibid., pp.246–7.
11. Waley, *The Opium War Through Chinese Eyes*, p.159 et seq.
12. Ouchterlony, *The Chinese War*, p.209.
13. *The Times*, 23 Nov. 1842.
14. Ouchterlony, *The Chinese War*, p.220.
15. Waley, *The Opium War Through Chinese Eyes*, p.165.
16. John Keegan, in *The Face of Battle* (London: J. Cape, 1976), quotes a US study showing that in the Second World War, and with good troops under pressure, only some 25 per cent would actually fire their weapons.
17. For example, Jocelyn, *Six Months with the Chinese Expedition*, pp.140–1.
18. An extensive account based on Pei can be found in Waley, *The Opium War Through Chinese Eyes*, pp.159 et seq.
19. Henry Knollys (ed.) *Incidents in the China War of 1860* (compiled from the private journals of General Sir Hope Grant) (Edinburgh: William Blackwood and Sons, 1865), p.99–100n.
20. Fay, *The Opium War*, p.325.
21. Ibid., p.331.
22. *Chinese Repository*, June 1842; Ouchterlony, *The Chinese War*.
23. Kipling, 'The Irish Guards', 1915. Lt-Colonel Tomlinson's face can still be seen on the marble memorial plaque put up for him and the other Royal Irish casualties on the wall of St Patrick's Cathedral, Dublin.
24. Letter of 8 May 1842, quoted in Fay, *The Opium War*, p.348.

25. Ouchterlony, *The Chinese War*, p.329.
26. Cited in Holt, *The Opium Wars in China*, p.145.
27. Note of 1 July 1842 from Pottinger to Gough, quoted in Pottinger, *Sir Henry Pottinger*, p.98 and footnote 12.
28. Rait, *The Life and Campaigns of Hugh, First Viscount Gough*, p.275.
29. Jack Beeching, *The Chinese Opium Wars*, (London: Hutchinson, 1975), p.152.
30. Morse, *The Period of Conflict*, pp.661–2.
31. Quoted in Hansard, House of Commons, 4 April 1843, cols 419–20.
32. Captain Granville G. Loch, *The Closing Events of the Campaign in China* (London: John Murray, 1843), pp.172–3.
33. Mountain, *Memoirs and Letters*, p.211.
34. Her note to Sir Robert Peel 26 Dec. 1842, in Letters, vol.1, p.446.
35. Letter of 4 Jan. 1843 from Lord Aberdeen to Sir Henry Pottinger: Morse, *The Period of Conflict*, Appendix O.

8 Almost a Settlement

1. Treaty Article II.
2. *Chinese Repository*, Oct. 1842.
3. Later, when it came to include Japan and Thailand, it changed its name to Far Eastern Service.
4. Quoted in Hansard, House of Commons, 4 April 1843, cols 418–19.
5. *Chinese Repository*, May 1843.
6. See Pottinger's proclamation of 1 Aug. 1843, *Chinese Repository*, Aug. 1843.
7. Jonathan D. Spence, *The Search for Modern China* (New York: Norton, 1990), pp.161–2.
8. Treaty of Wangxia, 1844, Article 32.
9. John K. Fairbank, *Trade and Diplomacy on the China Coast. The opening of the treaty ports, 1842–1854* (Cambridge, MA: Harvard University Press, 1953) vol.1, pp.137, 141.
10. Webster letter to Cushing of 8 May 1843, *The Letters of Daniel Webster*, ed. C.H. Van Tyne (New York: McClure, Phillips and Co., 1902); *Chinese Repository*, Aug. 1845.
11. Earl Swisher (ed.), *China's Management of the American Barbarians* (New Haven: Yale University Press, 1953), p.13.
12. *Chinese Repository*, Aug. 1845.
13. *Chinese Repository*, Sept. 1845; Morse, *The Period of Conflict*, p.325n29.
14. Cushing to Qiying, 2 June 1844, *Chinese Repository*, Sept. 1845.
15. Cushing letter of 22 June to Qiying, *Chinese Repository*, Oct. 1845.
16. Qiying to Cushing, 28 June 1844, *Chinese Repository*, Oct. 1847.
17. *Chinese Repository*, Nov. 1845.
18. Article 21.
19. Article 34.
20. Foster, *American Diplomacy in the Orient*, p.87.
21. Treaty of Whampoa, Article 27.
22. *Chinese Repository* 1842, pp.274–89; also Edgar Holt, *The Opium Wars in China*, pp.101–2.
23. *The Times*, 3 March 1857, p.9 (leader).

9   Clashes Continue: Britain and China after the War

1. Quoted in Asa Briggs, *Victorian People* (rev. edn) (Chicago: University of Chicago Press, 1970), Ch.V. It is a sentiment that might well have been echoed by Britain's Presbyterian Chancellor of the Exchequer, Gordon Brown, a century and a half later.
2. Quoted in Evan Luard, *Britain and China* (London: Chatto and Windus, 1962), p.11.
3. Donald Southgate, *The Most English Minister: The Politics and Policies of Palmerston*, p.146.
4. *Edinburgh Review*, Jan. 1860, pp.103–4.
5. Palmerston's letter of 3 Oct. 1846 to the Superintendent, Sir J.F. Davis, quoted in Morse, *The Period of Conflict*, p.385.
6. Palmerston, private letter of 9 Jan. 1847 to Davis, extracts in Kenneth Bourne, *The Foreign Policy of Victorian England 1830–1902* (Oxford: Clarendon Press, 1970), p.274; also Bulwer, *The Life of Henry John Temple, Viscount Palmerston*, vol.III, pp.376–8.
7. Palmerston note to Bonham in Hong Kong, 18 Aug. 1849, quoted in Costin, *Great Britain and China 1833–1860*, p.142.
8. Palmerston note of 29 Sept. 1850 quoted in Costin, *Great Britain and China 1833–1860*, pp.149–50.
9. Polachek, *The Inner Opium War*, p.52.
10. In 1853, when Shanghai was occupied by rebels, the Imperial Customs House shut down. The British consul, Alcock, ordered traders to pay to him, in cash or bills, the tariff dues owed to the Chinese. The imperial authorities then accepted that customs duties might be collected by foreigners.
11. Nathan A. Pelcovits, *Old China Hands and the Foreign Office* (New York: American Institute of Pacific Relations, 1948), pp.15–17.
12. Sir Clement Jones, *Chief Officer in China 1840–1853* (Liverpool: Charles Birchall and Sons, 1955), pp.70–1.
13. Letter of 10 April 1843 to Admiral Parker cited in Morse, *The Period of Conflict*, p.545n22.
14. Jones, *Chief Officer in China*, p.63.
15. His dispatch of 13 Feb. 1854 is printed in Morse, *The Period of Conflict*, Appendix Q, pp.670–3.
16. Clarendon to Elgin 20 April 1857.
17. Morse, *The Period of Conflict*, p.544.
18. Spence, The Search for Modern China, p.174; Morse, *The Period of Conflict*, p.445.
19. Frances Wood, *No Dogs and Not Many Chinese: Treaty Port Life in China 1843–1943* (London: John Murray, 1998), p.276.
20. Quoted in Costin, *Great Britain and China 1833–1860*, p.181.
21. J.W. Wong, *Deadly Dreams: Opium, Imperialism and the Arrow War (1856–1860) in China* (Cambridge: Cambridge University Press, 1998), pp.480–1.
22. A Western schooner with Chinese rigging.
23. Foster, *American Diplomacy in the Orient*, p.225.
24. See *The Times*, 2 Jan. 1857, pp.5–7. The paper included the texts of dispatches from Admiral Seymour, the Superintendent of Trade at Hong Kong, Sir John Bowring and the Consul at Canton, Harry Parkes.

25. *The Times*, 4 Feb. 1857, p.9.
26. Specifically, a treaty of 8 Oct. 1843 and a further agreement of 4 April 1846.
27. *The Times*, 8 Jan. 1857, p.8.
28. *The Globe*, 2 and 3 Jan. 1857.
29. Ibid., 13 Jan. 1857.
30. Ibid., 3 Feb. 1857.
31. *The Times*, 20 Feb. 1857, p.3.
32. John Bright and James E. Thorold Roberts, *Speeches on Questions of Public Policy by Richard Cobden M.P.*, 2 vols (London: Macmillan, 1870), vol. 1 pp.362–3; and Bourne, *The Foreign Policy of Victorian England*, document 38, pp.269–70.
33. J.A. Hobson, *Richard Cobden: The International Man* (London: Fisher Unwin, 1919), p.246.
34. Lewis diary 26 Feb.–7 May 1857, Bourne Papers, box 24.
35. Brian Connell, *Regina v Palmerston: The Correspondence between Queen Victoria and her Foreign and Prime Minister 1837–1865* (London: Evans Brothers, 1962), p.212.
36. Philip Guedalla, *Palmerston* (London: Ernest Benn, 1926), pp.391–2.
37. See a Bombay dispatch of 17 Dec. 1856 in *The Times* of 17 Jan. 1857.
38. Quoted in Masataka Banno, *China and the West 1858–1861* (Cambridge, MA: Harvard University Press), 1964, p.10.
39. Quoted in D.C.M. Platt, 'The Imperialism of Free Trade: Some Reservations', *Economic History Review*, 2nd series vol.XXI, 1968, p.301.
40. Quoted in Graham, *China Station*, pp.336–48.
41. Quoted in Costin, *Great Britain and China 1833–1860*, pp.279–80.
42. When the British, puzzled, cited the powers given to the Chinese negotiators at the time of the Treaty of Nanjing, the Chinese simply asserted that Qiying had forged his earlier credentials.
43. Quoted in Foster, *American Diplomacy in the Orient*, p.235.
44. Several junior officers in these actions were to have highly distinguished careers. One of them was John ('Jackie') Fisher, one of the later Victorian Navy's most remarkable and original minds and a critical figure in preparing the Navy for the First World War.
45. Quoted in Polachek, *The Inner Opium War*, p.172.
46. The English soldiers promptly made that into 'Sam Collinson'.
47. Russell letter to Bruce of 10.10.59, cited in Morse, *The Period of Conflict*, p.585.
48. Comments from Baron Gros, in Henri Cordier, *L'Expedition de Chine 1857–58* (Paris: F. Alcan, 1905), p.406n1.
49. Hurd, Douglas, *The Arrow War: An Anglo-Chinese Confusion 1856–60* (London: Collins, 1967), p.228.
50. G.J. Wolseley, *Narrative of the War with China in 1860* (London: Longman, Green, 1862), p.227.
51. Letter of 25 Nov. 1861 to Captain Butler, Guernsey, quoted in Alain Peyrefitte, *The Collision of Two Civilizations* (London: Harvill, 1993), p.530.
52. Letters and Journals of James, Eighth Earl of Elgin, ed. T. Walrond (London: John Murray, 1872), pp.213, 232.
53. Field Marshal Viscount Wolseley, *The Story of a Soldier's Life*, 2 vols (London: Archibald Constable, 1903), vol.2, p.2.
54. Hurd, *The Arrow War*, p.241.

10 China: Resentment Congeals into Nationalism

1. Some of this involved the question whether it was better to have a market economy or a state-owned and organized one; which was a replay, not for the first or last time, of disputes between legalists and Confucians going back to the sophisticated debates on salt and iron conducted under the Emperor Wu Di in 87 BC.
2. Teng and Fairbank, *China's Response to the West*, p.48.
3. Hart became Inspector General of the Service in 1863, at the age of 28, and held the post until 1908. Becoming adept at dealing with the Chinese bureaucracy, he also became a valued adviser to the Chinese government. Lord Clarendon, in line with the usual British refusal to accept direct responsibilities, had long before ruled that the foreign inspectors of the Service were clearly Chinese employees, for whom Beijing was entirely responsible.
4. Quoted in Morse, *The Period of Conflict*, vol.2, p.335.
5. Gray, *Rebellions and Revolutions*, p.80.
6. Jürgen Osterhammel, 'Britain and China 1842–1914', in A. Porter and A. Low (eds), *The Oxford History of the British Empire*, vol.III, Ch.8, p.149.
7. Even the name 'Japan' appears to come from 'Jipang', given to Japan by Marco Polo and stemming, in turn, from the South China pronunciation of the characters for 'Nihon' or Nippon.
8. E.W. Edwards, *British Diplomacy and Finance in China 1895–1914* (Oxford: Oxford University Press, 1987), p.158.
9. Niccolo Machiavelli finished the famous work of that name, written for the rulers of Florence, in 1514.
10. Garnet Wolseley, *Narrative of the War with China in 1860*, pp.243–4.
11. Teng and Fairbank, *China's Response to the West*, pp.47–9.
12. Paul A. Varg, *Missionaries, Chinese and Diplomats* (Princeton, NJ: Princeton University Press, 1958), p.324.
13. For instance, the Sino-American immigration treaty of 1880 – which came into force in 1887 – forbade each side's citizens to import opium into the other's country.
14. Domestic production may have been something over 100,000 piculs, one picul being around $133\frac{1}{3}$ English pounds. See Morse, *Trade and Administration of the Chinese Empire*, Ch.9.
15. On widespread opium cultivation in China, see G.E. Morrison, *An Australian in China* (London: H. Cox, 1895). Also Kathleen Lodwick, *Crusaders against Opium: Protestant Missionaries in China 1874–1917* (Lexington: University Press of Kentucky, 1996), p.6.
16. 'Opium and the Republic', *North China Daily News*, 11 May 1912.
17. W.G. Graham Apsland, 'China and Opium', *East and West*, Oct. 1924.
18. Richard Davenport-Hines, *The Pursuit of Oblivion: A Global History of Narcotics 1500–2000* (London: Weidenfeld and Nicolson, 2001), pp.211, 230.
19. Harrison E. Salisbury, *The Long March: The Untold Story* (New York/ Cambridge: Harper and Row, 1985), pp.107, 181, 305.
20. Cheng Yung-fa, 'The Blooming Poppy', in Tony Saich and Hans van den Ven (eds), *New Perspectives on the Chinese Communist Revolution* (Armonk, NY/ London: M.E. Sharpe, 1995), Ch.10.

21. See Frances Cairncross, 'A Survey of Illegal Drugs', *Economist* 28 July 2001, esp. p.4.

11 Britain: Evangelicals, Humanitarians and Guilt

1. Oliver MacDonagh, 'The Anti-Imperialism of Free Trade', *Economic History Review*, 2nd series, vol.XIV no.3, 1961–62, pp.489–501.
2. Andrew Porter, 'Trusteeship, Anti-Slavery and Humanitarianism', in A. Porter and A. Low (eds), *The Oxford History of the British Empire*, vol.III, Ch.10, p.200.
3. As well as academic reassessments which, over time, greatly expanded the concept of 'empire' and made it more amorphous. See the famous article by John Gallagher and Ronald Robinson, 'The Imperialism of Free Trade', *Economic History Review*, 1953, pp. 1–15.
4. Dona Torr (ed.), *Marx on China 1853–1860* (London: Lawrence and Wishart, 1968).
5. J.A. Hobson, *Imperialism: A Study*, p.224. See also V.I. Lenin, *Imperialism, The Highest State of Capitalism*.
6. Robin Renwick, *Fighting with Allies* (London: Macmillan, 1996), p.1.
7. *The Letters of Charles Dickens*, vol.12, 1868–1870, ed. Graham Storey (Oxford: Clarendon Press, 2001).
8. Davenport-Hines, *The Pursuit of Oblivion*, p.87.
9. Porter, *The Greatest Benefit to Mankind*.
10. Ibid., p.663.
11. Hansard, House of Lords, April 1843, col.363.
12. Fairbank, *The Creation of the Treaty System*, p.223.
13. See verbatim report in *The Times*, 4 March 1857, p.9.
14. The debate can be found in Hansard, House of Commons, 10 May 1870, cols 480–523.
15. Circulation of *The Times* rose from some 2500–3000 in 1801 to 7000 in 1820 and to around 60,000 by the late 1850s. By the early 1850s the *Anglican Record* boasted some 4000 per issue.
16. Andrew Porter, 'Religion, Missionary Enthusiasm and Empire', in A. Porter and A. Lowe (eds), *The Oxford History of the British Empire*, vol.III, Ch.11, pp.244–5.
17. In 1870 the Duke of Somerset asked in the House of Lords 'why British missionaries should travel to China to convert the Chinese in the middle of their country … for every missionary almost requires a gunboat.' Cited in Paul A. Cohen, *China and Christianity, The Missionary Movement and the Growth of Chinese Antiforeignism 1860–1870* (Cambridge, MA: Harvard University Press, 1963), p.194.
18. See, for instance, a pamphlet entitled 'No Opium! Or Commerce and Christianity Working Together for good in China', by 'a Minister and a Layman' and reviewed in *Gentleman's Magazine* March 1835, pp.265–6.
19. 'An Eye-Witness', *The Opium Trade in China: in four letters reprinted from the Leeds Mercury* (Leeds: Edward Baines and Sons, 1858).
20. V. Berridge and G. Edwards, *Opium and the People* (London: Allen Lane, 1981), pp.173–94.

21. Fox, 'Notes on China and the Chinese (Part I)', *The Friends' Quarterly Examiner*, 1883, p.502.
22. Ibid., Part II, 1884, pp.118–39.
23. The Commission's Final Report 6, p.141.
24. The title of his book, published in London by Elliot Stock.
25. Convocation of Canterbury, Record of Proceedings, 5 Feb. 1907, pp.48–52.
26. For instance, Luard, *Britain and China*, p.28.
27. Beecher, *A Treatise on Domestic Economy*, quoted in Hunter, *The Gospel of Gentility*, p.1.
28. See the remarks of even so sophisticated a scholar as Polachek on Britain's use of Indian soldiers, *The Inner Opium War*, p.201.
29. Hunter, *The Gospel of Gentility*, p.1.
30. Theodore Roosevelt, The Awakening of China, *The Outlook*, issue of 28 Nov. 1908, p.666, quoted in Varg, *Missionaries, Chinese and Diplomats*, p.78.
31. Good judges have said that Mao's calligraphy – and he was a devoted calligrapher – was redolent of a sense of history and tradition.
32. 'On Protracted War', May 1938, in *Selected Works of Mao Tse-tung*, vol.II (Peking: Foreign Languages Press, 1965), pp.113–94. The quotation is on p.125.
33. For example Beverley Hooper, *China Stands Up* (London: Allen and Unwin, 1986).
34. Li Zhisui, *The Private Life of Chairman Mao* (New York: Random House, 1994), p.567.

Select Bibliography

Newspapers, journals, parliamentary and state papers

Morning Post
The Times
Blackwood's Edinburgh Magazine, esp. vol.XLVII January–June
Chinese Repository, May 1832–December 1851, ed. E.C. Bridgman and S.W. Williams, 20 vols, Canton 1833–51
Edinburgh Review
Gentleman's Magazine
Parliamentary reports, Hansard
Quarterly Review, esp. vol.65, p.537 'Chinese Affairs'
State Papers, British and Foreign, London

Books

Airlie, Mabell, Countess of, *In Whig Society 1775–1818: compiled from the hitherto unpublished correspondence of Elizabeth, Viscountess Melbourne, and Emily Lamb, Countess Cowper, afterwards Viscountess Palmerston.* London/New York, Hodder and Stoughton, 1921.

Alexander, J.G., *Has the Opium Trade been Forced on China?* London, Society for the Suppression of the Opium Traffic, 1894.

Anderson, Lindsay, *A Cruise in an Opium Clipper* (1891). London, George Allen and Unwin, 1935.

Anonymous, Confessions of a Young Lady Laudanum-drinker, *Journal of Mental Sciences*, January 1889.

Anonymous, *Points and Pickings of Information about China and the Chinese.* London, Grant and Griffith, 1844.

Anonymous, *Review of the Management of our affairs in China, since the opening of the trade in 1834; with an analysis of the Government despatches from the assumption of office by Captain Elliot on the 14th Of December, 1836, to the 22nd March 1839.* London, Smith Elder and Co., 1840.

Ashley Evelyn, *The Life of Henry John Temple, Viscount Palmerston 1846–1865. With Selections from his Speeches and Correspondence*, 2 vols. London, R. Bentley and Son, 1876.

Aspinall, A., *Politics and the Press 1780–1850.* London, Home and Van Thal, 1949.

Bachmann, Chistian and Coppel, Anne, *Le dragon domestique: Deux siècles de relations étranges entre l'Occident et la drogue.* Paris, Albin Michel, 1989.

Baines, Edward, *History of the Cotton Manufacture in Great Britain.* London, H. Fisher, R. Fisher and P. Jackson, 1835.

Banno, Masatake, *China and the West 1858–1861*, Cambridge, MA, Harvard University Press, 1964.

Barbosa, Duarte, *A Description of the Coasts of East Africa and Malabar in the Beginning of the Sixteenth Century* (trans. Henry E.J. Stanley). London, Hakluyt Society, 1866.

Baudelaire, Charles, *Artificial Paradise* (trans. Ellen Fox). New York, Herder and Herder, 1971 (orig. *Les Paradis artificiels*, 1860).

Beattie, Hilary J., Protestant Missions and Opium in China 1858–1895, in *Papers on China* 22A (1969) pp.104–33.

Beeching Jack, *The Chinese Opium Wars*. London, Hutchinson and New York, Harcourt Brace Jovanovich, 1975.

Bell, Herbert C., *Lord Palmerston*, 2 vols. London, Longmans Green, 1936.

Bentham, Jeremy, *The Works of Jeremy Bentham* (published under the superintendence of his executor John Bowring) Edinburgh W. Tait, London, Simpkin Marshall, 1843 (esp. vol.IV).

Bernard, W.D., *Narrative of the Voyages and the Services of the Nemesis from 1840 to 1843* (from the notes of Commander W.H. Hall, RN), 2 vols. London, Henry Coulburn, 1844.

Berridge, Virginia and G. Edwards, *Opium and the People* (3rd rev. edn). London, Free Association Books, 1999.

Bingham, J. Elliot, *Narrative of the Expedition to China from the Commencement of the War to the Present Period*, 2 vols. London, Henry Coulburn, 1842.

Black, Jeremy, *The English Press, 1621–1861*. London, Sutton Publishing, 2001.

Booth, Martin, *Opium: A History*. London, Simon and Schuster, 1996.

Bourne, K., *The Foreign Policy of Victorian England 1830–1902*. Oxford, Clarendon Press, 1970.

Bourne, Kenneth, *Palmerston; the Early Years 1784–1841*. London, Allen Lane, 1982.

'Bourne Papers': various papers left by Prof. Kenneth Bourne, collection in the Library of the London School of Economics.

Bowring, J., *Autobiographical Recollections of Sir J. Bowring*. London, H.S. King and Co., 1877.

Bright, John and James E. Thorold Roberts (eds), *Speeches on Questions of Public Policy by Richard Cobden M.P.*, 2 vols. London, Macmillan, 1970.

Broughton, Baron (J.C.Hobhouse) *Recollections of a Long Life* (ed. Lady Dorchester) (6 vols). London, J. Murray, 1910.

Brown, Lucy, *Victorian News and Newspapers*. Oxford, Clarendon Press, 1985.

Brownlow, Kevin, *Behind the Mask of Innocence*. New York, Alfred A. Knopf, 1990.

Buell, R.L., *The International Opium Conferences*. Boston, World Peace Foundation, 1925.

Bull, Hedley and Adam Watson (eds), *The Expansion of International Society*. Oxford, Clarendon Press, 1985.

Bulwer, Sir Henry Lytton, *The Life of Henry John Temple, Viscount Palmerston: with Selections from his Diaries and Correspondence*, 3 vols. London, Richard Bentley, 1870.

Cady, J.F., *The Roots of French Imperialism in Eastern Asia*. Ithaca, NY, Cornell University Press, 1954.

Cambridge History of British Foreign Policy (ed. Sir A.W. Ward and G.P. Gooch), 3 vols. Cambridge, Cambridge University Press, 1922–23.

Cambridge History of China (gen. eds Denis Twitchett and John K. Fairbank), vol.10 Pt I, Late Ch'ing, 1800–1911 (ed. John K. Fairbank). Cambridge, Cambridge University Press, 1978, esp.

Ch.2: Joseph Fletcher, 'Ch'ing Inner Asia'
Ch.4: Frederic Wakeman Jr, 'The Canton Trade and the Opium War'
Ch.5: John K. Fairbank, 'The Creation of the Treaty System'
Ch.7: Joseph Fletcher, 'Sino-Russian Relations 1800–1862'
Ch.10: Ting-Yee Kuo and Kwang-Ching Liu, 'Self-strengthening: The Pursuit of Western Technology.'
Ch.11: Paul A. Cohen, 'Christian Missions and their Impact to 1900'
Carnwath, Tom and Ian Smith, *Heroin Century*. London, Routledge, 2002.
Cecil A, *Queen Victoria and her Prime Ministers*. London, Eyre and Spottiswoode, 1952.
Chang Hsin-Pao, *Commissioner Lin and the Opium War*. Cambridge, MA, Harvard University Press, 1964.
Cheng Pei-kai and Michal Lestz (eds) with Jonathan D. Spence, *The Search for Modern China: A Documentary Collection*. New York, Norton, 1999, pp.123–7.
Cheng Yung-fa, 'The Blooming Poppy' in Tony Saich and Hans van de Ven (eds), *New Perspectives on the Chinese Communist Revolutions: Conference Papers*.
Cheong, W.E., *Mandarins and Merchants: Jardine Matheson and Co, a China Agency of the Early Nineteenth Century*. London, Curzon Press, 1979.
Christian Union for the Severance of the British Empire with the Opium Traffic, *Our National Sin Against the Government and People of China*. London, Morgan and Scott, 1906.
Cleife, H.H.T., *England's Greatest National Sin: Being Selections and Reflections on our Asiatic Opium Policy and Traffic*. London, Elliot Stock, 1892.
Clyde, Paul H. and Burton Floyd Beers, *The Far East: A History of Western Impacts and Eastern Responses 1830–1973* (6th edn). Englewood Cliffs, New Jersey, Prentice-Hall, 1975.
Cohen, Paul A., *China and Christianity: The Missionary Movement and the Growth of Chinese Antiforeignism 1860–1870*. Cambridge, MA, Harvard University Press, 1963.
Cohen, Warren I., *America's Response to China; an Interpretative History of Sino-American Relations*. New York, John Wiley and Sons, 1971.
Collis, Maurice, *Foreign Mud*. London, Faber and Faber, 1946.
Committee on the Modern History of China, *The Opium War*. Peking, Foreign Language Press, 1979.
Connell, Brian, *Regina v Palmerston; The Correspondence Between Queen Victoria and her Foreign and Prime Minister 1837–1865*. London, Evans Brothers, 1962.
Cooke G.W., *China: Being the 'Times' Special Correspondence from China in the Years 1857–58*. London, G. Routledge and Co., 1858.
Cordier, Henri, *L'Expedition de Chine 1857–58*. Paris, F. Alcan, 1905.
Costin, W.C., *Great Britain and China 1833–1860*. Oxford, Oxford University Press, 1937.
Courtwright, David T., *Dark Paradise; Opiate Addiction in America before 1940*. Cambridge, MA, Harvard University Press, 1982.
Cranmer-Byng, J.L. (ed.), *An Embasy to China: Lord Macartney's Journal 1793–94*. London, Routledge, 2000.
Cunynghame, Arthur, *An ADC's Recollections of Service in China, a Residence in Hong Kong, and Visits to Other Islands in the Chinese Seas*. London, Saunders and Otley, 1844.

Davenport-Hines, Richard, *The Pursuit of Oblivion: a Global History of Narcotics 1500–2000*. London, Weidenfeld and Nicolson, 2001.

Davis, Sir John Francis, *China: during the War and since the Peace*, 2 vols. London, Longmans, 1852.

Dawson, Raymond, *The Chinese Chameleon*. Oxford, Oxford University Press, 1967.

Dickens, Charles, *The Letters of Charles Dickens*, vol.12 1868–1870 (ed. Madeline House, Graham Storey and Kathleen Tillotson). Oxford, Clarendon Press, 2001.

Driault, Éduard, *La question d'Extrême-Orient*. Paris, 1908.

Dukes, Edwin Joshua, *Everyday Life in China*. London, Religious Tract Society, 1885.

Eames, James B., *The English in China*. London, Pitman, 1909.

Edkins, J., *Opium: Historical Note, or the Poppy in China*. Shanghai American Presbyterian Mission Press, 1898.

Edwards, E.W., *British Diplomacy and Finance in China 1895–1914*. Oxford, Clarendon Press, 1987.

Edwards, Ruth Dudley, *The Pursuit of Reason: The Economist 1843–1993*. London, H. Hamilton, 1993.

Elgin, *Letters and Journals of James, Eighth Earl of Elgin* (ed. T. Walrond). London, John Murray, 1872.

Ellenborough, Edward (First Earl of), *India under Lord Ellenborough March 1842–June 1844: A selection from the hitherto unpublished papers and secret despatches of Edward, Earl of Ellenborough*. London, John Murray, 1926.

Fairbank, John K., *Trade and Diplomacy on the China Coast. The opening of the treaty ports, 1842–1854*, 2 vols. Cambridge, MA, Harvard University Press, 1953; reprinted Stanford University Press, 1969.

Fairbank, John K. (ed.), *The Chinese World Order: Traditional China's Foreign Relations*. Cambridge, MA, Harvard University Press, 1968.

Fay, Peter Ward, *The Opium War 1840–1842. Barbarians in the celestial empire in the early part of the nineteenth century and the war by which they forced her gates ajar*. Chapel Hill, NC, University of North Carolina Press, 1975.

'Field Officer', *The Last Year in China to the Peace of Nanking*. London, Longman, Brown, Green and Longmans, 1843.

Fisher, Arthur A'Court, *Personal Narrative of Three Years' Service in China*. London, Bentley, 1863.

Forbes, F.E., *Five Years in China: From 1842 to 1847*. London, Richard Bentley, 1848

Fortescue, J.W., *History of the British Army*, vol.12: 1839–1852. London, Macmillan, 1927.

Fortune Robert, *Three Years' Wanderings in the Northern Provinces of China* (2nd edn). London, John Murray, 1847.

Foster, John W., *American Diplomacy in the Orient*. Boston, MA, Houghton Mifflin, 1903; reprinted New York, Da Capo Press, 1970.

Gallagher, John and Robinson, Ronald, The Imperialism of Free Trade, *Economic History Review*, 2nd series vol.V, 1953, pp.1–15.

Garnet, J., *China and the Christian Impact*. Cambridge, Cambridge University Press, 1985.

Gautier, Théophile, The Opium Pipe, in *Hashish, Wine, Opium* (trans. Maurice Stang). London, Calder and Boyars, 1972 (original title *La Pipe d'Opium*, 1838).

Goldsmith, Margaret, *The Trail of Opium: The Eleventh Plague*. London, Robert Hale, 1939.

Gong, Gerritt, China's Entry into International Society, in Hedley Bull and Adam Watson, *The Expansion of International Society*.

Gough, General Sir Hugh, *Old Memories*. Edinburgh/London, W. Blackwood and Sons, 1897.

Graham, Gerald S., *The China Station: War and Diplomacy 1830–1860*. Oxford, Clarendon Press, 1978.

Grant, Hope and Henry Knollys, *Incidents in the China War of 1860*. Edinburgh, W. Blackwood, 1875.

Gray, Jack, *Rebellions and Revolutions: China from the 1800s to the 1980s*. Oxford, Oxford University Press, 1990.

Greenberg, Michael, *British Trade and the Opening of China 1800–1842*, New York, Monthly Review Press, 1979.

Greville, Charles C.F., *The Greville Memoirs*, 8 vols. London, Longmans Green, 1874–88.

Grey, Henry George, 3rd Earl, *The Colonial Policy of Lord John Russell's Administration*, 2 vols. London, 1853.

Guedalla, Philip, *Palmerston*. London, Ernest Benn, 1926.

Harding, G., *Opiate Addiction, Morality and Medicine: From Moral Illness to Pathological Disease*. London, Macmillan, 1988.

Hayter, Alethea, *Opium and the Romantic Imagination*. London, Faber and Faber, 1968.

Hevia, James, *Cherishing Men from Afar: Qing Guest Ritual and the Macartney Embassy of 1793*. Durham, NC, and London, Duke University Press, 1995.

Hobson, J.A., *Imperialism: A Study*. London, J. Nisbet, 1902.

Hobson, J.A., *Richard Cobden: The International Man*. London, Fisher Unwin, 1919.

Hoe, Susanna and Derek Roebuck, *The Taking of Hong Kong; Charles and Clara Elliot in China Waters*. Richmond, Surrey, Curzon Press, 1999.

Holt, Edgar, *The Opium Wars in China*. London, Putnam, 1964.

Hooper, Beverley, *China Stands Up*. London, Allen and Unwin, 1986.

Hsu, I.C.Y., *The Rise of Modern China* (5th edn). New York, Oxford University Press, 1995.

Huc, M., *The Chinese Empire: A Sequel to 'Recollections of a journey through Tartary and Thibet'*. London, Longman, Brown, Green, Longmans and Roberts, 1859.

Hunter, Jane, *The Gospel of Gentility*. New Haven, Yale University Press, 1984.

Hurd, Douglas, *The Arrow War: An Anglo-Chinese Confusion 1856–60*. London, Collins, 1967.

Jen Yu-wen, *The Taiping Revolutionary Movement*. New Haven, Yale University Press, 1973.

Jocelyn, Lord, *Six Months with the Chinese Expedition*. London, John Murray, 1841.

Jones, Sir Clement, *Chief Officer in China 1840–1853*. Liverpool, Charles Birchall and Sons, 1955.

Kane, Harry, *Opium-Smoking in America and China*. New York, G.P. Putnam, 1882.

Keegan, John, *The Face of Battle*. London, Jonathan Cape, 1976.

Knollys, Henry (ed.), *Incidents in the China War of 1860* (compiled from the private journals of General Sir Hope Grant). Edinburgh, William Blackwood and Sons, 1865.

Kuo, Pin-chia, *A Critical Study of the First Anglo-Chinese War, with Documents*. Shanghai, Commercial Press, 1935.

La Motte, Ellen N., *The Opium Monopoly*. New York, Macmillan, 1920.

Lane-Poole, Stanley, *The Life of Sir Harry Parkes*. London, Macmillan, 1894.

Lederer, I.J. (ed.), *Russian Foreign Policy*. New Haven, CT, Yale University Press, 1962.

Lenin, V.I., Imperialism, *The Highest State of Capitalism*. Moscow, Foreign Languages Publishing House, n.d.

Leavenworth, Charles, S., *The Arrow War with China*. London, Sampson Low, 1901.

Levenson, J.R., *Confucian China and its Modern Fate*, 3 vols. London, Routledge and Kegan Paul, 1958–65.

Li Zhisui, *The Private Life of Chairman Mao*. New York, Random House, 1994.

Liedekerke, Arnould de, *La Belle époque de l'opium*. Paris, Aux éditions de la difference, 1984.

Lindsay, H. Hamilton, *Letter to the Rt Hon. Viscount Palmerston on British Relations with China*. London, Saunders and Otley, 1836.

Lindsay, H. Hamilton, *Remarks on Occurrences in China since the Opium Seizure in March 1839, by a Resident in China*. London, Sherwood, Gilbert and Piper, 1840.

Lindsay, H. Hamilton, *Is the War with China a Just One?* London, James Ridgway, 1840.

List, Friedrich, *The National System of Political Economy* (trans. Sampson S. Lloyd), Longmans Green 1885 (from the original *Das Nationale System der Politischen Oekonomie*, Stuttgart, 1841).

Loch, Captain Granville G., *The Closing Events of the Campaign in China*. London, John Murray, 1843.

Loch, Henry Brougham, *Personal Narrative of Occurrences during Lord Elgin's Second Embassy to China in 1860*. London, John Murray, 1900.

Lodwick, Kathleen, *Crusaders Against Opium: Protestant Missionaries in China 1874–1917*. Lexington, University Press of Kentucky, 1996.

Lowe, C.J., *The Reluctant Imperialists: British Foreign Policy 1878–1902*, 2 vols. London, Routledge and Kegan Paul, 1967.

Lowe, Peter, *Britain in the Far East: A Survey from 1819 to the Present*. London, Longman, 1981.

Luard, Evan, *Britain and China*. London, Chatto and Windus, 1962.

Lubbock, Basil, *The China Clippers*. London, Brown, Son and Ferguson, 1914.

Lumby, E.W.R., Lord Elgin and the Burning of the Summer Palace, *History Today*, vol.10, January–December 1960, pp.479–87.

Lynn, Martin, British Policy, Trade, and Informal Empire in the Mid-Nineteenth Century, in Andrew Porter and Alaine Lowe (eds), *The Oxford History of the British Empire*, vol.III, Ch.6.

McCarthy, Justin, *A History of Our Own Times*, vol.1. London, Chatto and Windus, 1881.

MacDonagh, Oliver, The Anti-imperialism of Free Trade, *Economic History Review* 2nd series vol.XIV, 1961–62, no.3, pp.489–501.

Mackenzie, Keith Stewart, *Narrative of the Second Campaign in China*. London, Richard Bentley, 1842.

McPherson, Surgeon, *Two Years in China: Narrative of the China Expedition 1840–1842*. London, 1842.

Marsh, Peter (ed.), *The Conscience of the Victorian State*. New York, Syracuse, 1979.

Martin, W.A.P., *The Wakening of China*. London, Hodder and Stoughton, 1907.

Matheson, Sir James, *The Present Position and Prospects of the British Trade with China*. London, Smith Elder, 1836.

Merlin, Mark David, *On the Trail of the Ancient Opium Poppy*. Rutherford, NJ, Farleigh Dickinson University Press, 1984.

Morrison, Eliza, *Memoirs of the Life and Labours of Robert Morrison DD*, 2 vols. London, Longman, Orme, Brown, Green and Longmans, 1839.

Morrison, G.E., *An Australian in China*. London, H. Cox, 1895.

Morley, John, *Life of Gladstone*, 3 vols. London, Macmillan, 1903.

Morse, Hosea Ballou, *Trade and Administration of the Chinese Empires*. London, Longmans, Green, 1913.

Morse, Hosea Ballou, *The International Relations of the Chinese Empire*, 3 vols, vol.1, *The Period of Conflict 1834–1860*. London, Longmans Green and Co., 1910–18; Taipei reprint, Book World, 1963.

Morse, H.B. and Harley F. McNair, *Far Eastern International Relations*. Boston, Houghton Mifflin, 1931.

Moule, A.E., *The Responsibility of the Church as Regards the Opium Traffic with China*. London, Society for the Suppression of the Opium Trade, 1881.

Mountain, Armine S.H., *Memoirs and Letters*. London, Longman, Brown, Green, Longman and Roberts, 1857.

Nye, Gideon, *The Morning of my Life in China*. Canton, 1873.

Nye, Gideon, *The Rationale of the China Question: Comprising an Inquiry into the Repressive Policy of the Imperial Government*. Wilmington, DE, Scholarly Resources, 1872.

Nye, Gideon, *Peking, the Goal – the Sole Hope of Peace*. Canton, 1873.

Oliphant, Laurence, *Narrative of the Earl of Elgin's Mission to China and Japan in the Years 1857–58–59*, 2 vols. Edinburgh, Blackwood, 1860.

Ormerod, W.E., *The Opium Trade with China and England's Injustice towards the Chinese*. London, Anglo-Oriental Society for the Suppression of the Opium Trade, 1875.

Osterhammel, Jürgen *China und die Weltgesellschaft: vom 18 Jahrhundert bis in unsere Zeit*. Munich, C.H. Beck, 1989.

Osterhammel, Jürgen, Britain and China 1842–1914, in Andrew Porter and A. Low (eds), *The Oxford History of the British Empire*, vol.III, Ch.8.

Ouchterlony, John, *The Chinese War*. London, Saunders and Otley, 1844.

Owen, David Edward, *British Opium Policy in China and India*. New Haven, CT, Yale University Press, 1934.

Palmerston, Viscount (Henry John Temple), *Opinions and Policy of Viscount Palmerston as Minister, Diplomatist and Statesman, with a Memoir by George Henry Francis*. London, Colburn and Co., 1852.

Parssinen, Terry M., *Secret Passions, Secret Remedies: Narcotic Drugs in British Society 1820–1930*. Manchester, Manchester University Press, 1983.

Pelcovits, Nathan A., *Old China Hands and the Foreign Office*. New York, American Institute of Pacific Relations, 1948.

Pemberton, W. Baring, *Lord Palmerston*. London, Batchworth Press, 1954.

Peyrefitte, Alain, *The Collision of Two Civilisations*. London, Harvill, 1993.

Phipps, J., *A Practical Treatise on China and the Eastern Trade*. London, W.H. Allen, 1836.

Platt, D.C.M., *Finance, Trade, and Politics in British Foreign Policy 1815–1914*. Oxford, Clarendon Press, 1968.

Platt, D.C.M., The Imperialism of Free Trade: Some Reservations, *Economic History Review*, 2nd series vol.XXI, 1968, pp.296–306.

Polachek, James M., *The Inner Opium War*. Cambridge, MA, Harvard University Press, for the Council on East Asian Studies, Harvard University, 1992.

Porter, Andrew and Lowe Alaine (eds), *The Oxford History of the British Empire* (Wm Roger Louis, gen. ed.), vol.III, *The Nineteenth Century*. Oxford, Oxford University Press, 1999.

Porter, Roy, *The Greatest Benefit to Mankind: A Medical History of Humanity from Antiquity to the Present*. London, Fontana Press, 1999.

Pottinger, George, *Sir Henry Pottinger, First Governor of Hong Kong*. Stroud, Glos. Sutton Publishing, 1997.

Rait, Sir Robert S., *The Life and Campaigns of Hugh, First Viscount Gough, Field-Marshal*, 2 vols. London, A. Constable, 1903.

Read, Donald, *Cobden and Bright: A Victorian Political Partnership*. London, E. Arnold, 1967.

Rennie, D.F., *British Arms in North China and Japan*. London, J. Murray, 1864.

Rich, Paul, *Race and Empire in British Politics* (2nd edn). Cambridge, Cambridge University Press, 1990.

Royal Commission on Opium, Reports and Minutes of Evidence, Parliamentary Papers, 1894/95, vols 60, 61, 62.

Rush, James, *Opium to Java: Revenue Farming and Chinese Enterprise in Colonial Indonesia 1860–1910*. Ithaca, NY, Cornell University Press, 1990.

Russell, Lord John (later Earl Russell), *Early Correspondence* (ed. Rollo Russell), 2 vols. London, T. Fisher Unwin, 1913.

Saich, Tony and Hans van den Ven (eds), *New Perspectives on the Chinese Communist Revolution*. Armonk, NY/London, M.E. Sharpe, 1995.

Salisbury, Harrison E., *The Long March: The Untold Story*. NY/Cambridge, Harper and Row, 1985.

Sargent, A.J., *Anglo-Chinese Commerce and Diplomacy*. Oxford, Clarendon Press, 1907.

Semmel, Bernard, *The Rise of Free Trade Imperialism*. Cambridge, Cambridge University Press, 1970.

Sirr, Henry Charles, *China and the Chinese: Their Religion, Character, Customs and Manufactures; The Evils Arising from the Opium Trade*, vols I and II. London, Wm. S. Orr, 1849.

Slade, John, *Narrative of the late Proceedings and Events in China*. Canton Register Press, 1839; Wilmington, DE, Scholarly Resources, 1872 (Slade was editor of the Canton Register).

Smith, Rev. George, *Narrative of an Exploratory Visit to each of the Consular Cities of China ... in the Years 1844–45–46*. New York, Harpers, 1847.

Soothill, W.E., *China and the West*. London, Oxford University Press, 1925.

Southgate, Donald, *'The Most English Minister ...': The Policies and Politics of Palmerston*. London, Macmillan, 1966.

Spence, Jonathan, *The Search for Modern China* (2nd edn). New York, Norton, 1999.

Spence, Jonathan, Opium smoking in Ch'ing China in Frederic Wakeman Jr and Carolyn Grant (eds), *Conflict and Control in Late Imperial China*, pp.143–73.

Staunton, Sir G.T., *Memoirs of the Chief Incidents of the Public Life of Sir G.T. Staunton*. London, L. Booth, 1856.

Stephan, John J., *The Russian Far East: A History*. Stanford, CA, Stanford University Press, 1994.

Sudley, Lord (ed.), *The Lieven-Palmerston Correspondence 1828–1856*. London, John Murray, 1943.

Swinhoe, Robert, *Narrative of the North China Campaign of 1860*. London, Smith, Elder, 1861.

Taylor, Sir Henry, *Autobiography*. London, Harrison and Sons, 1874.

Taylor, T.C., *A Great Moral Wrong: Crisis in the Chinese Opium Trade*. London, Christian Commonwealth, 1912.

Teng Ssu-yu, *Chang Hsi and the Treaty of Nanking, 1842*. Chicago, University of Chicago Press, 1944.

Teng Ssu-yu and John K. Fairbank, *China's Response to the West*. Cambridge, MA, Harvard University Press, 1954.

Thomson, John, *The Land and the Peoples of China*. London, Society for Promoting Christian Knowledge, 1876.

Torr, Dona (ed.), *Marx on China 1853–1860*. London, Lawrence and Wishart, 1968.

Tuck, Patrick (ed.), *The East India Company: 1600–1858*; vol.VI, *C.H. Phillips, The East India Company 1784–1834*. Manchester, Manchester University Press, 1940.

Varg, Paul A., *Missionaries, Chinese and Diplomats*. Princeton, NJ, Princeton University Press, 1958.

Victoria, Queen, *The Letters of Queen Victoria* (ed. Arthur C. Benson and Viscount Esher), vol.1, 1837–43. London, J. Murray, 1908.

Wakeman, F. E., and Grant Carolyn (eds), *Conflict and Control in Late Imperial China*. Berkeley, CA, University of California Press, 1975.

Waley, Arthur, *The Opium War through Chinese Eyes*. London, Allen and Unwin, 1958.

Webster, Sir Charles, *The Foreign Policy of Palmerston 1830–1841: Britain, the Liberal Movement and the Eastern Question*, 2 vols. London, G. Bell and Sons, 1951.

Webster, *The Letters of Daniel Webster* (ed. C.H. Van Tyne). New York, McClure, Phillips and Co., 1902.

Wilson, Andrew, *The 'Ever Victorious Army': A History of the ... Suppression of the Taiping Rebellion*. Edinburgh, Blackwood, 1868.

Wilson, Daniel, *An Inaugural Dissertation on the Morbid Effects of Opium upon the Human Body*. Philadelphia, Solomon W. Conrad, 1803.

Wolseley, Garnet Joseph, *Narrative of the War with China in 1860*. London, Longmans, 1862.

Wolseley, Field Marshal Viscount, *The Story of a Soldier's Life*, 2 vols. London, A. Constable, 1903.

Wong, J.Y., *Deadly Dreams; Opium, Imperialism and the Arrow War (1856–1860) in China*. Cambridge, Cambridge University Press, 1998.

Wood, Frances, *No Dogs and Not Many Chinese: Treaty Port Life in China 1843–1943*. London, John Murray, 1998.

Wu Wen-tsao, *The Chinese Opium Question in British Opinion and Action*. New York, Academy Press, 1928.

Young, L.K., *British Policy in China 1895–1902*. Oxford, Oxford University Press, 1970.

Yvorel, Jean-Jacques, *Les Poisons de l'esprit: drogues et drogués au XIXe siècle*. Paris, Quai Voltaire, 1992.

Zheng Yongnian, *Discovering Chinese Nationalism in China*. Cambridge, Cambridge University Press, 1999.

Index